TRAVELING LIGHT

THE GREAT HOUSE OF GOD

Max Lucado

THOMAS NELSON
Since 1798

NASHVILLE DALLAS MEXICO CITY RIO DE JANEIRO BEIJING

Published in Nashville, Tennessee, by Thomas Nelson. Thomas Nelson is a registered trademark of Thomas Nelson, Inc.

Thomas Nelson, Inc., titles may be purchased in bulk for educational, business, fund-raising, or sales promotional use. For information, please e-mail SpecialMarkets@ThomasNelson.com.

ISBN: 978-0-8499-2107-0

Printed in the United States
08 09 10 11 12 QW 5 4 3 2 1

TRAVELING LIGHT

Contents

THE GREAT HOUSE OF GOD

CONTENTS

TRAVELING LIGHT

Releasing the Burdens
You Were Never Intended to Bear

To my dear friend Joey Paul,
celebrating thirty years of words at Word,
sharing the Word

Acknowledgments

Here are well-deserved pats on some sturdy backs:

To Liz Heaney and Karen Hill—my editors and my assistant, midwives of the manuscript. Sorry I groaned so much.

To Steve and Cheryl Green—my representative and my friends. Because of you, contracts are read, and bills are paid, and this old boy sleeps well at night.

To Greg Pruett—Bible translator and Hebrew student. Thanks for the great insights.

To Eugene Peterson—Bible translator, author, and hero to many. Thanks for letting me use the title. And, much more, thanks for sharing your heart.

To Steve Halliday—study guide author par excellence.

To my friends at Thomas Nelson. Once again, you're the best.

To Laura Kendall and Carol Bartley—the great sleuths of the English language. Thanks for making me look smart.

To Jenna, Andrea, and Sara—my delightful daughters. I couldn't be prouder.

To Denalyn—my wife of two decades. Before you were born, where did poets go for inspiration?

To you—the reader. May the real Author speak to you.

And, most of all, to you, Jesus. The only reason we can release a burden is because you are there to take it. All the applause is yours.

1

The Luggage of Life

I've never been one to travel light.

I've tried. Believe me, I've tried. But ever since I stuck three fingers in the air and took the Boy Scout pledge to be prepared, I've been determined to be exactly that—prepared.

Prepared for a bar mitzvah, baby dedication, or costume party. Prepared to parachute behind enemy lines or enter a cricket tournament. And if, perchance, the Dalai Lama might be on my flight and invite me to dine in Tibet, I carry snowshoes. One has to be prepared.

I don't know how to travel light.

Fact is, there's a lot about travel I don't know. I don't know how to interpret the restrictions of a supersaver seat—*half price if you leave on Wednesdays during duck-hunting season and return when the moon is full in a nonelection year.* I don't know why they don't build the whole plane out of the same metal they use to build the little black box. I don't know how to escape the airplane toilet without sacrificing one of my extremities to the jaws of the folding door. And I don't know what to say to guys like the taxi driver in Rio who learned I was an American and asked me if I knew his cousin Eddie who lives in the U.S.

There's a lot about traveling I don't know.

I don't know why we men would rather floss a crocodile than ask for directions. I don't know why vacation slides aren't used to treat insomnia, and I don't know when I'll learn not to eat food whose names I can't pronounce.

But most of all, I don't know how to travel light.

I don't know how to travel without granola bars, sodas, and rain gear. I don't know how to travel without flashlights and a generator and a global tracking system. I don't know how to travel without an ice chest of wieners. What if I stumble upon a backyard barbecue? To bring nothing to the party would be rude.

Every travel-catalog company in the world has my credit-card number. I've got an iron that doubles as a paperweight, a hair dryer the size of a coach's whistle, a Swiss Army knife that expands into a pup tent, and a pair of pants that inflate upon impact. (On one flight my wife, Denalyn, gave me a swat on the leg, and I couldn't get out of my seat.)

I don't know how to travel light. But I need to learn. Denalyn refuses to give birth to any more children even though the airlines allow each passenger three checked bags and two carry-ons.

I need to learn to travel light.

You're wondering why I can't. *Loosen up!* you're thinking. *You can't enjoy a journey carrying so much stuff. Why don't you just drop all that luggage?*

Funny you should ask. I'd like to inquire the same of you. Haven't you been known to pick up a few bags?

Odds are, you did this morning. Somewhere between the first step on the floor and the last step out the door, you grabbed some luggage. You stepped over to the baggage carousel and loaded up. Don't remember doing so? That's because you did it without thinking. Don't remember seeing a baggage terminal? That's because the carousel is not the one in the airport; it's the one in the mind. And the bags we grab are not made of leather; they're made of burdens.

The suitcase of guilt. A sack of discontent. You drape a duffel bag of weariness on one shoulder and a hanging bag of grief on the other. Add on a backpack of doubt, an overnight bag of loneliness, and a trunk of fear. Pretty soon you're pulling more stuff than a skycap. No wonder you're so tired at the end of the day. Lugging luggage is exhausting.

What you were saying to me, God is saying to you, "Set that stuff down! You're carrying burdens you don't need to bear."

"Come to me," he invites, "all of you who are weary and carry heavy burdens, and I will give you rest" (Matt. 11:28 NLT).

If we let him, God will lighten our loads . . . but how do we let him? May I invite an old friend to show us? The Twenty-third Psalm.

> The LORD is my shepherd;
> I shall not want.
> He makes me to lie down in green pastures;
> He leads me beside the still waters.
> He restores my soul;
> He leads me in the paths of righteousness
> For His name's sake.
>
> Yea, though I walk through the valley of the shadow of death,
> I will fear no evil;
> For You are with me;
> Your rod and Your staff, they comfort me.
>
> You prepare a table before me in the presence of my enemies;
> You anoint my head with oil.
> My cup runs over.
> Surely goodness and mercy shall follow me
> All the days of my life;
> And I will dwell in the house of the LORD
> Forever. (NKJV)

Do more beloved words exist? Framed and hung in hospital halls, scratched on prison walls, quoted by the young, and whispered by the dying. In these lines sailors have found a harbor, the frightened have found a father, and strugglers have found a friend.

And because the passage is so deeply loved, it is widely known. Can you find ears on which these words have never fallen? Set to music in a hundred songs, translated into a thousand tongues, domiciled in a million hearts.

One of those hearts might be yours. What kinship do you feel with these words? Where do the verses transport you? To a fireside? Bedside? Graveside?

Hardly a week passes that I don't turn to them. This passage is to the minister what balm is to the physician. I recently applied them to the heart of a dear friend. Summoned to his house with the words "The doctors aren't giving him more than a few days," I looked at him and understood. Face pale. Lips stretched and parched. Skin draping between bones like old umbrella cloth between spokes. The cancer had taken so much: his appetite, his strength, his days. But the cancer hadn't touched his faith. Pulling a chair to his bed and squeezing his hand, I whispered, "Bill, 'The Lord is my shepherd; I shall not want.'" He rolled his head toward me as if to welcome the words.

"He makes me to lie down in green pastures; He leads me beside the still waters. He restores my soul; He leads me in the paths of righteousness for His name's sake."

Reaching the fourth verse, fearful that he might not hear, I leaned forward until I was a couple of inches from his ear and said, "Though I walk through the valley of the shadow of death, I will fear no evil; for You are with me; Your rod and Your staff, they comfort me."

He didn't open his eyes, but he arched his brows. He didn't speak, but his thin fingers curled around mine, and I wondered if the Lord was helping him set down some luggage, the fear of dying.

Do you have some luggage of your own? Do you think God might use David's psalm to lighten your load? *Traveling light means trusting God with the burdens you were never intended to bear.*

Why don't you try traveling light? Try it for the sake of those you love. Have you ever considered the impact that excess baggage has on relationships? We've made this point at our church by virtue of a drama. A wedding is reenacted in which we hear the thoughts of the bride and groom. The groom enters, laden with luggage. A bag dangles from every appendage. And each bag is labeled: guilt, anger, arrogance, insecurities. This fellow is loaded. As he stands at the altar, the audience hears him thinking, *Finally, a woman who will help me carry all my burdens. She's so strong, so stable, so . . .*

As his thoughts continue, hers begin. She enters, wearing a wedding gown but, like her fiancé, covered with luggage. Pulling a hanging bag, shouldering a carry-on, hauling a makeup kit, paper sack—everything you could imagine and everything labeled. She has her own bags: prejudice, loneliness, disappointments. And her expectations? Listen to what she is thinking: *Just a few more minutes and I've got me a man. No more counselors. No more group sessions. So long, discouragement and worry. I won't be seeing you anymore. He's going to fix me.*

Finally they stand at the altar, lost in a mountain of luggage. They smile their way through the ceremony, but when given the invitation to kiss each other, they can't. How do you embrace someone if your arms are full of bags?

For the sake of those you love, learn to set them down.

And, for the sake of the God you serve, do the same. He wants to use you, you know. But how can he if you are exhausted? This truth came home to me yesterday afternoon on a run. Preparing for a jog, I couldn't decide what to wear. The sun was out, but the wind was chilly. The sky was clear, but the forecast said rain. Jacket or sweatshirt? The Boy Scout within me prevailed. I wore both.

I grabbed my Walkman but couldn't decide which tape to bring. A sermon or music? You guessed it, I took both. Needing to stay in touch with my kids, I carried a cell phone. So no one would steal my car, I pocketed my keys. As a precaution against thirst, I brought along some drink money in a pouch. I looked more like a pack mule than a runner! Within half a mile I was peeling off the jacket and hiding it in a bush. That kind of weight will slow you down.

What's true in jogging is true in faith. God has a great race for you to run. Under his care you will go where you've never been and serve in ways you've never dreamed. But you have to drop some stuff. How can you share grace if you are full of guilt? How can you offer comfort if you are disheartened? How can you lift someone else's load if your arms are full with your own?

For the sake of those you love, travel light.

For the sake of the God you serve, travel light.

For the sake of your own joy, travel light.

There are certain weights in life you simply cannot carry. Your Lord is asking you to set them down and trust him. He is the father at the baggage claim. When a dad sees his five-year-old son trying to drag the family trunk off the carousel, what does he say? The father will say to his son what God is saying to you.

"Set it down, child. I'll carry that one."

What do you say we take God up on his offer? We just might find ourselves traveling a little lighter.

By the way, I may have overstated my packing problems. (I don't usually take snowshoes.) But I can't overstate God's promise: "Unload all your worries onto him, since he is looking after you" (1 Pet. 5:7 JB).

2

The Middle C of Life

The Burden of a Lesser God

The LORD . . .

PSALM 23:1

I'm only five feet from an eagle. His wings are spread, and his talons are lifted above the branch. White feathers cap his head, and black eyes peer at me from both sides of a golden beak. He is so close I could touch him. So near I could stroke him. With only a lean and a stretch of my right arm, I could cover the eagle's crown with my hand.

But I don't. I don't reach. Why not? Am I afraid of him?

Hardly. He hasn't budged in two years. When I first opened the box, he impressed me. When I first set him on the shelf, I admired him. Man-made eagles are nice for a while, but you quickly get used to them.

David is concerned that you and I don't make the same mistake with God. His pen has scarcely touched papyrus, and he's urging us to avoid gods of our own making. With his very first words in this psalm, David sets out to deliver us from the burden of a lesser deity.

One might argue that he seeks to do nothing else. For though he will speak of green pastures, his thesis is not rest. He will describe death's somber valley, but this poem is not an ode to dying. He will tell of the Lord's forever house, but his theme is not heaven. Why did David write the Twenty-third Psalm? To build our trust in God . . . to remind us of who he is.

In this psalm David devotes one hundred and fifteen words to explaining the first two:[1] "The LORD." In the arena of unnecessary luggage, the psalmist begins with the weightiest: the refashioned god. One who looks nice but does little. God as . . .

A genie in a bottle. Convenient. Congenial. Need a parking place, date, field goal made or missed? All you do is rub the bottle and *poof*— it's yours. And, what's even better, this god goes back into the bottle after he's done.

A sweet grandpa. So soft hearted. So wise. So kind. But very, very, very old. Grandpas are great when they are awake, but they tend to doze off when you need them.

A busy dad. Leaves on Mondays, returns on Saturdays. Lots of road trips and business meetings. He'll show up on Sunday, however, so clean up and look spiritual. On Monday, be yourself again. He'll never know.

Ever held these views of God? If so, you know the problems they cause. A busy dad doesn't have time for your questions. A kind grandpa is too weak to carry your load. And if your god is a genie in a bottle, then you are greater than he is. He comes and goes at your command.

A god who looks nice but does little.

Reminds me of a briefcase I own. Though I'd like to fault the salesman, I can't. The purchase was my decision. But he certainly made it easy. I didn't need a new satchel. The one I had was fine. Scarred and scratched but fine. The paint was worn off the zippers, and the edges were scuffed, but the bag was fine.

Oh, but this new one, to use the words of the college-age boy in the leather store, was "really fine." Loaded with features: copper covers on the corners, smooth leather from Spain, and, most of all, an Italian name near the handle. The salesman gave his line and handed me the bag, and I bought them both.

I left the store with a briefcase that I have used maybe twice. What was I thinking? It carries so little. My old bag had no copper-covered corners, but it had a belly like a beluga. This new one reminds me of a high-fashion model: slim, stiff, and tight-lipped. A book and a newspaper, and this Italian satchel is *"fullisimo."*

The bag looks nice but does nothing.

Is that the kind of God you want? Is that the kind of God we have?

David's answer is a resounding no. "You want to know who God really is?" he asks. "Then read this." And he writes the name *Yahweh.* "Yahweh is my shepherd."

Though foreign to us, the name was rich to David. So rich, in fact, that David chose *Yahweh* over *El Shaddai* (God Almighty), *El Elyon* (God Most High), and *El Olam* (God the Everlasting). These and many other titles for God were at David's disposal. But when he considered all the options, David chose *Yahweh.*

Why *Yahweh?* Because *Yahweh* is God's name. You can call me preacher or writer or half-baked golfer—these are accurate descriptions, but these aren't my names. I might call you dad, mom, doctor, or student, and those terms may describe you, but they aren't your name. If you want to call me by my name, say *Max.* If I call you by your name, I say it. And if you want to call God by his name, say *Yahweh.*

God has told us his name. (How he must long to be close to us.)

Moses was the first to learn it. Seven centuries prior to David, the eighty-year-old shepherd was tending sheep when the bush began to blaze and his life began to change. Moses was told to return to Egypt and rescue the enslaved Hebrews. He raised more excuses than a kid at bedtime, but God trumped each one. Finally Moses asked,

> "When I go to the Israelites, I will say to them, 'The God of your fathers sent me to you.' What if the people say, 'What is his name?' What should I tell them?"
>
> Then God said to Moses, "I AM WHO I AM. When you go to the people of Israel, tell them, 'I AM sent me to you.'" (Exod. 3:13–14)

God would later remind Moses: "I am Yahweh. To Abraham and Isaac and Jacob I appeared as El Shaddai; I did not make myself known to them by my name Yahweh" (Exod. 6:2–3 JB).

The Israelites considered the name too holy to be spoken by human lips. Whenever they needed to say *Yahweh,* they substituted the word *Adonai,* which means "Lord." If the name needed to be written, the scribes would take a bath before they wrote it and destroy the pen afterward.[2]

God never gives a definition of the word *Yahweh,* and Moses never requests one. Many scholars wish he had, for the study of the name has raised some healthy discussions.

The name I AM sounds strikingly close to the Hebrew verb *to be—havah.* It's quite possibly a combination of the present tense form (I am) and the causative tense (I cause to be). *Yahweh,* then, seems to mean "I AM" and "I cause." God is the "One who is" and the "One who causes."

Why is that important? Because we need a big God. And if God is the "One who is," then he is an unchanging God.

Think about it. Do you know anyone who goes around saying, "I am"? Neither do I. When we say "I am," we always add another word. "I am *happy.*" "I am *sad.*" "I am *strong.*" "I am *Max.*" God, however, starkly states, "I AM" and adds nothing else.

"You are what?" we want to ask. "I AM," he replies. God needs no descriptive word because he never changes. God is what he is. He is what he has always been. His immutability motivated the psalmist to declare, "But thou art the same" (Ps. 102:27 KJV). The writer is saying, "You are the One who is. You never change."[3] Yahweh is an unchanging God.

He is also an uncaused God.

Though he creates, God was never created. Though he makes, he was never made. Though he causes, he was never caused. Hence the psalmist's proclamation: "Before the mountains were born or you brought forth the earth and the world, from everlasting to everlasting you are God" (Ps. 90:2 NIV).

God is Yahweh—an unchanging God, an uncaused God, and an ungoverned God.

You and I are governed. The weather determines what we wear. The terrain tells us how to travel. Gravity dictates our speed, and health determines our strength. We may challenge these forces and alter them slightly, but we never remove them.

God—our Shepherd—doesn't check the weather; he makes it. He doesn't defy gravity; he created it. He isn't affected by health; he has no body. Jesus said, "God is spirit" (John 4:24). Since he has no body, he has no limitations—equally active in Cambodia as he is in Connecticut. "Where can I go to get away from your Spirit?" asked David. "Where can I run from you? If I go up to the heavens, you are there. If I lie down in the grave, you are there" (Ps. 139:7–8).

Unchanging. Uncaused. Ungoverned. These are only a fraction of God's qualities, but aren't they enough to give you a glimpse of your Father? Don't we need this kind of shepherd? Don't we need an unchanging shepherd?

When Lloyd Douglas, author of *The Robe* and other novels, attended college, he lived in a boardinghouse. A retired, wheelchair-bound music professor resided on the first floor. Each morning Douglas would stick his head in the door of the teacher's apartment and ask the same question, "Well, what's the good news?" The old man would pick up his tuning fork, tap it on the side of the wheelchair, and say, "That's middle C! It was middle C yesterday; it will be middle C tomorrow; it will be middle C a thousand years from now. The tenor upstairs sings flat. The piano across the hall is out of tune, but, my friend, that is middle C."[4]

You and I need a middle C. Haven't you had enough change in your life? Relationships change. Health changes. The weather changes. But the Yahweh who ruled the earth last night is the same Yahweh who rules it today. Same convictions. Same plan. Same mood. Same love. He never changes. You can no more alter God than a pebble can alter the rhythm of the Pacific. Yahweh is our middle C. A still point in a turning world. Don't we need a still point? Don't we need an unchanging shepherd?

We equally need an uncaused shepherd. No one breathed life into Yahweh. No one sired him. No one gave birth to him. No one caused him. No act brought him forth.

And since no act brought him forth, no act can take him out. Does he fear an earthquake? Does he tremble at a tornado? Hardly. Yahweh sleeps through storms and calms the winds with a word. Cancer does not trouble him, and cemeteries do not disturb him. He was here before they came. He'll be here after they are gone. He is uncaused.

And he is ungoverned. Counselors can comfort you *in* the storm, but you need a God who can *still* the storm. Friends can hold your hand at your deathbed, but you need a Yahweh who has defeated the grave. Philosophers can debate the meaning of life, but you need a Lord who can declare the meaning of life.

You need a Yahweh.

You don't need what Dorothy found. Remember her discovery in *The Wonderful Wizard of Oz*? She and her trio followed the yellow-brick road only to discover that the wizard was a wimp! Nothing but smoke and mirrors and tin-drum thunder. Is that the kind of god you need?

You don't need to carry the burden of a lesser god . . . a god on a shelf, a god in a box, or a god in a bottle. No, you need a God who can place 100 billion stars in our galaxy and 100 billion galaxies in the universe. You need a God who can shape two fists of flesh into 75 to 100 billion nerve cells, each with as many as 10,000 connections to other nerve cells, place it in a skull, and call it a brain.[5]

And you need a God who, while so mind-numbingly mighty, can come in the soft of night and touch you with the tenderness of an April snow.

You need a Yahweh.

And, according to David, you have one. He is your shepherd.

3

I'll Do It My Way

The Burden of Self-Reliance

The LORD is my shepherd.

PSALM 23:1 NKJV

You say you can swing a club like Tiger Woods? That's saying a lot.

You hope to score touchdowns like Joe Montana? You'll have to work hard.

And you, young lady? You aspire to be the next Mia Hamm? Good for you.

And me? Well, actually there is one fellow who's caught my attention. He reminds me of me. You've probably never heard of him. Did you see the British Open in '99? Yeah, the one in Carnoustie, Scotland? Remember the player who had a seven-stroke lead with one hole to go?

That's right, the Frenchman. Jean Van de Velde. He was six strokes and 480 yards away from a major championship, a wad of cash, and a place in history. All he needed to do was score a six on a par four.

I could shoot a six on a par four. My mother could make a six on a par four. This guy could shoot a six with a waffle iron and a banana. Tell the trophy engraver to warm up the pen and practice his *V*s. He'll need two to write "Jean Van de Velde."

Granted the hole was not easy. Bisected three times by a "wee burn," the Scottish term for a marshy creek. No sweat. Hit three short shots . . . putt three times if you have to. Just take a six, win the hole, and smile for the cameras. Besides it's windy, and the "wee burn" is wee deep. Don't flirt with it.

Oh, but the French love to flirt. Van de Velde pulls out his driver, and somewhere in Des Moines an armchair duffer who'd been lured to sleep by the seven-stroke lead opens one eye. *He's holding a driver?*

Van de Velde's caddie was a thirty-year-old Parisian named Christopher with untidy English and a paintbrush on his chin and bleached hair under his hat. "I think he and I—we want too much show," he later confessed.

Van de Velde pushes his drive halfway to the Eiffel Tower. Now he has 240 yards to the green with nothing but deep grass and heartache in between. Surely he will hit a short shot back in the fairway.

Logic says, "Don't go for the green."

Golf 101 says, "Don't go for the green."

Every Scot in the gallery says, "Aye, laddie. Don't go for the green."

Van de Velde says, "I'm going for the green."

He pulls out a two iron, and the armchair golfer in Des Moines opens the other eye. *A two iron!? Maybe if you're teed up on the beach, trying to hit into the Caribbean!* The spectators are silent. Most out of respect. A few in prayer. Van de Velde's two iron becomes a FORE! iron. *Whack. Clang. Plop.* The ball caroms off the bleachers and disappears into marsh tall enough to hide a lawn gnome.

His lie would've made Pinocchio's nose grow. The next shot lands in the water and the next in the sand. Tally the damage, and you've got four strokes plus a penalty. He's lying five and not on the green. So much for winning the hole. By now he's praying for a seven and a tie. To the great relief of the civilized world, Van de Velde makes the seven. You've got to wonder if he ever recovered from the "wee burn." He lost the play-off.

Golf, like nylon running shorts, reveals a lot about a person. What the eighteenth hole revealed about Van de Velde reminds me of me.

I've done the same thing. The same blasted thing. All he needed was a five iron, but he had to go and pull out the driver. Or, in my case:

All I needed to do was apologize, but I had to argue.

All I needed to do was listen, but I had to open my big mouth.

All I needed to do was be patient, but I had to take control.

All I had to do was give it to God, but I tried to fix it myself.

Why don't I leave the driver in the bag? I know how Christopher the caddie would answer: "I think he and I and Max—we want too much show."

Too much stubbornness. Too much independence. Too much self-reliance.

I don't need advice—*Whack.*

I can handle this myself—*Clang.*

I don't need a shepherd, thank you—*Plop.*

Can you relate? Are Jean and I the only ones to make an anthem out of Sinatra's song "I Did It My Way"? Are we the only two dragging around the cast-iron chest of self-reliance? I don't think so.

We humans want to do things our way. Forget the easy way. Forget the common way. Forget the best way. Forget God's way. We want to do things *our* way.

And, according to the Bible, that's precisely our problem. "We all have wandered away like sheep; each of us has gone his own way" (Isa. 53:6).

You wouldn't think sheep would be obstinate. Of all God's animals, the sheep is the least able to take care of himself.

Sheep are dumb! Have you ever met a sheep trainer? Ever seen sheep tricks? Know anyone who has taught his sheep to roll over? Ever witnessed a circus sideshow featuring "Mazadon and his jumping sheep"? No. Sheep are just too dumb.

And defenseless. They have no fangs or claws. They can't bite you or outrun you. That's why you never see sheep as team mascots. We've heard of the St. Louis Rams and the Chicago Bulls and the Seattle

Seahawks, but the New York Lambs? Who wants to be a lamb? You couldn't even stir up a decent yell for the cheerleaders.

> We are the sheep.
> We don't make a peep.
> Victory is yours to keep.
> But count us if you want to sleep.

What's more, sheep are dirty. A cat can clean itself. So can a dog. We see a bird in a birdbath or a bear in a river. But sheep? They get dirty and stay that way.

Couldn't David have thought of a better metaphor? Surely he could have. After all, he outran Saul and outgunned Goliath. Why didn't he choose something other than sheep?

How about:

"The Lord is my commander in chief, and I am his warrior." There. We like that better. A warrior gets a uniform and a weapon, maybe even a medal.

Or, "The Lord is my inspiration, and I am his singer." We are in God's choir; what a flattering assignment.

Or, "The Lord is my king, and I am his ambassador." Who wouldn't like to be a spokesperson for God?

Everyone stops when the ambassador speaks. Everyone listens when God's minstrel sings. Everyone applauds when God's warrior passes.

But who notices when God's sheep show up? Who notices when the sheep sing or speak or act? Only one person notices. The shepherd. And that is precisely David's point.

When David, who was a warrior, minstrel, and ambassador for God, searched for an illustration of God, he remembered his days as a shepherd. He remembered how he lavished attention on the sheep day and night. How he slept with them and watched over them.

And the way he cared for the sheep reminded him of the way God cares for us. David rejoiced to say, "The LORD is my shepherd," and in so doing he proudly implied, "I am his sheep."

Still uncomfortable with being considered a sheep? Will you humor me and take a simple quiz? See if you succeed in self-reliance. Raise your hand if any of the following describe you.

You can control your moods. You're never grumpy or sullen. You can't relate to Jekyll and Hyde. You're always upbeat and upright. Does that describe you? No? Well, let's try another.

You are at peace with everyone. Every relationship as sweet as fudge. Even your old flames speak highly of you. Love all and are loved by all. Is that you? If not, how about this description?

You have no fears. Call you the Teflon toughie. Wall Street plummets—no problem. Heart condition discovered—yawn. World War III starts—what's for dinner? Does this describe you?

You need no forgiveness. Never made a mistake. As square as a game of checkers. As clean as grandma's kitchen. Never cheated, never lied, never lied about cheating. Is that you? No?

Let's evaluate this. You can't control your moods. A few of your relationships are shaky. You have fears and faults. Hmmm. Do you really want to hang on to your chest of self-reliance? Sounds to me as if you could use a shepherd. Otherwise, you might end up with a Twenty-third Psalm like this:

> I am my own shepherd. I am always in need.
>
> I stumble from mall to mall and shrink to shrink, seeking relief but never finding it.
>
> I creep through the valley of the shadow of death and fall apart.

I fear everything from pesticides to power lines, and I'm starting to act like my mother.

I go down to the weekly staff meeting and am surrounded by enemies. I go home, and even my goldfish scowls at me.

I anoint my headache with extra-strength Tylenol.

My Jack Daniel's runneth over.

Surely misery and misfortune will follow me, and I will live in self-doubt for the rest of my lonely life.

Why is it that the ones who most need a shepherd resist him so?

Ah, now there is a question for the Van de Veldes of life. Scripture says, "Do it God's way." Experience says, "Do it God's way." Every Scot in heaven begs, "Aye, laddie, do it God's way."

And, every so often, we do. And when we do, when we follow the lead of *Notre Dieu* and keep the driver in the bag, somehow the ball stays in the fairway.

Yes, Van de Velde reminds me of me.

After losing the play-off hole, he kept his composure for the crowds. But once he sat in the scorer's tent, he buried his face in his hands. "Next time I'll hit zee wedge," he sobbed. "You'll say I'm a coward, but next time I'll hit zee wedge."

You and me both, Jean.[1]

4

The Prison of Want

The Burden of Discontent

The LORD is my shepherd; I shall not want.

PSALM 23:1 NKJV

Come with me to the most populated prison in the world. The facility has more inmates than bunks. More prisoners than plates. More residents than resources.

Come with me to the world's most oppressive prison. Just ask the inmates; they will tell you. They are overworked and underfed. Their walls are bare and bunks are hard.

No prison is so populated, no prison so oppressive, and, what's more, no prison is so permanent. Most inmates never leave. They never escape. They never get released. They serve a life sentence in this overcrowded, underprovisioned facility.

The name of the prison? You'll see it over the entrance. Rainbowed over the gate are four cast-iron letters that spell out its name:

W-A-N-T

The prison of want. You've seen her prisoners. They are "in want." They want something. They want something bigger. Nicer. Faster. Thinner. They want.

They don't want much, mind you. They want just one thing. One new job. One new car. One new house. One new spouse. They don't want much. They want just one.

And when they have "one," they will be happy. And they are right—

they will be happy. When they have "one," they will leave the prison. But then it happens. The new-car smell passes. The new job gets old. The neighbors buy a larger television set. The new spouse has bad habits. The sizzle fizzles, and before you know it, another ex-con breaks parole and returns to jail.

Are you in prison? You are if you feel better when you have more and worse when you have less. You are if joy is one delivery away, one transfer away, one award away, or one makeover away. If your happiness comes from something you deposit, drive, drink, or digest, then face it—you are in prison, the prison of want.

That's the bad news. The good news is, you have a visitor. And your visitor has a message that can get you paroled. Make your way to the receiving room. Take your seat in the chair, and look across the table at the psalmist David. He motions for you to lean forward. "I have a secret to tell you," he whispers, "the secret of satisfaction. 'The LORD is my shepherd; I shall not want'" (Ps. 23:1 NKJV).

David has found the pasture where discontent goes to die. It's as if he is saying, "What I have in God is greater than what I don't have in life."

You think you and I could learn to say the same?

Think for just a moment about the things you own. Think about the house you have, the car you drive, the money you've saved. Think about the jewelry you've inherited and the stocks you've traded and the clothes you've purchased. Envision all your stuff, and let me remind you of two biblical truths.

Your stuff isn't yours. Ask any coroner. Ask any embalmer. Ask any funeral-home director. No one takes anything with him. When one of the wealthiest men in history, John D. Rockefeller, died, his accountant was asked, "How much did John D. leave?" The accountant's reply? "All of it."[1]

"Naked a man comes from his mother's womb, and as he comes, so he departs. He takes nothing from his labor that he can carry in his hand" (Eccles. 5:15 NIV).

All that stuff—it's not yours. And you know what else about all that stuff? *It's not you.* Who you are has nothing to do with the clothes you wear or the car you drive. Jesus said, "Life is not defined by what you have, even when you have a lot" (Luke 12:15 MSG). Heaven does not know you as the fellow with the nice suit or the woman with the big house or the kid with the new bike. Heaven knows your heart. "The LORD does not look at the things man looks at. Man looks at the outward appearance, but the LORD looks at the heart" (1 Sam. 16:7 NIV). When God thinks of you, he may see your compassion, your devotion, your tenderness or quick mind, but he doesn't think of your things.

And when you think of you, you shouldn't either. Define yourself by your stuff, and you'll feel good when you have a lot and bad when you don't. Contentment comes when we can honestly say with Paul: "I have learned to be satisfied with the things I have. . . . I know how to live when I am poor, and I know how to live when I have plenty" (Phil. 4:11–12).

Doug McKnight could say those words. At the age of thirty-two he was diagnosed with multiple sclerosis. Over the next sixteen years it would cost him his career, his mobility, and eventually his life. Because of MS, he couldn't feed himself or walk; he battled depression and fear. But through it all, Doug never lost his sense of gratitude. Evidence of this was seen in his prayer list. Friends in his congregation asked him to compile a list of requests so they could intercede for him. His response included eighteen blessings for which to be grateful and six concerns for which to be prayerful. His blessings outweighed his needs by three times. Doug McKnight had learned to be content.[2]

So had the leper on the island of Tobago. A short-term missionary met her on a mission trip. On the final day, he was leading worship in a leper colony. He asked if anyone had a favorite song. When he did, a woman turned around, and he saw the most disfigured face he'd ever seen. She had no ears and no nose. Her lips were gone. But she raised a fingerless hand and asked, "Could we sing 'Count Your Many Blessings'?"

The missionary started the song but couldn't finish. Someone later commented, "I suppose you'll never be able to sing the song again." He answered, "No, I'll sing it again. Just never in the same way."[3]

Are you hoping that a change in circumstances will bring a change in your attitude? If so, you are in prison, and you need to learn a secret of traveling light. *What you have in your Shepherd is greater than what you don't have in life.*

May I meddle for a moment? What is the one thing separating you from joy? How do you fill in this blank: "I will be happy when ____________________"? When I am healed. When I am promoted. When I am married. When I am single. When I am rich. How would you finish that statement?

Now, with your answer firmly in mind, answer this. If your ship never comes in, if your dream never comes true, if the situation never changes, could you be happy? If not, then you are sleeping in the cold cell of discontent. You are in prison. And you need to know what you have in your Shepherd.

You have a God who hears you, the power of love behind you, the Holy Spirit within you, and all of heaven ahead of you. If you have the Shepherd, you have grace for every sin, direction for every turn, a candle for every corner, and an anchor for every storm. You have everything you need.

And who can take it from you? Can leukemia infect your salvation? Can bankruptcy impoverish your prayers? A tornado might take your earthly house, but will it touch your heavenly home?

And look at your position. Why clamor for prestige and power? Are you not already privileged to be part of the greatest work in history?

According to Russ Blowers, we are. He is a minister in Indianapolis. Knowing he would be asked about his profession at a Rotary Club meeting, he resolved to say more than "I'm a preacher."

Instead he explained, "Hi, I'm Russ Blowers. I'm with a global enterprise. We have branches in every country in the world. We have representatives in nearly every parliament and boardroom on earth. We're into motivation and behavior alteration. We run hospitals, feeding stations, crisis-pregnancy centers, universities, publishing houses, and nursing homes. We care for our clients from birth to death. We are into life insurance and fire insurance. We perform spiritual heart transplants. Our original Organizer owns all the real estate on earth plus an assortment of galaxies and constellations. He knows everything and lives everywhere. Our product is free for the asking. (There's not enough money to buy it.) Our CEO was born in a hick town, worked as a carpenter, didn't own a home, was misunderstood by his family and hated by his enemies, walked on water, was condemned to death without a trial, and arose from the dead. I talk with him every day."[4]

If you can say the same, don't you have reason to be content?

A man once went to a minister for counseling. He was in the midst of a financial collapse. "I've lost everything," he bemoaned.

"Oh, I'm so sorry to hear that you've lost your faith."

"No," the man corrected him, "I haven't lost my faith."

"Well, then I'm sad to hear that you've lost your character."

"I didn't say that," he corrected. "I still have my character."

"I'm so sorry to hear that you've lost your salvation."

"That's not what I said," the man objected. "I haven't lost my salvation."

"You have your faith, your character, your salvation. Seems to me," the minister observed, "that you've lost none of the things that really matter."

We haven't either. You and I could pray like the Puritan. He sat down to a meal of bread and water. He bowed his head and declared, "All this and Jesus too?"

Can't we be equally content? Paul says that "godliness with contentment is great gain" (1 Tim. 6:6 NIV). When we surrender to God the cumbersome sack of discontent, we don't just give up something; we gain something. God replaces it with a lightweight, tailor-made, sorrow-resistant attaché of gratitude.

What will you gain with contentment? You may gain your marriage. You may gain precious hours with your children. You may gain your self-respect. You may gain joy. You may gain the faith to say, "The LORD is my shepherd; I shall not want."

Try saying it slowly. "The LORD is my shepherd; I shall not want."

Again, "The LORD is my shepherd; I shall not want."

Again, "The LORD is my shepherd; I shall not want."

Shhhhhhh. Did you hear something? I think I did. I'm not sure . . . but I think I heard the opening of a jail door.

5

I Will Give You Rest

The Burden of Weariness

He makes me to lie down in green pastures.

PSALM 23:2 NKJV

I'll give you the consequences of the burden; you guess the cause.

- It afflicts 70 million Americans and is faulted for 38,000 deaths each year.
- The condition annually costs the U.S. $70 billion worth of productivity.
- Teenagers suffer from it. Studies show that 64 percent of teens blame it for poor school performance.
- Middle agers face it. Researchers say the most severe cases occur between ages thirty and forty.
- Senior citizens are afflicted by it. One study suggests that the condition impacts 50 percent of the over-sixty-five population.
- Treatments involve everything from mouth guards to herbal teas to medication.[1]

Any idea what's being described?

Chemical abuse? Divorce? Long sermons? None of those answers are correct, though the last one was a good hunch. The answer may surprise you. Insomnia. America can't get to sleep.

For most of my life I secretly snickered at the thought of sleep difficulties. My problem was not in going to sleep. My problem was staying awake. But a few years ago I went to bed one night, closed my eyes, and nothing happened. I didn't fall asleep. Rather than slow to a halt, my mind kicked into high gear. A thousand and one obligations rushed at me. Midnight passed, and I was still awake. I drank some milk, returned to bed. I was still awake. I woke up Denalyn, using the blue ribbon of dumb questions, "Are you awake?" She told me to quit thinking about things. So I did. I quit thinking about things and started thinking about people. But as I thought of people, I thought of what those people were doing. They were sleeping. That made me mad and kept me awake. Finally, somewhere in the early hours of the morning, having been initiated into the fraternity of 70 million sleepless Americans, I dozed off.

I don't snicker at the thought of sleep difficulties anymore. Nor do I question the inclusion of the verse about rest in the Twenty-third Psalm.

People with too much work and too little sleep step over to the baggage claim of life and grab the duffel bag of weariness. You don't carry this one. You don't hoist it onto your shoulder and stride down the street. You drag it as you would a stubborn St. Bernard. Weariness wearies.

Why are we so tired? Have you read a newspaper lately? We long to have the life of Huck and Tom on the Mississippi, but look at us riding the white waters of the Rio Grande. Forks in the river. Rocks in the water. Heart attacks, betrayal, credit-card debt, and custody battles. Huck and Tom didn't have to face these kinds of things. We do, however, and they keep us awake. And since we can't sleep, we have a second problem.

Our bodies are tired. Think about it. If 70 million Americans aren't sleeping enough, what does that mean? That means one-third of our country is dozing off at work, napping through class, or sleeping at the wheel. (Fifteen hundred road deaths per year are blamed on heavy-eyed truckdrivers.) Some even snooze while reading Lucado books.

(Hard to fathom, I know.) Thirty tons of aspirins, sleeping pills, and tranquilizers are consumed every day![2] The energy gauge on the dashboard of our forehead says empty.

Were we to invite an alien to solve our problem, he'd suggest a simple solution—everybody go to sleep. We'd laugh at him. He doesn't understand the way we work. Literally. He doesn't understand *the way* we work. We work hard. There is money to be made. Degrees to be earned. Ladders to be climbed. In our book, busyness is next to godliness. We idolize Thomas Edison, who claimed he could live on fifteen-minute naps. Somehow we forget to mention Albert Einstein, who averaged eleven hours of sleep a night.[3] In 1910 Americans slept nine hours a night; today we sleep seven and are proud of it. And we are tired because of it. Our minds are tired. Our bodies are tired. But much more important, our souls are tired.

We are eternal creatures, and we ask eternal questions: Where did I come from? Where am I going? What is the meaning of life? What is right? What is wrong? Is there life after death? These are the primal questions of the soul. And left unanswered, such questions will steal our rest.

Only one other living creature has as much trouble resting as we do. Not dogs. They doze. Not bears. They hibernate. Cats invented the catnap, and the sloths slumber twenty hours a day. (So that's what I was rooming with my sophomore year in college.) Most animals know how to rest. There is one exception. These creatures are woolly, simpleminded, and slow. No, not husbands on Saturday—sheep! Sheep can't sleep.

For sheep to sleep, everything must be just right. No predators. No tension in the flock. No bugs in the air. No hunger in the belly.[4] Everything has to be just so.

Unfortunately, sheep cannot find safe pasture, nor can they spray insecticide, deal with the frictions, or find food. They need help. They need a shepherd to "lead them" and help them "lie down in green pastures." Without a shepherd, they can't rest.

Without a shepherd, neither can we.

In the second verse of the Twenty-third Psalm, David the poet becomes David the artist. His quill becomes a brush, his parchment a canvas, and his words paint a picture. A flock of sheep on folded legs, encircling a shepherd. Bellies nestled deep in the long shoots of grass. A still pond on one side, the watching shepherd on the other. "He makes me to lie down in green pastures; He leads me beside the still waters" (Ps. 23:2 NKJV).

Note the two pronouns preceding the two verbs. *He* makes me . . . *He* leads me . . .

Who is the active one? Who is in charge? The shepherd. The shepherd selects the trail and prepares the pasture. The sheep's job—our job—is to watch the shepherd. With our eyes on our Shepherd, we'll be able to get some sleep. "You will keep him in perfect peace, whose mind is stayed on You" (Isa. 26:3 NKJV).

May I show you something? Flip to the back of this book, and look at an empty page. When you look at it, what do you see? What you see is a white piece of paper. Now place a dot in the center of the sheet. Look at it again. Now what do you see? You see the dot, don't you? And isn't that our problem? We let the dark marks eclipse the white space.

We see the waves of the water rather than the Savior walking through them. We focus on our paltry provisions rather than on the One who can feed five thousand hungry people. We concentrate on the dark Fridays of crucifixion and miss the bright Sundays of resurrection.

Change your focus and relax.

And while you are at it, change your schedule and rest!

The other day my wife met a friend at a restaurant for coffee. The two entered the parking lot at the same time. When Denalyn stepped out of her car, she saw her friend waving her over. Denalyn thought she was saying something, but she couldn't hear a word. A jack-hammer was pounding pavement only a few feet away. She walked toward her friend, who, as it turned out, was just saying hello, and the two entered the restaurant.

When it came time to leave, my wife couldn't find her keys. She looked in her purse, on the floor, in her friend's car. Finally when she went to her car, there they were. Not only were the keys in the ignition, the car was running. It had been running the entire time she and her friend were in the café.

Denalyn blames the oversight on the noise. "Everything was so loud, I forgot to turn it off."

The world gets that way. Life can get so loud we forget to shut it down. Maybe that's why God made such a big deal about rest in the Ten Commandments.

Since you did so well on the dot exercise, let me give you another. Of the ten declarations carved in the tablets, which one occupies the most space? Murder? Adultery? Stealing? You'd think so. Certainly each is worthy of ample coverage. But curiously, these commands are tributes to brevity. God needed only five English words to condemn adultery and four to denounce thievery and murder.

But when he came to the topic of rest, one sentence would not suffice.

> Remember the Sabbath day, to keep it holy. Six days you shall labor and do all your work, but the seventh day is the Sabbath of the LORD your God. In it you shall do no work: you, nor your son, nor your daughter, nor your manservant, nor your maidservant, nor your cattle, nor your stranger who is within your gates. For in six days the LORD made the heavens and the earth, the sea, and all that is in them, and rested the

> seventh day. Therefore the LORD blessed the Sabbath day and hallowed it. (Exod. 20:8–11 NKJV)

God knows us so well. He can see the store owner reading this verse and thinking, "Somebody needs to work that day. If I can't, my son will." So God says, *Nor your son.* "Then my daughter will." *Nor your daughter.* "Then maybe an employee." *Nor them.* "I guess I'll have to send my cow to run the store, or maybe I'll find some stranger to help me." *No,* God says. *One day of the week you will say no to work and yes to worship. You will slow and sit down and lie down and rest.*

Still we object. "But . . . but . . . but . . . who is going to run the store?" "What about my grades?" "I've got my sales quota." We offer up one reason after another, but God silences them all with a poignant reminder: "In six days the LORD made the heavens and the earth, the sea, and all that is in them, and rested the seventh day." God's message is plain: "If creation didn't crash when I rested, it won't crash when you do."

Repeat these words after me: It is not my job to run the world.

A century ago Charles Spurgeon gave this advice to his preaching students:

> Even beasts of burden must be turned out to grass occasionally; the very sea pauses at ebb and flood; earth keeps the Sabbath of the wintry months; and man, even when exalted to God's ambassador, must rest or faint, must trim his lamp or let it burn low; must recruit his vigor or grow prematurely old. . . . In the long run we shall do more by sometimes doing less.[5]

The bow cannot always be bent without fear of breaking. For a field to bear fruit, it must occasionally lie fallow. And for you to be healthy, you must rest. Slow down, and God will heal you. He will bring rest to your mind, to your body, and most of all to your soul. He will lead you to green pastures.

Green pastures were not the natural terrain of Judea. The hills around Bethlehem where David kept his flock were not lush and green. Even today they are white and parched. Any green pasture in Judea is the work of some shepherd. He has cleared the rough, rocky land. Stumps have been torn out, and brush has been burned. Irrigation. Cultivation. Such are the work of a shepherd.

Hence, when David says, "He makes me to lie down in green pastures," he is saying, "My shepherd makes me lie down in his finished work." With his own pierced hands, Jesus created a pasture for the soul. He tore out the thorny underbrush of condemnation. He pried loose the huge boulders of sin. In their place he planted seeds of grace and dug ponds of mercy.

And he invites us to rest there. Can you imagine the satisfaction in the heart of the shepherd when, with work completed, he sees his sheep rest in the tender grass?

Can you imagine the satisfaction in the heart of God when we do the same? His pasture is his gift to us. This is not a pasture that you have made. Nor is it a pasture that you deserve. It is a gift of God. "For it is by grace you have been saved, through faith—and this not from yourselves, it is the gift of God" (Eph. 2:8 NIV).

In a world rocky with human failure, there is a land lush with divine mercy. Your Shepherd invites you there. He wants you to lie down. Nestle deeply until you are hidden, buried, in the tall shoots of his love, and there you will find rest.

6

Whaddifs and Howells

The Burden of Worry

He leads me beside the still waters.

PSALM 23:2 NKJV

Your ten-year-old is worried. So anxious he can't eat. So worried he can't sleep. "What's wrong?" you inquire. He shakes his head and moans, "I don't even have a pension plan."

Or your four-year-old is crying in bed. "What's wrong, sweetheart?" She whimpers, "I'll never pass college chemistry."

Your eight-year-old's face is stress-struck. "I'll be a rotten parent. What if I set a poor example for my kids?"

How would you respond to such statements? Besides calling a child psychologist, your response would be emphatic: "You're too young to worry about those things. When the time comes, you'll know what to do."

Fortunately, most kids don't have such thoughts.

Unfortunately, we adults have more than our share. Worry is the burlap bag of burdens. It's overflowing with "whaddifs" and "howells." "Whaddif it rains at my wedding?" "Howell I know when to discipline my kids?" "Whaddif I marry a guy who snores?" "Howell we pay our baby's tuition?" "Whaddif, after all my dieting, they learn that lettuce is fattening and chocolate isn't?"

The burlap bag of worry. Cumbersome. Chunky. Unattractive. Scratchy. Hard to get a handle on. Irritating to carry and impossible to give away. No one wants your worries.

The truth be told, you don't want them either. No one has to remind you of the high cost of anxiety. (But I will anyway.) Worry divides the mind. The biblical word for *worry (merimnao)* is a compound of two Greek words, *merizo* ("to divide") and *nous* ("the mind"). Anxiety splits our energy between today's priorities and tomorrow's problems. Part of our mind is on the now; the rest is on the not yet. The result is half-minded living.

That's not the only result. Worrying is not a disease, but it causes diseases. It has been connected to high blood pressure, heart trouble, blindness, migraine headaches, thyroid malfunctions, and a host of stomach disorders.

Anxiety is an expensive habit. Of course, it might be worth the cost if it worked. But it doesn't. Our frets are futile. Jesus said, "You cannot add any time to your life by worrying about it" (Matt. 6:27). Worry has never brightened a day, solved a problem, or cured a disease.

How can a person deal with anxiety? You might try what one fellow did. He worried so much that he decided to hire someone to do his worrying for him. He found a man who agreed to be his hired worrier for a salary of $200,000 per year. After the man accepted the job, his first question to his boss was, "Where are you going to get $200,000 per year?" To which the man responded, "That's your worry."

Sadly, worrying is one job you can't farm out, but you can overcome it. There is no better place to begin than in verse two of the shepherd's psalm.

"He leads me beside the still waters," David declares. And, in case we missed the point, he repeats the phrase in the next verse: "He leads me in the paths of righteousness."

"He leads me." God isn't behind me, yelling, "Go!" He is ahead of me, bidding, "Come!" He is in front, clearing the path, cutting the brush, showing the way. Just before the curve, he says, "Turn here."

Prior to the rise, he motions, "Step up here." Standing next to the rocks, he warns, "Watch your step here."

He leads us. He tells us what we need to know when we need to know it. As a New Testament writer would affirm: "We will find grace to help us *when we need it*" (Heb. 4:16 NLT, emphasis mine).

Listen to a different translation: "Let us therefore boldly approach the throne of our gracious God, where we may receive mercy and in his grace find *timely help*" (Heb. 4:16 NEB, emphasis mine).

God's help is timely. He helps us the same way a father gives plane tickets to his family. When I travel with my kids, I carry all our tickets in my satchel. When the moment comes to board the plane, I stand between the attendant and the child. As each daughter passes, I place a ticket in her hand. She, in turn, gives the ticket to the attendant. Each one receives the ticket in the nick of time.

What I do for my daughters God does for you. He places himself between you and the need. And at the right time, he gives you the ticket. Wasn't this the promise he gave his disciples? "When you are arrested and judged, don't worry ahead of time about what you should say. Say whatever *is given you to say at that time,* because it will not really be you speaking; it will be the Holy Spirit" (Mark 13:11, emphasis mine).

Isn't this the message God gave the children of Israel? He promised to supply them with manna each day. But he told them to collect only one day's supply at a time. Those who disobeyed and collected enough for two days found themselves with rotten manna. The only exception to the rule was the day prior to the Sabbath. On Friday they could gather twice as much. Otherwise, God would give them what they needed, in their time of need.

God leads us. God will do the right thing at the right time. And what a difference that makes.

Since I know his provision is timely, I can enjoy the present.

"Give your entire attention to what God is doing right now, and don't get worked up about what may or may not happen tomorrow. God will help you deal with whatever hard things come up when the time comes" (Matt. 6:34 MSG).

That last phrase is worthy of your highlighter: "when the time comes."

"I don't know what I'll do if my husband dies." You will, *when the time comes.*

"When my children leave the house, I don't think I can take it." It won't be easy, but strength will arrive *when the time comes.*

"I could never lead a church. There is too much I don't know." You may be right. Or you may be wanting to know everything too soon. Could it be that God will reveal answers to you *when the time comes?*

The key is this: Meet today's problems with today's strength. Don't start tackling tomorrow's problems until tomorrow. You do not have tomorrow's strength yet. You simply have enough for today.

More than eighty years ago a great Canadian man of medicine, Sir William Osler, delivered a speech to the students of Yale University entitled "A Way of Life." In the message he related an event that occurred while he was aboard an ocean liner.

One day while he was visiting with the ship's captain, a loud, piercing alarm sounded, followed by strange grinding and crashing sounds below the deck. "Those are our watertight compartments closing," the captain explained. "It's an important part of our safety drill. In case of real trouble, water leaking into one compartment would not affect the rest of the ship. Even if we should collide with an iceberg, as did the *Titanic,* water rushing in will fill only that particular ruptured compartment. The ship, however, will still remain afloat."

When he spoke to the students at Yale, Osler remembered the captain's description of the boat:

> Each one of you is certainly a much more marvelous organization than that great liner and bound on a far longer voyage. What I urge is that you learn to master your life by living each day in a day-tight compartment and this will certainly ensure your safety throughout your entire journey of life. Touch a button and hear, at every level of your life, the iron doors shutting out the Past—the dead yesterdays. Touch another and shut off, with a metal curtain, the Future—the unborn tomorrows. Then you are safe—safe for today.
>
> Think not of the amount to be accomplished, the difficulties to be overcome, but set earnestly at the little task near your elbow, letting that be sufficient for the day; for surely our plain duty is not to see what lies dimly at a distance but to do what lies clearly at hand.[1]

Jesus made the same point in fewer words: "So don't worry about tomorrow, because tomorrow will have its own worries. Each day has enough trouble of its own" (Matt. 6:34).

Easy to say. Not always easy to do, right? We are so prone to worry. Just last night I was worrying in my sleep. I dreamed that I was diagnosed with ALS, a degenerative muscle disease, which took the life of my father. I awakened from the dream and, right there in the middle of the night, began to worry. Then Jesus' words came to my mind, "Don't worry about tomorrow." And for once, I decided not to. I dropped the burlap sack. After all, why let tomorrow's imaginary problem rob tonight's rest? Can I prevent the disease by staying awake? Will I postpone the affliction by thinking about it? Of course not. So I did the most spiritual thing I could have done. I went back to sleep.

Why don't you do the same? God is leading you. Leave tomorrow's problems until tomorrow.

Arthur Hays Sulzberger was the publisher of the *New York Times* during the Second World War. Because of the world conflict, he found it almost impossible to sleep. He was never able to banish worries from his mind until he adopted as his motto these five words—"one step enough for me"—taken from the hymn "Lead Kindly Light."[2]

> Lead, kindly Light . . .
> Keep Thou my feet; I do not ask to see
> The distant scene; one step enough for me.

God isn't going to let you see the distant scene either. So you might as well quit looking for it. He promises a lamp unto our feet, not a crystal ball into the future.[3] We do not need to know what will happen tomorrow. We only need to know he leads us and "we will find grace to help us when we need it" (Heb. 4:16 NLT).

7

It's a Jungle Out There

The Burden of Hopelessness

He restores my soul.

PSALM 23:3 NKJV

I wonder if you could imagine yourself in a jungle. A dense jungle. A dark jungle. Your friends convinced you it was time for a once-in-a-lifetime trip, and here you are. You paid the fare. You crossed the ocean. You hired the guide and joined the group. And you ventured where you had never ventured before—into the thick, strange world of the jungle.

Sound interesting? Let's take it a step farther. Imagine that you are in the jungle, lost and alone. You paused to lace your boot, and when you looked up, no one was near. You took a chance and went to the right; now you're wondering if the others went to the left. (Or did you go left and they go right?)

Whatever, you are alone. And you have been alone for, well, you don't know how long it has been. Your watch was attached to your pack, and your pack is on the shoulder of the nice guy from New Jersey who volunteered to hold it while you tied your boots. You didn't intend for him to walk off with it. But he did. And here you are, stuck in the middle of nowhere.

You have a problem. First, you were not made for this place. Drop you in the center of avenues and buildings, and you could sniff your way home. But here in sky-blocking foliage? Here in trail-hiding thickets? You are out of your element. You weren't made for this jungle.

What's worse, you aren't equipped. You have no machete. No knife.

No matches. No flares. No food. You aren't equipped, but now you are trapped—and you haven't a clue how to get out.

Sound like fun to you? Me either. Before moving on, let's pause and ask how you would feel. Given such circumstances, what emotions would surface? With what thoughts would you wrestle?

Fear? Of course you would.

Anxiety? To say the least.

Anger? I could understand that. (You'd like to get your hands on those folks who convinced you to take this trip.)

But most of all, what about hopelessness? No idea where to turn. No hunch what to do. Who could blame you for sitting on a log (better check for snakes first), burying your face in your hands, and thinking, *I'll never get out of here.* You have no direction, no equipment, no hope.

Can you freeze frame that emotion for a moment? Can you sense, for just a second, how it feels to be out of your element? Out of solutions? Out of ideas and energy? Can you imagine, just for a moment, how it feels to be out of hope?

If you can, you can relate to many people in this world.

For many people, life is—well, life is a jungle. Not a jungle of trees and beasts. Would that it were so simple. Would that our jungles could be cut with a machete or our adversaries trapped in a cage. But our jungles are comprised of the thicker thickets of failing health, broken hearts, and empty wallets. Our forests are framed with hospital walls and divorce courts. We don't hear the screeching of birds or the roaring of lions, but we do hear the complaints of neighbors and the demands of bosses. Our predators are our creditors, and the brush that surrounds us is the rush that exhausts us.

It's a jungle out there.

And for some, even for many, hope is in short supply. Hopelessness is an odd bag. Unlike the others, it isn't full. It is empty, and its emptiness creates the burden. Unzip the top and examine all the pockets. Turn it upside down and shake it hard. The bag of hopelessness is painfully empty.

Not a very pretty picture, is it? Let's see if we can brighten it up. We've imagined the emotions of being lost; you think we can do the same with being rescued? What would it take to restore your hope? What would you need to reenergize your journey?

Though the answers are abundant, three come quickly to mind.

The first would be a person. Not just any person. You don't need someone equally confused. You need someone who knows the way out.

And from him you need some vision. You need someone to lift your spirits. You need someone to look you in the face and say, "This isn't the end. Don't give up. There is a better place than this. And I'll lead you there."

And, perhaps most important, you need direction. If you have only a person but no renewed vision, all you have is company. If he has a vision but no direction, you have a dreamer for company. But if you have a person with direction—who can take you from this place to the right place—ah, then you have one who can restore your hope.

Or, to use David's words, "He restores my soul."

Our Shepherd majors in restoring hope to the soul. Whether you are a lamb lost on a craggy ledge or a city slicker alone in a deep jungle, everything changes when your rescuer appears.

Your loneliness diminishes, because you have fellowship.

Your despair decreases, because you have vision.

Your confusion begins to lift, because you have direction.

Please note: You haven't left the jungle. The trees still eclipse the sky, and the thorns still cut the skin. Animals lurk and rodents scurry. The jungle is still a jungle. It hasn't changed, but you have. You have changed because you have hope. And you have hope because you have met someone who can lead you out.

Your Shepherd knows that you were not made for this place. He knows you are not equipped for this place. So he has come to guide you out.

He has come to restore your soul. He is the perfect one to do so.

He has the right vision. He reminds you that "you are like foreigners and strangers in this world" (1 Pet. 2:11). And he urges you to lift your eyes from the jungle around you to the heaven above you. "Don't shuffle along, eyes to the ground, absorbed with the things right in front of you. Look up, and be alert to what is going on around Christ. . . . See things from his perspective" (Col. 3:2 MSG).

David said it this way, "I lift up my eyes to the hills—where does my help come from? My help comes from the LORD, the Maker of heaven and earth. He will not let your foot slip—he who watches over you will not slumber. . . . The LORD watches over you . . . the sun will not harm you by day, nor the moon by night. The LORD will keep you from all harm—he will watch over your life" (Ps. 121:1–7 NIV).

God, your rescuer, has the right vision. He also has the right direction. He made the boldest claim in the history of man when he declared, "I am the way" (John 14:6). People wondered if the claim was accurate. He answered their questions by cutting a path through the underbrush of sin and death . . . and escaping alive. He's the only One who ever did. And he is the only One who can help you and me do the same.

He has the right vision: He has seen the homeland. He has the right directions: He has cut the path. But most of all, he is the right person, for he is our God. Who knows the jungle better than the One who made it? And who knows the pitfalls of the path better than the One who has walked it?

The story is told of a man on an African safari deep in the jungle. The guide before him had a machete and was whacking away the tall weeds and thick underbrush. The traveler, wearied and hot, asked in frustration, "Where are we? Do you know where you are taking me? Where is the path?!" The seasoned guide stopped and looked back at the man and replied, "I am the path."

We ask the same questions, don't we? We ask God, "Where are you taking me? Where is the path?" And he, like the guide, doesn't tell us. Oh, he may give us a hint or two, but that's all. If he did, would we understand? Would we comprehend our location? No, like the traveler, we are unacquainted with this jungle. So rather than give us an answer, Jesus gives us a far greater gift. He gives us himself.

Does he remove the jungle? No, the vegetation is still thick.

Does he purge the predators? No, danger still lurks.

Jesus doesn't give hope by changing the jungle; he restores our hope by giving us himself. And he has promised to stay until the very end. "I am with you always, to the very end of the age" (Matt. 28:20 NIV).

We need that reminder. We all need that reminder. For all of us need hope.

Some of you don't need it right now. Your jungle has become a meadow and your journey a delight. If such is the case, congratulations. But remember—we do not know what tomorrow holds. We do not know where this road will lead. You may be one turn from a cemetery, from a hospital bed, from an empty house. You may be a bend in the road from a jungle.

And though you don't need your hope restored today, you may tomorrow. And you need to know to whom to turn.

Or perhaps you do need hope today. You know you were not made for this place. You know you are not equipped. You want someone to lead you out.

If so, call out for your Shepherd. He knows your voice. And he's just waiting for your request.

8

A Heavenly Exchange

The Burden of Guilt

He leads me in the paths of righteousness for His name's sake.

PSALM 23:3 NKJV

A friend organized a Christmas cookie swap for our church office staff. The plan was simple. Price of admission was a tray of cookies. Your tray entitled you to pick cookies from the other trays. You could leave with as many cookies as you brought.

Sounds simple, if you know how to cook. But what if you can't? What if you can't tell a pan from a pot? What if, like me, you are culinarily challenged? What if you're as comfortable in an apron as a bodybuilder in a tutu? If such is the case, you've got a problem.

Such was the case, and I had a problem. I had no cookies to bring; hence I would have no place at the party. I would be left out, turned away, shunned, eschewed, and dismissed. (Are you feeling sorry for me yet?)

This was my plight.

And, forgive me for bringing it up, but your plight's even worse.

God is planning a party . . . a party to end all parties. Not a cookie party, but a feast. Not giggles and chitchat in the conference room, but wide-eyed wonder in the throne room of God.

Yes, the guestlist is impressive. Your question to Jonah about undergoing a gut check in a fish gut? You'll be able to ask him. But more impressive than the names of the guests is the nature of the guests. No egos, no power plays. Guilt, shame, and sorrow will be checked at the gate. Disease, death, and depression will be the Black Plagues of a distant past. What we now see daily, there we will never see.

And what we now see vaguely, there we will see clearly. We will see God. Not by faith. Not through the eyes of Moses or Abraham or David. Not via Scripture or sunsets or summer rains. We will see not God's work or words, but we will see him! For he is not the host of the party; he is the party. His goodness is the banquet. His voice is the music. His radiance is the light, and his love is the endless topic of discussion.

There is only one hitch. The price of admission is somewhat steep. In order to come to the party, you need to be righteous. Not good. Not decent. Not a taxpayer or churchgoer.

Citizens of heaven are righteous. R-i-g-h-t.

All of us *occasionally* do what is right. A few *predominantly* do what is right. But do any of us *always* do what is right? According to Paul we don't. "There is none righteous, no, not one" (Rom. 3:10 NKJV).

Paul is adamant about this. He goes on to say, "No one anywhere has kept on doing what is right; not one" (Rom. 3:12 TLB).

Some may beg to differ. "I'm not perfect, Max, but I'm better than most folks. I've led a good life. I don't break the rules. I don't break hearts. I help people. I like people. Compared to others, I think I could say I'm a righteous person."

I used to try that one on my mother. She'd tell me my room wasn't clean, and I'd ask her to go with me to my brother's room. His was always messier than mine. "See, my room is clean; just look at his."

Never worked. She'd walk me down the hall to her room. When it came to tidy rooms, my mom was righteous. Her closet was just right. Her bed was just right. Her bathroom was just right. Compared to hers, my room was, well, just wrong. She would show me her room and say, "This is what I mean by clean."

God does the same. He points to himself and says, "This is what I mean by righteousness."

Righteousness is who God is.

"Our God and Savior Jesus Christ does what is right" (2 Pet. 1:1).

"God is a righteous judge" (Ps. 7:11 NIV).

"The LORD is righteous, he loves justice" (Ps. 11:7 NIV).

God's righteousness "endures forever" (Ps. 112:3 NIV) and "reaches to the skies" (Ps. 71:19 NIV).

Isaiah described God as "a righteous God and a Savior" (Isa. 45:21 NIV).

On the eve of his death, Jesus began his prayer with the words "Righteous Father" (John 17:25 NIV).

Get the point? God is righteous. His decrees are righteous (Rom. 1:32). His judgment is righteous (Rom. 2:5). His requirements are righteous (Rom. 8:4). His acts are righteous (Dan. 9:16). Daniel declared, "Our God is right in everything he does" (Dan. 9:14).

God is never wrong. He has never rendered a wrong decision, experienced the wrong attitude, taken the wrong path, said the wrong thing, or acted the wrong way. He is never too late or too early, too loud or too soft, too fast or too slow. He has always been and always will be right. He is righteous.

When it comes to righteousness, God runs the table without so much as a bank shot. And when it comes to righteousness, we don't know which end of the cue stick to hold. Hence, our plight.

Will God, who is righteous, spend eternity with those who are not? Would Harvard admit a third-grade dropout? If it did, the act might be benevolent, but it wouldn't be right. If God accepted the unrighteous, the invitation would be even nicer, but would he be right? Would he be right to overlook our sins? Lower his standards? No. He wouldn't be right. And if God is anything, he is right.

He told Isaiah that righteousness would be his plumb line, the standard by which his house is measured (Isa. 28:17). If we are unrighteous, then, we are left in the hallway with no cookies. Or to use Paul's analogy, "we're sinners, every one of us, in the same sinking boat with everybody else" (Rom. 3:19 MSG). Then what are we to do?

Carry a load of guilt? Many do. So many do.

What if our spiritual baggage were visible? Suppose the luggage in our hearts was literal luggage on the street. You know what you'd see most of all? Suitcases of guilt. Bags bulging with binges, blowups, and compromises. Look around you. The fellow in the gray-flannel suit? He's dragging a decade of regrets. The kid with the baggy jeans and nose ring? He'd give anything to retract the words he said to his mother. But he can't. So he tows them along. The woman in the business suit? Looks as if she could run for senator? She'd rather run for help, but she can't run at all. Not hauling that carpetbag of cagmag everywhere she goes.

Listen. The weight of weariness pulls you down. Self-reliance misleads you. Disappointments discourage you. Anxiety plagues you. But guilt? Guilt consumes you.

So what do we do? Our Lord is right, and we are wrong. His party is for the guiltless, and we are anything but. What do we do?

I can tell you what I did. I confessed my need. Remember my cookie dilemma? This is the e-mail I sent to the whole staff. "I can't cook, so I can't be at the party."

Did any of the assistants have mercy on me? No.

Did any of the staff have mercy on me? No.

Did any of the Supreme Court justices have mercy upon me? No.

But a saintly sister in the church did have mercy on me. How she heard of my problem, I do not know. Perhaps my name found its way on an emergency prayer list. But I do know this. Only moments before the celebration, I was given a gift, a plate of cookies, twelve circles of kindness.

And by virtue of that gift, I was privileged a place at the party.

Did I go? You bet your cookies I did. Like a prince carrying a crown on a pillow, I carried my gift into the room, set it on the table, and stood tall. And because some good soul heard my plea, I was given a place at the table.

And because God hears your plea, you'll be given the same. Only, he did more—oh, so much more—than bake cookies for you.

It was, at once, history's most beautiful and most horrible moment. Jesus stood in the tribunal of heaven. Sweeping a hand over all creation, he pleaded, "Punish me for their mistakes. See the murderer? Give me his penalty. The adulteress? I'll take her shame. The bigot, the liar, the thief? Do to me what you would do to them. Treat me as you would a sinner."

And God did. "For Christ died for sins once for all, the righteous for the unrighteous, to bring you to God" (1 Pet. 3:18 NIV).

Yes, righteousness is what God is, and, yes, righteousness is what we are not, and, yes, righteousness is what God requires. But "God has a way to make people right with him" (Rom. 3:21).

David said it like this: "He leads me in the paths of righteousness" (Ps. 23:3 NKJV).

The path of righteousness is a narrow, winding trail up a steep hill. At the top of the hill is a cross. At the base of the cross are bags. Countless bags full of innumerable sins. Calvary is the compost pile for guilt. Would you like to leave yours there as well?

One final thought about the Christmas cookie party. Did everyone know I didn't cook the cookies? If they didn't, I told them. I told them I was present by virtue of someone else's work. My only contribution was my own confession.

We'll be saying the same for eternity.

9

Get Over Yourself

The Burden of Arrogance

For His name's sake . . .

PSALM 23:3 NKJV

Humility is such an elusive virtue. Once you think you have it, you don't, or you wouldn't think you did. You've heard the story of the boy who received the "Most Humble" badge and had it taken away because he wore it?

Something similar happened to me just the other morning. I had retreated to a nearby town to work on this book. The village is a perfect hideaway; it is quaint, quiet, and has great food.

I'd gone to a café for breakfast when I noticed that people were staring at me. As I parked, two fellows turned and looked in my direction. A woman did a double take as I entered, and several patrons looked up as I passed. When I took my seat, the waitress gave me a menu but not before she'd given me a good study.

Why the attention? Couldn't be my fly; I was wearing sweats. After some thought I took the mature posture and assumed they recognized me from my book jackets. *Why, this must be a town of readers. And,* I shrugged to myself, *they know a good author when they see one.* My appreciation for the village only increased.

Giving a smile to the folks at the other tables, I set about to enjoy my meal. When I walked to the cash register, the heads turned again. *I'm sure Steinbeck had the same problem.* The woman who took my money started to say something but then paused. Overwhelmed, I guessed.

It was only when I stopped in the rest room that I saw the real reason for the attention—a ribbon of dried blood on my chin. My patch job on the shaving nick hadn't worked, and I was left with my own turkey wattle.

So much for feeling famous. They probably thought I was an escapee from a Texas prison.

Oh, the things God does to keep us humble. He does it for our own good, you know. Would you set a saddle on the back of your five-year-old? Would God let you be saddled with arrogance? No way.

This is one piece of luggage God hates. He doesn't dislike arrogance. He doesn't disapprove of arrogance. He's not unfavorably disposed toward arrogance. God hates arrogance. What a meal of maggots does for our stomach, human pride does for God's.

"I hate pride and arrogance" (Prov. 8:13 NIV).

"The LORD despises pride" (Prov. 16:5 NLT).

God says, "Do nothing out of . . . vain conceit" (Phil. 2:3 NIV). And, "Do not let arrogance come out of your mouth" (1 Sam. 2:3 NASB). And, in the same way that he gives grace to the humble, "God opposes the proud" (1 Pet. 5:5 NIV). As humility goes before honor, "pride goes . . . before a fall" (Prov. 16:18 NIV).

Ever wonder why churches are powerful in one generation but empty the next? Perhaps the answer is found in Proverbs 15:25: "The LORD will tear down the house of the proud" (NASB).

God hates arrogance. He hates arrogance because we haven't done anything to be arrogant about. Do art critics give awards to the canvas? Is there a Pulitzer for ink? Can you imagine a scalpel growing smug after a successful heart transplant? Of course not. They are only tools, so they get no credit for the accomplishments.

And the message of the Twenty-third Psalm is that we have nothing to be proud about either. We have rest, salvation, blessings, and a home in heaven—and we did nothing to earn any of it. Who did? Who did the work? The answer threads through the psalm like a silk thread through pearls.

"He makes me . . ."

"He leads me . . ."

"He restores my soul . . ."

"You are with me . . ."

"Your rod and Your staff . . . comfort me . . ."

"You prepare a table . . ."

"You anoint my head . . ."

We may be the canvas, the paper, or the scalpel, but we are not the ones who deserve the applause. And just to make sure we get the point, right smack-dab in the middle of the poem, David declares who does. The shepherd leads his sheep, not for our names' sake, but "for His name's sake."

Why does God have anything to do with us? *For his name's sake.* No other name on the marquee. No other name up in lights. No other name on the front page. This is all done for God's glory.

Why? What's the big deal? Does God have an ego problem?

No, but we do. We are about as responsible with applause as I was with the cake I won in the first grade. In the grand finale of the musical chairs competition, guess who had a seat? And guess what the little red-headed, freckle-faced boy won? A tender, moist coconut cake. And guess what the boy wanted to do that night in one sitting? Eat the whole thing! Not half of it. Not a piece of it. All of it! After all, I'd won it.

But you know what my folks did? They rationed the cake. They gave me only what I could handle. Knowing that today's binge is tomorrow's bellyache, they made sure I didn't get sick on my success.

God does the same. He takes the cake. He takes the credit, not because he needs it, but because he knows we can't handle it. We aren't content with a bite of adulation; we tend to swallow it all. It messes with our systems. The praise swells our heads and shrinks our brains, and pretty soon we start thinking we had something to do with our survival. Pretty soon we forget we were made out of dirt and rescued from sin.

Pretty soon we start praying like the fellow at the religious caucus: "God, I thank you that the world has people like me. The man on the corner needs welfare—I don't. The prostitute on the street has AIDS—I don't. The drunk at the bar needs alcohol—I don't. The gay caucus needs morality—I don't. I thank you that the world has people like me."

Fortunately, there was a man in the same meeting who had deflected all the applause. Too contrite even to look to the skies, he bowed and prayed, "God, have mercy on me, a sinner. Like my brother on welfare, I'm dependent on your grace. Like my sister with AIDS, I'm infected with mistakes. Like my friend who drinks, I need something to ease my pain. And as you love and give direction to the gay, grant some to me as well. Have mercy on me, a sinner."

After telling a story like that, Jesus said, "I tell you, when this man went home, he was right with God, but the Pharisee was not. All who make themselves great will be made humble, but all who make themselves humble will be made great" (Luke 18:14).

With the same intensity that he hates arrogance, God loves humility. The Jesus who said, "I am gentle and humble in heart" (Matt. 11:29 NASB) loves those who are gentle and humble in heart. "Though the LORD is supreme, he takes care of those who are humble" (Ps. 138:6). God says, "I live with people who are . . . humble" (Isa. 57:15). He also says, "To this one I will look, to him who is humble and contrite" (Isa. 66:2 NASB). And to the humble, God gives great treasures:

He gives honor: "Humility goes before honor" (Prov. 15:33 NRSV).

He gives wisdom: "With the humble is wisdom" (Prov. 11:2 NASB).

He gives direction: "He teaches the humble His way" (Ps. 25:9 NASB).

And most significantly, he gives grace: "God . . . gives grace to the humble" (1 Pet. 5:5).

And this reassurance: "He crowns the humble with salvation" (Ps. 149:4 NIV).

The mightiest of the saints were known for their humility. Though Moses had served as prince of Egypt and emancipator of the slaves, the Bible says, "Moses was . . . more humble than anyone else" (Num. 12:3 NIV).

The apostle Paul was saved through a personal visit from Jesus. He was carried into the heavens and had the ability to raise the dead. But when he introduced himself, he mentioned none of these. He simply said, "I, Paul, am God's slave" (Titus 1:1 MSG).

John the Baptist was a blood relative of Jesus and the first evangelist in history, but he is remembered in Scripture as the one who resolved, "He must increase, but I must decrease" (John 3:30 NKJV).

God loves humility. Could that be the reason he offers so many tips on cultivating it? May I, ahem, humbly articulate a few?

1. Assess yourself honestly. Humility isn't the same as low self-esteem. Being humble doesn't mean you think you have nothing to offer; it means you know exactly what you have to offer and no more. "Don't cherish exaggerated ideas of yourself or your importance, but try to have a sane estimate of your capabilities by the light of the faith that God has given to you" (Rom. 12:3 PHILLIPS).

2. Don't take success too seriously. Scripture gives this warning: "When your . . . silver and gold increase, . . . your heart will become proud" (Deut. 8:13–14). Counteract this pride with reminders of the brevity of life and the frailty of wealth.

Ponder your success and count your money in a cemetery, and remember that neither of the two is buried with you. "People come into this world with nothing, and when they die they leave with nothing" (Eccles. 5:15). I saw a reminder of this in a cemetery. Parked next to the entrance was a nice recreational boat with a For Sale sign. You had to wonder if the fisherman realized he couldn't take it with him.

3. *Celebrate the significance of others.* "In humility consider others better than yourselves" (Phil. 2:3 NIV). Columnist Rick Reilly gave this advice to rookie professional athletes: "Stop thumping your chest. The line blocked, the quarterback threw you a perfect spiral while getting his head knocked off, and the *good* receiver blew the double coverage. Get over yourself."[1]

The truth is, every touchdown in life is a team effort. Applaud your teammates. An elementary-age boy came home from the tryouts for the school play. "Mommy, Mommy," he announced, "I got a part. I've been chosen to sit in the audience and clap and cheer." When you have a chance to clap and cheer, do you take it? If you do, your head is starting to fit your hat size.

4. *Don't demand your own parking place.* This was the instruction of Jesus to his followers: "Go sit in a seat that is not important. When the host comes to you, he may say, 'Friend, move up here to a more important place.' Then all the other guests will respect you" (Luke 14:10).

Demanding respect is like chasing a butterfly. Chase it, and you'll never catch it. Sit still, and it may light on your shoulder. The French philosopher Blaise Pascal asked, "Do you wish people to speak well of you? Then never speak well of yourself."[2] Maybe that's why the Bible says, "Don't praise yourself. Let someone else do it" (Prov. 27:2).

5. *Never announce your success before it occurs.* Or as one of the kings of Israel said, "One who puts on his armor should not boast like one who takes it off" (1 Kings 20:11 NIV). Charles Spurgeon trained many young ministers. On one occasion a student stepped up to preach with great confidence but failed miserably. He came down, humbled and

meek. Spurgeon told him, "If you had gone up as you came down, you would have come down as you went up."[3] If humility precedes an event, then confidence may follow.

6. Speak humbly. "Let no arrogance come from your mouth" (1 Sam. 2:3 NKJV). Don't be cocky. People aren't impressed with your opinions. Take a tip from Benjamin Franklin.

> [I developed] the habit of expressing myself in terms of modest diffidence, never using when I advance any thing that may possibly be disputed, the words certainly, undoubtedly, or any others that give the air of positiveness to an opinion; but rather I say, I conceive or I apprehend a thing to be so or so. . . . This habit I believe has been a great advantage to me.[4]

It would be a great advantage to us as well.

One last thought to foster humility.

7. Live at the foot of the cross. Paul said, "The cross of our Lord Jesus Christ is my only reason for bragging" (Gal. 6:14). Do you feel a need for affirmation? Does your self-esteem need attention? You don't need to drop names or show off. You need only pause at the base of the cross and be reminded of this: The maker of the stars would rather die for you than live without you. And that is a fact. So if you need to brag, brag about that.

And check your chin occasionally.

10

I Will Lead You Home

The Burden of the Grave

Yea, though I walk through the valley of the shadow of death, I will fear no evil; for You are with me; Your rod and Your staff, they comfort me.

PSALM 23:4 NKJV

Summer in ancient Palestine. A woolly bunch of bobbing heads follow the shepherd out of the gate. The morning sun has scarcely crested the horizon, and he is already leading his flock. Like every other day, he guides them through the gate and out into the fields. But unlike most days, the shepherd will not return home tonight. He will not rest on his bed, and the sheep will not sleep in their fenced-in pasture. This is the day the shepherd takes the sheep to the high country. Today he leads his flock to the mountains.

He has no other choice. Springtime grazing has left his pasture bare, so he must seek new fields. With no companion other than his sheep and no desire other than their welfare, he leads them to the deep grass of the hillsides. The shepherd and his flock will be gone for weeks, perhaps months. They will stay well into the autumn, until the grass is gone and the chill is unbearable.

Not all shepherds make this journey. The trek is long. The path is dangerous. Poisonous plants can infect the flock. Wild animals can attack the flock. There are narrow trails and dark valleys. Some shepherds choose the security of the barren pasture below.

But the good shepherd doesn't. He knows the path. He has walked this trail many times. Besides, he is prepared. Staff in hand

and rod attached to his belt. With his staff he will nudge the flock; with his rod he will protect and lead the flock. He will lead them to the mountains.

David understood this annual pilgrimage. Before he led Israel, he led sheep. And could his time as a shepherd be the inspiration behind one of the greatest verses in the Bible? "Yea, though I walk through the valley of the shadow of death, I will fear no evil; for You are with me; Your rod and Your staff, they comfort me" (Ps. 23:4 NKJV).

For what the shepherd does with the flock, our Shepherd will do with us. He will lead us to the high country. When the pasture is bare down here, God will lead us up there. He will guide us through the gate, out of the flatlands, and up the path of the mountain.

As one shepherd writes:

> Every mountain has its valleys. Its sides are scarred by deep ravines and gulches and draws. And the best route to the top is always through these valleys.
>
> Any sheepman familiar with the high country knows this. He leads his flock gently, but persistently up the paths that wind through the dark valleys.[1]

Someday our Shepherd will do the same with us. He will take us to the mountain by way of the valley. He will guide us to his house through the valley of the shadow of death.

Many years ago when I lived in Miami, our church office received a call from a nearby funeral home. A man had identified the body of an indigent as his brother and wanted a memorial service. He didn't know any ministers in the area. Would we say a few words? The senior minister and I agreed. When we arrived, the brother of the deceased had selected a text from a Spanish Bible: "Yea, though I walk through the valley of the shadow of death, I will fear no evil; for You are with me; Your rod and Your staff, they comfort me" (Ps. 23:4 NKJV).

He needed assurance that, though his brother had lived alone, he did not die alone. And for that assurance, he turned to this verse. You've likely done the same.

If you've attended a memorial service, you've heard the words. If you've walked through a cemetery, you've read them. They're quoted at the gravesides of paupers, carved on the headstones of kings. Those who know nothing of the Bible know this part of the Bible. Those who quote no scripture can remember this scripture, the one about the valley and the shadow and the shepherd.

Why? Why are these words so treasured? Why is this verse so beloved? I can think of a couple of reasons. By virtue of this psalm, David grants us two important reminders that can help us surrender our fear of the grave.

We all have to face it. In a life marked by doctor appointments, dentist appointments, and school appointments, there is one appointment that none of us will miss, the appointment with death. "Everyone must die once, and after that be judged by God" (Heb. 9:27 TEV). Oh, how we'd like to change that verse. Just a word or two would suffice. "*Nearly* everyone must die . . ." or "*Everyone but me* must die . . ." or "*Everyone who forgets to eat right and take vitamins* must die . . ." But those are not God's words. In his plan everyone must die, even those who eat right and take their vitamins.

I could have gone all day without reminding you of that. We do our best to avoid the topic. One wise man, however, urges us to face it squarely: "We all must die, and everyone living should think about this" (Eccles. 7:2). Solomon isn't promoting a morbid obsession with death. He is reminding us to be honest about the inevitable.

Moses gave the same exhortation. In the only psalm attributed to his pen, he prayed, "Teach us how short our lives really are so that we may be wise" (Ps. 90:12).

The wise remember the brevity of life. Exercise may buy us a few more heartbeats. Medicine may grant us a few more breaths. But in the end, there is an end. And the best way to face life is to be honest about death.

David was. He may have slain Goliath, but he had no illusions about sidestepping the giant of death. And though his first reminder sobers us, his second reminder encourages us: *We don't have to face death alone.*

Don't miss the shift in David's vocabulary. Up to this point, you and I have been the audience and God has been the topic. "The LORD is my shepherd." "He makes me to lie down." "He leads me beside the still waters." "He restores my soul." "He leads me in the paths of righteousness." For the first three verses, David speaks to us and God listens.

But suddenly in verse four, David speaks to God and we listen. It's as if David's face, which was on us, now lifts toward God. His poem becomes a prayer. Rather than speak to us, he speaks to the Good Shepherd. "You are with me; Your rod and Your staff, they comfort me."

David's implied message is subtle but crucial. Don't face death without facing God. Don't even speak of death without speaking to God. He and he alone can guide you through the valley. Others may speculate or aspire, but only God knows the way to get you home. And only God is committed to getting you there safely.

Years after David wrote these words, another Bethlehem Shepherd would say: "There are many rooms in my Father's house; I would not tell you this if it were not true. I am going there to prepare a place for you. After I go and prepare a place for you, I will come back and take you to be with me so that you may be where I am" (John 14:2–3).

Note the promise of Jesus. "I will come back and take you to be with me." He pledges to take us home. He does not delegate this task. He may send missionaries to teach you, angels to protect you, teachers to guide you, singers to inspire you, and physicians to heal you, but he sends no one to take you. He reserves this job for himself. "I will come back and take you home." He is your personal Shepherd. And he is personally responsible to lead you home. And because he is present when any of his sheep dies, you can say what David said, "I will fear no evil."

When my daughters were younger, we enjoyed many fun afternoons in the swimming pool. Just like all of us, they had to overcome their fears in order to swim. One of the final fears they had to face was the fear of the deep. It's one thing to swim on the surface; it's another to plunge down to the bottom. I mean, who knows what kind of dragons and serpents dwell in the depths of an eight-foot pool? You and I know there is no evil to fear, but a six-year-old doesn't. A child feels the same way about the deep that you and I feel about death. We aren't sure what awaits us down there.

I didn't want my daughters to be afraid of the deep end, so with each I played Shamu the whale. My daughter would be the trainer. I would be Shamu. She would pinch her nose and put her arm around my neck, then down we would go. Deep, deep, deep until we could touch the bottom of the pool. Then up we would explode, breaking the surface. After several plunges they realized they had nothing to fear. They feared no evil. Why? Because I was with them.

And when God calls us into the deep valley of death, he will be with us. Dare we think that he would abandon us in the moment of death? Would a father force his child to swim the deep alone? Would the shepherd require his sheep to journey to the highlands alone? Of course not. Would God require his child to journey to eternity alone? Absolutely not! He is with you!

What God said to Moses, he says to you: "My Presence will go with you, and I will give you rest" (Exod. 33:14 NIV).

What God said to Jacob, he says to you: "I am with you and will watch over you wherever you go" (Gen. 28:15 NIV).

What God said to Joshua, he says to you: "As I was with Moses, so I will be with you; I will never leave you nor forsake you" (Josh. 1:5 NIV).

What God said to the nation of Israel, he says to you: "When you pass through the waters, I will be with you" (Isa. 43:2 NIV).

The Good Shepherd is with you. And because he is with you, you can say what David said: "I will fear no evil; for You are with me; Your rod and Your staff, they comfort me."

Years ago a chaplain in the French army used the Twenty-third Psalm to encourage soldiers before battle. He would urge them to repeat the opening clause of the psalm, ticking it off, one finger at a time. The little finger represented the word *the;* the ring finger represented the word *LORD;* the middle finger, *is;* the index finger, *my;* and the thumb, *shepherd*. Then he asked every soldier to write the words on the palm of his hand and to repeat the verse whenever he needed strength.

The chaplain placed special emphasis on the message of the index finger—*my*. He reminded the soldiers that God is a personal shepherd with a personal mission—to get them home safely.

Did the chaplain's words find their mark? In the life of one man they did. After a battle one of the young soldiers was found dead, his right hand clutching the index finger of the left. "The LORD is my shepherd . . ."[2]

I pray that your final hours will find you clutching the same hope.

11

When Mourning Comes

The Burden of Grief

Though I walk through the valley of the shadow of death . . .

PSALM 23:4 NKJV

Carlos Andres Baisdon-Niño lay down with his favorite Bible storybook. He began with the first chapter and turned every page until the end. When he finished, he blew his good-night kisses to Mami and Papi, to his three *"niñas,"* and then, as always, he blew one to Papa Dios. He closed his eyes, drifted off to sleep, and awoke in heaven.

Carlos was three years old.

When Tim and Betsa, his parents, and I met to plan the funeral, they wanted me to watch a video of Carlos. "You've got to see him dancing," Tim told me. One look and I could see why. What little Carlos did to the rhythm of a Latin song can't be described with words. He shook from top to bottom. His feet moved, his hands bounced, his head swayed. You got the impression that his heart rate had switched over to his native Colombian beat.

We laughed, the three of us did. And in the laughter, for just a moment, Carlos was with us. For just a moment there was no leukemia, syringes, blankets, or chemotherapy. There was no stone to carve or grave to dig. There was just Carlos. And Carlos was just dancing.

But then the video stopped, and so did the laughter. And this mom and dad resumed their slow walk through the valley of the shadow of death.

Are you passing through the same shadow? Is this book being held by the same hands that touched the cold face of a friend? And the eyes that fall upon this page, have they also fallen upon the breathless figure of a husband, wife, or child? Are you passing through the valley? If not, this chapter may seem unnecessary. Feel free to move on—it will be here when you need it.

If so, however, you know that the black bag of sorrow is hard to bear.

It's hard to bear because not everyone understands your grief. They did at first. They did at the funeral. They did at the graveside. But they don't now; they don't understand. Grief lingers.

As silently as a cloud slides between you and the afternoon sun, memories drift between you and joy, leaving you in a chilly shadow. No warning. No notice. Just a whiff of the cologne he wore or a verse of the song she loved, and you are saying good-bye all over again.

Why won't the sorrow leave you alone?

Because you buried more than a person. You buried some of yourself. Wasn't it John Donne who said, "Any man's death diminishes me"? It's as if the human race resides on a huge trampoline. The movements of one can be felt by all. And the closer the relationship, the more profound the exit. When someone you love dies, it affects you.

It affects your dreams.

Some years ago my wife and I served with other missionaries in Rio de Janeiro, Brazil. Our team consisted of several young couples who, by virtue of being far away from home, became very close. We rejoiced greatly when two of our team members, Marty and Angela, announced that she was pregnant with their first child.

The pregnancy was difficult, however, and the joy became concern. Angela was told to stay in bed, and we were urged to stay in prayer. We did. And the Lord answered our prayers, though not as we desired. The baby died in the womb.

I've never forgotten Marty's comment. "More than a baby died, Max. A dream died."

Why does grief linger? Because you are dealing with more than memories—you are dealing with unlived tomorrows. You're not just battling sorrow—you're battling disappointment. You're also battling anger.

It may be on the surface. It may subterranean. It may be a flame. It may be a blowtorch. But anger lives in sorrow's house. Anger at self. Anger at life. Anger at the military or the hospital or the highway system. But most of all, anger at God. Anger that takes the form of the three-letter question—why? Why him? Why her? Why now? Why us?

You and I both know I can't answer that question. Only God knows the reasons behind his actions. But here is a key truth on which we can stand.

Our God is a good God.

"You are good, LORD. The LORD is good and right" (Ps. 25:7–8).

"Taste and see that the LORD is good" (Ps. 34:8 NIV).

God is a good God. We must begin here. Though we don't understand his actions, we can trust his heart.

God does only what is good. But how can death be good? Some mourners don't ask this question. When the quantity of years has outstripped the quality of years, we don't ask how death can be good.

But the father of the dead teenager does. The thirty-year-old widow does. The parents of Carlos did. My friends in Rio did. How could death be good?

Part of the answer may be found in Isaiah 57:1–2: "Good people are taken away, but no one understands. Those who do right are being taken away from evil and are given peace. Those who live as God wants find rest in death."

Death is God's way of taking people away from evil. From what kind of evil? An extended disease? An addiction? A dark season of rebellion? We don't know. But we know that no person lives one day more or less than God intends. "All the days planned for me were written in your book before I was one day old" (Ps. 139:16).

But her days here were so few . . .

His life was so brief . . .

To us it seems that way. We speak of a short life, but compared to eternity, who has a long one? A person's days on earth may appear as a drop in the ocean. Yours and mine may seem like a thimbleful. But compared to the Pacific of eternity, even the years of Methuselah filled no more than a glass. James was not speaking just to the young when he said, "Your life is like a mist. You can see it for a short time, but then it goes away" (James 4:14).

In God's plan every life is long enough and every death is timely. And though you and I might wish for a longer life, God knows better.

And—this is important—though you and I may wish a longer life for our loved ones, they don't. Ironically, the first to accept God's decision of death is the one who dies.

While we are shaking heads in disbelief, they are lifting hands in worship. While we are mourning at a grave, they are marveling at heaven. While we are questioning God, they are praising God.

But, Max, what of those who die with no faith? My husband never prayed. My grandpa never worshiped. My mother never opened a Bible, much less her heart. What about the one who never believed?

How do we know he didn't?

Who among us is privy to a person's final thoughts? Who among us knows what transpires in those final moments? Are you sure no prayer was offered? Eternity can bend the proudest knees. Could a person stare into the yawning canyon of death without whispering a plea for mercy? And could our God, who is partial to the humble, resist it?

He couldn't on Calvary. The confession of the thief on the cross was both a first and final one. But Christ heard it. Christ received it. Maybe you never heard your loved one confess Christ, but who's to say Christ didn't?

We don't know the final thoughts of a dying soul, but we know this. We know our God is a good God. He is "not willing that any should perish but that all should come to repentance" (2 Pet. 3:9 NKJV). He wants your loved one in heaven more than you do. And he usually gets what he wants.

You know what else God wants? He wants you to face your sorrow. Denial and dismissal are not a part of God's grief therapy.

David faced his. When he learned of the death of Saul and Jonathan, David and the entire army tore their clothing, wept aloud, and fasted until sunset. His lament was intense and public. "May there be no dew or rain on the mountains of Gilboa," he mourned, "and may their fields produce no grain. . . . We loved Saul and Jonathan and enjoyed them while they lived. They are together even in death. They were faster than eagles. They were stronger than lions" (2 Sam. 1:21–23).

David not only sang this dirge, he "ordered that the people of Judah be taught this song" (v. 18). Death was not soft-pedaled or passed over. Face it, fight it, question it, or condemn it, but don't deny it. As his son Solomon explained, "There is . . . a time to mourn" (Eccles. 3:1, 4 NIV). Don't heed, but do forgive, those who urge you not to.

God will lead you *through,* not around, the valley of the shadow of death. And, by the way, aren't you glad it's just a shadow?

Dr. Donald Grey Barnhouse told of the occasion of his first wife's death. He and his children were driving home from the burial, overcome with grief. He searched for a word of comfort to offer but could think of nothing. Just then, a large moving van drove by. As it passed, the shadow of the truck swept over the car. An inspiration came to Dr. Barnhouse. He turned to his family and asked, "Children, would you rather be run over by a truck or by its shadow?"

The children said, "Well, of course, Dad, we'd rather be run over by the shadow. That can't hurt us at all."

Dr. Barnhouse explained, "Did you know that two thousand years ago the truck of death ran over the Lord Jesus . . . in order that only its shadow might run over us?"[1]

We face death, but thanks to Jesus, we only face its shadow. And thanks to Jesus, we believe that our loved ones are happy and that the little Carloses of the world are dancing as never before.

12

From Panic to Peace

The Burden of Fear

I will fear no evil.

PSALM 23:4 NKJV

It's the expression of Jesus that puzzles us. We've never seen his face like this.

Jesus smiling, yes.

Jesus weeping, absolutely.

Jesus stern, even that.

But Jesus anguished? Cheeks streaked with tears? Face flooded in sweat? Rivulets of blood dripping from his chin? You remember the night.

> Jesus left the city and went to the Mount of Olives, as he often did, and his followers went with him. When he reached the place, he said to them, "Pray for strength against temptation."
>
> Then Jesus went about a stone's throw away from them. He kneeled down and prayed, "Father, if you are willing, take away this cup of suffering. But do what you want, not what I want." Then an angel from heaven appeared to him to strengthen him. Being full of pain, Jesus prayed even harder. His sweat was like drops of blood falling to the ground. (Luke 22:39–44)

The Bible I carried as a child contained a picture of Jesus in the Garden of Gethsemane. His face was soft, hands calmly folded as he knelt beside a rock and prayed. Jesus seemed peaceful. One reading of the Gospels disrupts that image. Mark says, "Jesus fell to the ground" (Mark 14:35). Matthew tells us Jesus was "very sad and troubled . . . to the point of death" (Matt. 26:37–38). According to Luke, Jesus was "full of pain" (Luke 22:44).

Equipped with those passages, how would you paint this scene? Jesus flat on the ground? Face in the dirt? Extended hands gripping grass? Body rising and falling with sobs? Face as twisted as the olive trees that surround him?

What do we do with this image of Jesus?

Simple. We turn to it when we look the same. We read it when we feel the same; we read it when we feel afraid. For isn't it likely that fear is one of the emotions Jesus felt? One might even argue that fear was the primary emotion. He saw something in the future so fierce, so foreboding that he begged for a change of plans. "Father, if you are willing, take away this cup of suffering" (Luke 22:42).

What causes you to pray the same prayer? Boarding an airplane? Facing a crowd? Public speaking? Taking a job? Taking a spouse? Driving on a highway? The source of your fear may seem small to others. But to you, it freezes your feet, makes your heart pound, and brings blood to your face. That's what happened to Jesus.

He was so afraid that he bled. Doctors describe this condition as hematidrosis. Severe anxiety causes the release of chemicals that break down the capillaries in the sweat glands. When this occurs, sweat comes out tinged with blood.

Jesus was more than anxious; he was afraid. Fear is worry's big brother. If worry is a burlap bag, fear is a trunk of concrete. It wouldn't budge.

How remarkable that Jesus felt such fear. But how kind that he told us about it. We tend to do the opposite. Gloss over our fears. Cover them up. Keep our sweaty palms in our pockets, our nausea and dry mouths a secret. Not so with Jesus. We see no mask of strength. But we do hear a request for strength.

"Father, if you are willing, take away this cup of suffering." The first one to hear his fear is his Father. He could have gone to his mother. He could have confided in his disciples. He could have assembled a prayer meeting. All would have been appropriate, but none were his priority. He went first to his Father.

Oh, how we tend to go everywhere else. First to the bar, to the counselor, to the self-help book or the friend next door. Not Jesus. The first one to hear his fear was his Father in heaven.

A millennium earlier David was urging the fear-filled to do the same. "I will fear no evil." How could David make such a claim? Because he knew where to look. "You are with me; Your rod and Your staff, they comfort me."

Rather than turn to the other sheep, David turned to the Shepherd. Rather than stare at the problems, he stared at the rod and staff. Because he knew where to look, David was able to say, "I will fear no evil."

I know a fellow who has a fear of crowds. When encircled by large groups, his breath grows short, panic surfaces, and he begins to sweat like a sumo wrestler in a sauna. He received some help, curiously, from a golfing buddy.

The two were at a movie theatre, waiting their turn to enter, when fear struck again. The crowd closed in like a forest. He wanted out and out fast. His buddy told him to take a few deep breaths. Then he helped manage the crisis by reminding him of the golf course.

"When you are hitting your ball out of the rough, and you are surrounded by trees, what do you do?"

"I look for an opening."

"You don't stare at the trees?"

"Of course not. I find an opening and focus on hitting the ball through it."

"Do the same in the crowd. When you feel the panic, don't focus on the people; focus on the opening."

Good counsel in golf. Good counsel in life. Rather than focus on the fear, focus on the solution.

That's what Jesus did.

That's what David did.

And that's what the writer of Hebrews urges us to do. "Let us run with endurance the race that is set before us, looking unto Jesus, the author and finisher of our faith" (Heb. 12:1–2 NKJV).

The writer of Hebrews was not a golfer, but he could have been a jogger, for he speaks of a runner and a forerunner. The forerunner is Jesus, the "author and finisher of our faith." He is the author—that is to say he wrote the book on salvation. And he is the finisher—he not only charted the map, he blazed the trail. He is the forerunner, and we are the runners. And we runners are urged to keep our eyes on Jesus.

I'm a runner. More mornings than not I drag myself out of bed and onto the street. I don't run fast. And compared to marathoners, I don't run far. But I run. I run because I don't like cardiologists. Nothing personal, mind you. It's just that I come from a family that keeps them in business. One told my dad he needed to retire. Another opened the chests of both my mom and brother. I'd like to be the one family member who doesn't keep a heart surgeon's number on speed dial.

Since heart disease runs in our family, I run in our neighborhood. As the sun is rising, I am running. And as I am running, my body is groaning. It doesn't want to cooperate. My knee hurts. My hip is stiff. My ankles complain. Sometimes a passerby laughs at my legs, and my ego hurts.

Things hurt. And as things hurt, I've learned that I have three options. Go home. (Denalyn would laugh at me.) Meditate on my hurts until I start imagining I'm having chest pains. (Pleasant thought.) Or I can keep running and watch the sun come up. My trail has just enough easterly bend to give me a front-row seat for God's morning miracle. If I watch God's world go from dark to golden, guess what? The same happens to my attitude. The pain passes and the joints loosen, and before I know it, the run is half over and life ain't half bad. Everything improves as I fix my eyes on the sun.

Wasn't that the counsel of the Hebrew epistle—"looking unto Jesus"? What was the focus of David? "You are with me; Your rod and Your staff, they comfort me."

How did Jesus endure the terror of the crucifixion? He went first to the Father with his fears. He modeled the words of Psalm 56:3: "When I am afraid, I put my trust in you" (NLT).

Do the same with yours. Don't avoid life's Gardens of Gethsemane. Enter them. Just don't enter them alone. And while there, be honest. Pounding the ground is permitted. Tears are allowed. And if you sweat blood, you won't be the first. Do what Jesus did; open your heart.

And be specific. Jesus was. "Take *this* cup," he prayed. Give God the number of the flight. Tell him the length of the speech. Share the details of the job transfer. He has plenty of time. He also has plenty of compassion.

He doesn't think your fears are foolish or silly. He won't tell you to "buck up" or "get tough." He's been where you are. He knows how you feel.

And he knows what you need. That's why we punctuate our prayers as Jesus did. "If you are willing . . ."

Was God willing? Yes and no. He didn't take away the cross, but he took the fear. God didn't still the storm, but he calmed the sailor.

Who's to say he won't do the same for you?

"Do not be anxious about anything, but in everything, by prayer and petition, with thanksgiving, present your requests to God" (Phil. 4:6 NIV).

Don't measure the size of the mountain; talk to the One who can move it. Instead of carrying the world on your shoulders, talk to the One who holds the universe on his. Hope is a look away.

Now, what were you looking at?

13

Silent Nights and Solitary Days

The Burden of Loneliness

You are with me.

Psalm 23:4 NKJV

A friend of mine worked at a pharmacy while attending the University of Texas. Steve's primary job was to deliver supplies to nursing homes in the Austin area. An additional task, however, involved a short trip next door.

Every four days he shouldered a large jug of water and carried it fifty or so feet to a building behind the pharmacy. The customer was an older woman, perhaps in her seventies, who lived alone in a dark, sparse, and tarnished apartment. A single light bulb hung from the ceiling. The wallpaper was stained and peeling. The shades were drawn, and the room was shadowy. Steve would deliver the jug, receive the payment, thank the woman, and leave.

Over the weeks he grew puzzled by her purchase. He learned that the woman had no other source of water. She would rely on his delivery for four days of washing, bathing, and drinking. Odd choice. Municipal water was cheaper. The city would have charged her twelve to fifteen dollars a month; her expense at the pharmacy added up to fifty dollars a month. Why didn't she choose the less expensive source?

The answer was in the delivery system. Yes, the city water cost less. But the city sent only the water; they didn't send a person. She preferred to pay more and see a human being than pay less and see no one.

Could anyone be that lonely?

It seems that David was. Some of his psalms have the feel of a lone oak on a winter prairie.

He wrote:

> Turn to me and be gracious to me,
>   for I am lonely and afflicted. (Ps. 25:16 NIV)

> I'm tired of all this—so tired. My bed
>   has been floating forty days and nights
> On the flood of my tears.
>   My mattress is soaked, soggy with tears.
> The sockets of my eyes are black holes;
>   Nearly blind, I squint and grope. (Ps. 6:6–7 MSG)

David knew what it feels like to be lonely . . . betrayed.

> When they were sick, I dressed in black;
>   instead of eating, I prayed.
> My prayers were like lead in my gut,
>   like I'd lost my best friend, my brother.
> I paced, distraught as a motherless child,
>   hunched and heavyhearted.

> But when I was down
>   they threw a party!
> All the nameless riffraff of the town came
>   chanting insults about me.
> Like barbarians desecrating a shrine,
>   they destroyed my reputation.

> YAHWEH, how long are you going
> to stand there doing nothing? (Ps. 35:13–17 MSG)

David knew the feeling of loneliness.

He knew it in his family. He was one of eight sons of Jesse. But when Samuel the prophet asked to see Jesse's boys, David was overlooked. The prophet counted and asked if there wasn't another child somewhere. Jesse snapped his fingers as if he'd forgotten his keys. "I still have the youngest son. He is out taking care of the sheep" (1 Sam. 16:11).

Jesse's term for "youngest son" was not complimentary. He literally said, "I still have the runt." Some of you were the runt in your family. The runt is the one the others have to put up with and keep an eye on. And on this day the runt was left out. How would you feel if a family meeting was called and your name wasn't?

Things didn't improve when he changed households.

His inclusion in the royal family was King Saul's idea. His exclusion was Saul's idea as well. Had David not ducked, he would have been pinned to the wall by the spear of the jealous king. But David did duck, and David did run. For ten years he ran. Into the wilderness he ran. Sleeping in caves, surviving on wild animals. He was hated and hunted like a jackal.

David was no stranger to loneliness.

You aren't either. By now you've learned that you don't have to be alone to feel lonely. Two thousand years ago 250 million people populated the earth. Now there are more than 5 billion. If loneliness could be cured by the presence of people, then surely there would be less loneliness today. But loneliness lingers.

Very early in my ministry I offered this Sunday morning prayer: "Thank you, Lord, for all our friends. We have so many we can't spend time with them all." After the service a successful businessman corrected me, "You may have more friends than you can see. Not me. I have none." A person can be surrounded by a church and still be lonely.

Loneliness is not the absence of faces. It is the absence of intimacy. Loneliness doesn't come from being alone; it comes from feeling alone. Feeling as if you are

facing death alone,

facing disease alone,

facing the future alone.

Whether it strikes you in your bed at night or on your drive to the hospital, in the silence of an empty house or the noise of a crowded bar, loneliness is when you think, *I feel so alone. Does anyone care?*

Bags of loneliness show up everywhere. They litter the floors of boardrooms and clubs. We drag them into parties and usually drag them back out. You'll spot them near the desk of the overworker, beside the table of the overeater, and on the nightstand of the one-night stand. We'll try anything to unload our loneliness. This is one bag we want to drop quickly.

But should we? Should we be so quick to drop it? Rather than turn from loneliness, what if we turned toward it? Could it be that loneliness is not a curse but a gift? A gift from God?

Wait a minute, Max. That can't be. Loneliness heavies my heart. Loneliness leaves me empty and depressed. Loneliness is anything but a gift.

You may be right, but work with me for a moment. I wonder if loneliness is God's way of getting our attention.

Here's what I mean. Suppose you borrow a friend's car. His radio doesn't work, but his CD player does. You rummage through his collection, looking for your style of music—let's say, country-western. But you find nothing. He has nothing but his style of music—let's say, classical.

It's a long trip. And you can talk to yourself for only so long. So eventually you reach for a CD. You'd prefer some steel guitar, but you're stuck with soaring tenors. Initially it's tolerable. At least it fills the air. But eventually it's enjoyable. Your heart picks up the pattern of the kettledrums, your head rolls with the cellos, and you even catch yourself attempting a little Italian aria. "Hey, this isn't so bad."

Now, let me ask you. Would you have made this discovery on your own? No. What led to it? What caused you to hear music you'd never heard before? Simple. You had no other choice, no other option. You had nowhere else to go. Finally, when the silence was too loud, you took a chance on a song you'd never heard.

Oh, how God wants you to hear his music.

He has a rhythm that will race your heart and lyrics that will stir your tears. You want to journey to the stars? He can take you there. You want to lie down in peace? His music can soothe your soul.

But first, he's got to get rid of that country-western stuff. (Forgive me, Nashville. Only an example.)

And so he begins tossing the CDs. A friend turns away. The job goes bad. Your spouse doesn't understand. The church is dull. One by one he removes the options until all you have left is God.

He would do that? Absolutely. "The Lord disciplines those he loves" (Heb. 12:6). If he must silence every voice, he will. He wants you to hear his music. He wants you to discover what David discovered and to be able to say what David said.

"You are with me."

Yes, you, Lord, are in heaven. Yes, you rule the universe. Yes, you sit upon the stars and make your home in the deep. But yes, yes, yes, you are with me.

The Lord is with me. The Creator is with me. Yahweh is with me.

Moses proclaimed it: "What great nation has a god as near to them as the LORD our God is near to us" (Deut. 4:7 NLT).

Paul announced it: "He is not far from each one of us" (Acts 17:27 NIV).

And David discovered it: "You are with me."

Somewhere in the pasture, wilderness, or palace, David discovered that God meant business when he said:

"I will not leave you" (Gen. 28:15).

"I will . . . not forsake My people" (1 Kings 6:13 NKJV).

"The LORD will not abandon His people" (Ps. 94:14 NASB).

"God . . . will never leave you nor forsake you" (Deut. 31:6 NIV).

The discovery of David is indeed the message of Scripture—*the Lord is with us.* And, since the Lord is near, everything is different. Everything!

You may be facing death, but you aren't facing death alone; the Lord is with you. You may be facing unemployment, but you aren't facing unemployment alone; the Lord is with you. You may be facing marital struggles, but you aren't facing them alone; the Lord is with you. You may be facing debt, but you aren't facing debt alone; the Lord is with you.

Underline these words: You are not alone.

Your family may turn against you, but God won't. Your friends may betray you, but God won't. You may feel alone in the wilderness, but you are not. He is with you. And because he is, everything is different. *You* are different.

God changes your *n* into a *v*. You go from *lonely* to *lovely.*

When you know God loves you, you won't be desperate for the love of others.

You'll no longer be a hungry shopper at the market. Have you ever gone to the grocery on an empty stomach? You're a sitting duck. You buy everything you don't need. Doesn't matter if it is good for you—you just want to fill your tummy. When you're lonely, you do the same in life, pulling stuff off the shelf, not because you need it, but because you are hungry for love.

Why do we do it? Because we fear facing life alone. For fear of not fitting in, we take the drugs. For fear of standing out, we wear the clothes. For fear of appearing small, we go into debt and buy the house. For fear of going unnoticed, we dress to seduce or to impress. For fear of sleeping alone, we sleep with anyone. For fear of not being loved, we search for love in all the wrong places.

But all that changes when we discover God's perfect love. And "perfect love casts out fear" (1 John 4:18 NKJV).

Loneliness. Could it be one of God's finest gifts? If a season of solitude is his way to teach you to hear his song, don't you think it's worth it?

So do I.

14

The Crowing Rooster and Me

The Burden of Shame

You prepare a table before me in the presence of my enemies.

PSALM 23:5 NKJV

See the fellow in the shadows? That's Peter. Peter the apostle. Peter the impetuous. Peter the passionate. He once walked on water. Stepped right out of the boat onto the lake. He'll soon preach to thousands. Fearless before friends and foes alike. But tonight the one who stepped on the water has hurried into hiding. The one who will speak with power is weeping in pain.

Not sniffling or whimpering, but weeping. Bawling. Bearded face buried in thick hands. His howl echoing in the Jerusalem night. What hurts more? The fact that he did it? Or the fact that he swore he never would?

"Lord, I am ready to go with you to prison and even to die with you!" he pledged only hours earlier. "But Jesus said, 'Peter, before the rooster crows this day, you will say three times that you don't know me'" (Luke 22:33–34).

Denying Christ on the night of his betrayal was bad enough, but did he have to boast that he wouldn't? And one denial was pitiful, but three? Three denials were horrific, but did he have to curse? "Peter began to place a curse on himself and swear, 'I don't know the man'" (Matt. 26:74).

And now, awash in a whirlpool of sorrow, Peter is hiding. Peter is weeping. And soon Peter will be fishing.

We wonder why he goes fishing. We know why he goes to Galilee.

He had been told that the risen Christ would meet the disciples there. The arranged meeting place is not the sea, however, but a mountain (Matt. 28:16). If the followers were to meet Jesus on a mountain, what are they doing in a boat? No one told them to fish, but that's what they did. "Simon Peter said, 'I am going out to fish.' The others said, 'We will go with you' " (John 21:3). Besides, didn't Peter quit fishing? Two years earlier, when Jesus called him to fish for men, didn't he drop his net and follow? We haven't seen him fish since. We never see him fish again. Why is he fishing now? Especially now! Jesus has risen from the dead. Peter has seen the empty tomb. Who could fish at a time like this?

Were they hungry? Perhaps that's the sum of it. Maybe the expedition was born out of growling stomachs.

Or then again, maybe it was born out of a broken heart.

You see, Peter could not deny his denial. The empty tomb did not erase the crowing rooster. Christ had returned, but Peter wondered, he must have wondered, "After what I did, would he return for someone like me?"

We've wondered the same. Is Peter the only person to do the very thing he swore he'd never do?

"Infidelity is behind me!"

"From now on, I'm going to bridle my tongue."

"No more shady deals. I've learned my lesson."

Oh, the volume of our boasting. And, oh, the heartbreak of our shame.

Rather than resist the flirting, we return it.

Rather than ignore the gossip, we share it.

Rather than stick to the truth, we shade it.

And the rooster crows, and conviction pierces, and Peter has a partner in the shadows. We weep as Peter wept, and we do what Peter did. We go fishing. We go back to our old lives. We return to our pre-Jesus practices. We do what comes naturally, rather than what comes spiritually. And we question whether Jesus has a place for folks like us.

Jesus answers that question. He answers it for you and me and all who tend to "Peter out" on Christ. His answer came on the shore of the sea in a gift to Peter. You know what Jesus did? Split the waters? Turn the boat to gold and the nets to silver? No, Jesus did something much more meaningful. He invited Peter to breakfast. Jesus prepared a meal.

Of course, the breakfast was one special moment among several that morning. There was the great catch of fish and the recognition of Jesus. The plunge of Peter and the paddling of the disciples. And there was the moment they reached the shore and found Jesus next to a fire of coals. The fish were sizzling, and the bread was waiting, and the defeater of hell and the ruler of heaven invited his friends to sit down and have a bite to eat.

No one could have been more grateful than Peter. The one Satan had sifted like wheat was eating bread at the hand of God. Peter was welcomed to the meal of Christ. Right there for the devil and his tempters to see, Jesus "prepared a table in the presence of his enemies."

OK, so maybe Peter didn't say it that way. But David did. "You prepare a table before me in the presence of my enemies" (Ps. 23:5 NKJV). What the shepherd did for the sheep sounds a lot like what Jesus did for Peter.

At this point in the psalm, David's mind seems to be lingering in the high country with the sheep. Having guided the flock through the valley to the alp lands for greener grass, he remembers the shepherd's added responsibility. He must prepare the pasture.

This is new land, so the shepherd must be careful. Ideally, the grazing area will be flat, a mesa or tableland. The shepherd searches for poisonous plants and ample water. He looks for signs of wolves, coyotes, and bears.

Of special concern to the shepherd is the adder, a small brown snake that lives underground. Adders are known to pop out of their holes and nip the sheep on the nose. The bite often infects and can even kill. As defense against the snake, the shepherd pours a circle of oil at the top of each adder's hole. He also applies the oil to the noses of the animals. The oil on the snake's hole lubricates the exit, preventing the snake from climbing out. The smell of the oil on the sheep's nose drives the serpent away. The shepherd, in a very real sense, has prepared the table.[1]

What if your Shepherd did for you what the shepherd did for his flock? Suppose he dealt with your enemy, the devil, and prepared for you a safe place of nourishment? What if Jesus did for you what he did for Peter? Suppose he, in the hour of your failure, invited you to a meal?

What would you say if I told you he has done exactly that?

On the night before his death, Jesus prepared a table for his followers.

> On the first day of the Festival of Unleavened Bread, the day the lambs for the Passover meal were killed, Jesus' disciples asked him, "Where do you want us to go and get the Passover meal ready for you?"
>
> Then Jesus sent two of them with these instructions: "Go into the city, and a man carrying a jar of water will meet you. Follow him to the house he enters, and say to the owner of the house: 'The Teacher says, Where is the room where my disciples and I will eat the Passover meal?' Then he will show you a large, upstairs room, fixed up and furnished, where you will get everything ready for us." (Mark 14:12–15 TEV)

Look who did the "preparing" here. Jesus reserved a large room and arranged for the guide to lead the disciples. Jesus made certain the room was furnished and the food set out. What did the disciples do? They faithfully complied and were fed.

The Shepherd prepared the table.

Not only that, he dealt with the snakes. You'll remember that only one of the disciples didn't complete the meal that night. "The devil had already persuaded Judas Iscariot, the son of Simon, to turn against Jesus" (John 13:2). Judas started to eat, but Jesus didn't let him finish. On the command of Jesus, Judas left the room. "'The thing that you will do—do it quickly.' . . . Judas took the bread Jesus gave him and immediately went out. It was night" (John 13:27, 30).

There is something dynamic in this dismissal. Jesus prepared a table in the presence of the enemy. Judas was allowed to see the supper, but he wasn't allowed to stay there.

You are not welcome here. This table is for my children. You may tempt them. You may trip them. But you will never sit with them. This is how much he loves us.

And if any doubt remains, lest there be any "Peters" who wonder if there is a place at the table for them, Jesus issues a tender reminder as he passes the cup. "Every one of you drink this. This is my blood which is the new agreement that God makes with his people. This blood is poured out for many to forgive their sins" (Matt. 26:27–28).

"*Every one* of you drink this." Those who feel unworthy, drink this. Those who feel ashamed, drink this. Those who feel embarrassed, drink this.

May I share a time when I felt all three?

By the age of eighteen I was well on my way to a drinking problem. My system had become so resistant to alcohol that a six-pack of beer had little or no impact on me. At the age of twenty, God not only saved me from hell after this life, he saved me from hell during it. Only he knows where I was headed, but I have a pretty good idea.

For that reason, part of my decision to follow Christ included no more beer. So I quit. But, curiously, the thirst for beer never left. It hasn't hounded me or consumed me, but two or three times a week the thought of a good beer sure entices me. Proof to me that I have to be careful is this—nonalcoholic beers have no appeal. It's not the flavor of the drink; it's the buzz. But for more than twenty years, drinking has never been a major issue.

A couple of years ago, however, it nearly became one. I lowered my guard a bit. *One beer with barbecue won't hurt.* Then another time with Mexican food. Then a time or two with no food at all. Over a period of two months I went from no beers to maybe one or two a week. Again, for most people, no problem, but for me it could become one.

You know when I began to smell trouble? One hot Friday afternoon I was on my way to speak at our annual men's retreat. Did I say the day was hot? Brutally hot. I was thirsty. Soda wouldn't do. So I began to plot. Where could I buy a beer and not be seen by anyone I knew?

With that thought, I crossed a line. What's done in secret is best not done at all. But I did it anyway. I drove to an out-of-the-way convenience store, parked, and waited until all patrons had left. I entered, bought my beer, held it close to my side, and hurried to the car.

That's when the rooster crowed.

It crowed because I was sneaking around. It crowed because I knew better. It crowed because, and this really hurt, the night before I'd scolded one of my daughters for keeping secrets from me. And now, what was I doing?

I threw the beer in the trash and asked God to forgive me. A few days later I shared my struggle with the elders and some members of the congregation and was happy to chalk up the matter to experience and move on.

But I couldn't. The shame plagued me. Of all the people to do such a thing. So many could be hurt by my stupidity. And of all the times to do such a thing. En route to minister at a retreat. What hypocrisy!

I felt like a bum. Forgiveness found its way into my head, but the elevator designed to lower it eighteen inches to my heart was out of order.

And, to make matters worse, Sunday rolled around. I found myself on the front row of the church, awaiting my turn to speak. Again, I had been honest with God, honest with the elders, honest with myself. But still, I struggled. Would God want a guy like me to preach?

The answer came in the Supper. The Lord's Supper. The same Jesus who'd prepared a meal for Peter had prepared one for me. The same Shepherd who had trumped the devil trumped him again. The same Savior who had built a fire on the shore stirred a few embers in my heart.

"*Every one* of you drink this." And so I did. It felt good to be back at the table.

15

Slippery Sheep and Healed Hurts

The Burden of Disappointment

You anoint my head with oil.

PSALM 23:5 NKJV

D*is* changes everything. With *dis,* "obey" becomes "*dis*obey." "Respect" is changed to "*dis*respect." "Regard" is suddenly "*dis*regard." What was an "ability" becomes a "*dis*ability." "Engage" is now "*dis*engage," and "grace" is transformed into "*dis*grace." All because of *dis.*

We'd be hard pressed to find a more potent trio of letters. And we'd be hard pressed to find a better example of their power than the word *appointment.*

Most of us like appointments. Even the organizationally inept like appointments. Appointments create a sense of predictability in an unpredictable world. Down deep we know we control the future as much as a caboose controls the train, yet our Day-Timers give us the illusion that we do.

A disappointment reminds us that we don't. A disappointment is a missed appointment. What we hoped would happen, didn't. We wanted health; we got disease. We wanted retirement; we got reassignment. Divorce instead of family. Dismissal instead of promotion. Now what? What do we do with our disappointments?

We could do what Miss Haversham did. Remember her in Charles Dickens's *Great Expectations*? Jilted by her fiancé just prior to the wedding, her appointment became a missed appointment and a disappointment. How did she respond? Not too well. She closed all the blinds in the house, stopped every clock, left the wedding cake on the table to gather cobwebs, and continued to wear her wedding dress until it hung in yellow decay around her shrunken form. Her wounded heart consumed her life.

We can follow the same course.

Or we can follow the example of the apostle Paul. His goal was to be a missionary in Spain. Rather than send Paul to Spain, however, God sent him to prison. Sitting in a Roman jail, Paul could have made the same choice as Miss Haversham, but he didn't. Instead he said, "As long as I'm here, I might as well write a few letters." Hence your Bible has the Epistles to Philemon, the Philippians, the Colossians, and the Ephesians.[1] No doubt Paul would have done a great work in Spain. But would it have compared with the work of those four letters?

You've sat where Paul sat. I know you have. You were hotter than a two-dollar pistol on the trail to Spain or college or marriage or independence . . . but then came the layoff or the pregnancy or the sick parent. And you ended up in prison. So long, Spain. Hello, Rome. So long, appointment. Hello, disappointment. Hello, pain.

How did you handle it? Better asked, how are you handling it? Could you use some help? I've got just what you need. Six words in the fifth verse of the Twenty-third Psalm: "You anoint my head with oil."

Don't see the connection? What does a verse on oil have to do with the hurts that come from the disappointments of life?

A little livestock lesson might help. In ancient Israel shepherds used oil for three purposes: to repel insects, to prevent conflicts, and to heal wounds.

Bugs bug people, but they can kill sheep. Flies, mosquitoes, and gnats can turn the summer into a time of torture for the livestock. Consider nose flies, for example. If they succeed in depositing their eggs into the soft membrane of the sheep's nose, the eggs become wormlike larvae, which drive the sheep insane. One shepherd explains: "For relief from this agonizing annoyance sheep will deliberately beat their heads against trees, rocks, posts, or brush. . . . In extreme cases of intense infestation a sheep may even kill itself in a frenzied endeavor to gain respite from the aggravation."[2]

When a swarm of nose flies appears, sheep panic. They run. They hide. They toss their heads up and down for hours. They forget to eat. They aren't able to sleep. Ewes stop milking, and lambs stop growing. The entire flock can be disrupted, even destroyed by the presence of a few flies.

For this reason, the shepherd anoints the sheep. He covers their heads with an oil-like repellent. The fragrance keeps the insects at bay and the flock at peace.

At peace, that is, until mating season. Most of the year, sheep are calm, passive animals. But during mating season, everything changes. The rams put the "ram" in *rambunctious*. They strut around the pasture and flex their necks, trying to win the attention of the new gal on the block. When a ram catches her eye, he tosses his head back and says, "I want ewe, baby." About that time her boyfriend shows up and tells her to go someplace safe. "Ewe better move, sweetie. This could get ugly." The two rams lower their heads and POW! An old-fashioned head butt breaks out.

To prevent injury, the shepherd anoints the rams. He smears a slippery, greasy substance over the nose and head. This lubricant causes them to glance off rather than crash into each other.

They still tend to get hurt, however. And these wounds are the third reason the shepherd anoints the sheep.

Most of the wounds the shepherd treats are simply the result of living in a pasture. Thorns prick or rocks cut or a sheep rubs its head too hard against a tree. Sheep get hurt. As a result, the shepherd regularly, often daily, inspects the sheep, searching for cuts and abrasions. He doesn't want the cut to worsen. He doesn't want today's wound to become tomorrow's infection.

Neither does God. Just like sheep, we have wounds, but ours are wounds of the heart that come from disappointment after disappointment. If we're not careful, these wounds lead to bitterness. And so just like sheep, we need to be treated. "He made us, and we belong to him; we are his people, the sheep he tends" (Ps. 100:3).

Sheep aren't the only ones who need preventive care, and sheep aren't the only ones who need a healing touch. We also get irritated with each other, butt heads, and then get wounded. Many of our disappointments in life begin as irritations. The large portion of our problems are not lion-sized attacks, but rather the day-to-day swarm of frustrations and mishaps and heartaches. You don't get invited to the dinner party. You don't make the team. You don't get the scholarship. Your boss doesn't notice your hard work. Your husband doesn't notice your new dress. Your neighbor doesn't notice the mess in his yard. You find yourself more irritable, more gloomy, more . . . well, more hurt.

Like the sheep, you don't sleep well, you don't eat well. You may even hit your head against a tree a few times.

Or you may hit your head against a person. It's amazing how hard-headed we can be with each other. Some of our deepest hurts come from butting heads with people.

Like the sheep, the rest of our wounds come just from living in the pasture. The pasture of the sheep, however, is much more appealing. The sheep have to face wounds from thorns and thistles. We have to face aging, loss, and illness. Some of us face betrayal and injustice. Live long enough in this world, and most of us will face deep, deep hurts of some kind or another.

So we, like the sheep, get wounded. And we, like the sheep, have a shepherd. Remember the words we read? "We belong to him; we are his people, the sheep he tends" (Ps. 100:3). He will do for you what the shepherd does for the sheep. He will tend to you.

If the Gospels teach us anything, they teach us that Jesus is a Good Shepherd. "I am the good shepherd," Jesus announces. "The good shepherd gives his life for the sheep" (John 10:11).

Didn't Jesus spread the oil of prevention on his disciples? He prayed for them. He equipped them before he sent them out. He revealed to them the secrets of the parables. He interrupted their arguments and calmed their fears. Because he was a good shepherd, he protected them against disappointments.

Not only did Jesus prevent wounds, he healed them. He touched the eyes of the blind man. He touched the disease of the leper. He touched the body of the dead girl. Jesus tends to his sheep. He touched the searching heart of Nicodemus. He touched the open heart of Zacchaeus. He touched the broken heart of Mary Magdalene. He touched the confused heart of Cleopas. And he touched the stubborn heart of Paul and the repentant heart of Peter. Jesus tends to his sheep. And he will tend to you.

If you will let him. How? How do you let him? The steps are so simple.

First, go to him. David would trust his wounds to no other person but God. He said, "*You* anoint my head with oil." Not, "your prophets," "your teachers," or "your counselors." Others may guide us to God. Others may help us understand God. But no one does the work of God, for only God can heal. God "heals the brokenhearted" (Ps. 147:3).

Have you taken your disappointments to God? You've shared them with your neighbor, your relatives, your friends. But have you taken them to God? James says, "Anyone who is having troubles should pray" (James 5:13).

Before you go anywhere else with your disappointments, go to God.

Maybe you don't want to trouble God with your hurts. *After all, he's got famines and pestilence and wars; he won't care about my little struggles,* you think. Why don't you let him decide that? He cared enough about a wedding to provide the wine. He cared enough about Peter's tax payment to give him a coin. He cared enough about the woman at the well to give her answers. "He cares about you" (1 Pet. 5:7).

Your first step is to go to the right person. Go to God. Your second step is to assume the right posture. Bow before God.

In order to be anointed, the sheep must stand still, lower their heads, and let the shepherd do his work. Peter urges us to "be humble under God's powerful hand so he will lift you up when the right time comes" (1 Pet. 5:6).

When we come to God, we make requests; we don't make demands. We come with high hopes and a humble heart. We state what we want, but we pray for what is right. And if God gives us the prison of Rome instead of the mission of Spain, we accept it because we know "God will always give what is right to his people who cry to him night and day, and he will not be slow to answer them" (Luke 18:7).

We go to him. We bow before him, and we *trust in him*.

The sheep doesn't understand why the oil repels the flies. The sheep doesn't understand how the oil heals the wounds. In fact, all the sheep knows is that something happens in the presence of the shepherd. And that's all we need to know as well. "LORD, I give myself to you; my God, I trust you" (Ps. 25:1–2).

Go.

Bow.

Trust.

Worth a try, don't you think?

16

Jam Session

The Burden of Envy

My cup overflows with blessings.

PSALM 23:5 NLT

A member of our church gave me a jar of homemade peach preserves a couple of weeks ago. Few delicacies in life compare with her peach preserves. Should I someday face a firing squad, I'll pass on the cigarette but be the first to perk up if Sarah's peach preserves are offered. Each spoonful is a celestial experience. The only problem with her gift was that it didn't last. I'm sad to report that the bottom of my jar is in sight. I'll soon be shaking out the last drop like a lost cowboy shakes his canteen.

To be quite honest, I'm dreading the moment. Its proximity has affected my behavior. Anyone who requests a taste of my peach preserves is met with a Clint Eastwood snarl, "Don't even think about it."

If I were Sarah's husband, Keith, I wouldn't have such a problem. He gets all the peach preserves he wants. Does the clinking of the spoon at the bottom of the jar trigger tears for Keith? Hardly, he has an unlimited supply. One might even say that he has more than he deserves. And one might wonder why he has so much and I have so little. Why should he have a pantryful and I just a jarful? Who gave him the key to the jam-and-jelly castle? Who made him the master of marmalades? Who crowned Keith the king of confitures? It's not fair. It's not right. In fact, the more I think about it . . .

Which is exactly what I shouldn't do. I shouldn't think about it. For resting at the end of this trail of thought is the deadly briefcase of envy.

If you haven't seen one in real life, you've seen one in the spy movies. The assassin carries it up the back stairs into the vacated room at the top of the building. When he is sure no one can see him, he opens the case. The disassembled rifle sits in cushioned slots. The scope, the barrel, the stock—all await the hand of the marksman. The marksman awaits the arrival of his victim.

Who is his victim? Anyone who has more than he has. More karats, more horsepower, more office space, more church members. Jealousy sets her cross hairs on the one who has more. "You want something you don't have, and you will do anything to get it. You will even kill!" (James 4:2 CEV).

Honestly, Max, I would never do that. I would never kill.

With a rifle, maybe not. But with your tongue? With your glare? Your gossip? "Jealousy," informs Proverbs 6:34, "enrages a man" (NASB). Are your sights set on someone? If so, be careful; "jealousy will rot your bones" (Prov. 14:30).

Need a deterrent for envy? An antidote for jealousy? The psalm we are studying offers one. Rather than bemoan the peach preserves you don't have, rejoice in the abundant cup you do. "My cup overflows with blessings" (Ps. 23:5 NLT).

Is an overflowing cup full? Absolutely. The wine reaches the rim and then tumbles over the edge. The goblet is not large enough to contain the quantity. According to David, our hearts are not large enough to contain the blessings that God wants to give. He pours and pours until they literally flow over the edge and down on the table. You'll like the paragraph penned a century ago by F. B. Meyer:

> Whatever the blessing is in our cup, it is sure to run over. With him the calf is always the fatted calf; the robe is always the best robe; the joy is unspeakable; the peace passeth understanding. . . . There is no

> grudging in God's benevolence; He does not measure out his goodness as an apothecary counts his drops and measures his drams, slowly and exactly, drop by drop. God's way is always characterized by multitudinous and overflowing bounty.[1]

The last thing we need to worry about is not having enough. Our cup overflows with blessings.

Let me ask a question—a crucial question. If focusing on our diminishing items leads to envy, what would happen if we focused on the unending items? If awareness of what we don't have creates jealousy, is it possible that an awareness of our abundance will lead to contentment? Let's give it a try and see what happens. Let's dedicate a few paragraphs to a couple of blessings that, according to the Bible, are overflowing in our lives.

Abounding grace. "The more we see our sinfulness, the more we see God's *abounding grace* forgiving us" (Rom. 5:20 TLB, emphasis mine). To abound is to have a surplus, an abundance, an extravagant portion. Should the fish in the Pacific worry that it will run out of ocean? No. Why? The ocean abounds with water. Need the lark be anxious about finding room in the sky to fly? No. The sky abounds with space.

Should the Christian worry that the cup of mercy will run empty? He may. For he may not be aware of God's abounding grace. Are you? Are you aware that the cup God gives you *overflows* with mercy? Or are you afraid your cup will run dry? Your warranty will expire? Are you afraid your mistakes are too great for God's grace?

We can't help but wonder if the apostle Paul had the same fear. Before he was Paul the apostle, he was Saul the murderer. Before he encouraged Christians, he murdered Christians. What would it be like to live with such a past? Did he ever meet children whom he had made orphans? Did their faces haunt his sleep? Did Paul ever ask, "Can God forgive a man like me?"

The answer to his and our questions is found in a letter he wrote to Timothy: "The grace of our Lord was poured out on me abundantly, along with the faith and love that are in Christ Jesus" (1 Tim. 1:14 NIV).

God is not a miser with his grace. Your cup may be low on cash or clout, but it is overflowing with mercy. You may not have the prime parking place, but you have sufficient pardon. "He will abundantly pardon" (Isa. 55:7 NKJV). Your cup overflows with grace.

Hope. And because it does, your cup overflows with hope. "God will help you overflow with hope in him through the Holy Spirit's power within you" (Rom. 15:13 TLB).

Heaven's hope does for your world what the sunlight did for my grandmother's cellar. I owe my love of peach preserves to her. She canned her own and stored them in an underground cellar near her West Texas house. It was a deep hole with wooden steps, plywood walls, and a musty smell. As a youngster I used to climb in, close the door, and see how long I could last in the darkness. Not even a slit of light entered that underground hole. I would sit silently, listening to my breath and heartbeats, until I couldn't take it anymore and then would race up the stairs and throw open the door. Light would avalanche into the cellar. What a change! Moments before I couldn't see anything—all of a sudden I could see everything.

Just as light poured into the cellar, God's hope pours into your world. Upon the sick, he shines the ray of healing. To the bereaved, he gives the promise of reunion. For the dying, he lit the flame of resurrection. To the confused, he offers the light of Scripture.

God gives hope. So what if someone was born thinner or stronger, lighter or darker than you? Why count diplomas or compare résumés?

What does it matter if they have a place at the head table? You have a place at God's table. And he is filling your cup to overflowing.

The overflowing cup was a powerful symbol in the days of David. Hosts in the ancient East used it to send a message to the guest. As long as the cup was kept full, the guest knew he was welcome. But when the cup sat empty, the host was hinting that the hour was late. On those occasions, however, when the host really enjoyed the company of the person, he filled the cup to overflowing. He didn't stop when the wine reached the rim; he kept pouring until the liquid ran over the edge of the cup and down on the table.[2]

Have you noticed how wet your table is? God wants you to stay. Your cup overflows with joy. Overflows with grace. Shouldn't your heart overflow with gratitude?

The heart of the boy did. Not at first, mind you. Initially he was full of envy. But, in time, he was full of gratitude.

According to the fable, he lived with his father in a valley at the base of a large dam. Every day the father would go to work on the mountain behind their house and return home with a wheelbarrow full of dirt. "Pour the dirt in the sacks, Son," the father would say. "And stack them in front of the house."

And though the boy would obey, he also complained. He was tired of dirt. He was weary of bags. Why didn't his father give him what other fathers gave their sons? They had toys and games; he had dirt. When he saw what the others had, he grew mad at them. "It's not fair," he said to himself.

And when he saw his father, he objected. "They have fun. I have dirt."

The father would smile and place his arm on the boy's shoulders and say, "Trust me, Son. I'm doing what is best."

But it was so hard for the boy to trust. Every day the father would bring the load. Every day the boy would fill bags. "Stack them as high as you can," the father would say as he went for more. And so the boy filled the bags and piled them high. So high he couldn't see over them.

"Work hard, Son," the father said one day. "We're running out of time." As the father spoke, he looked at the darkening sky. The boy stared at the clouds and turned to ask about them, but when he did, the thunder cracked and the sky opened. The rain poured so hard he could scarcely see his father through the water. "Keep stacking, Son!" And as he did, the boy heard a mighty crash.

The water of the river poured through the dam and toward the little village. In a moment the tide swept everything in its path, but the dike of dirt gave the boy and the father the time they needed. "Hurry, Son. Follow me."

They ran to the side of the mountain behind their house and into a tunnel. In a matter of moments they exited the other side and scampered up the hill and came upon a new cottage.

"We'll be safe here," the father said to the boy.

Only then did the son realize what the father had done. He had burrowed an exit. Rather than give him what he wanted, the father gave his boy what he needed. He gave him a safe passage and a safe place.

Hasn't our Father given us the same? A strong wall of grace to protect us? A sure exit to deliver us? Of whom can we be envious? Who has more than we do? Rather than want what others have, shouldn't we wonder if they have what we do? Instead of being jealous of them, how about zealous for them? For heaven's sake, drop the rifles and hold out the cup. There is enough to go around.

One thing is certain. When the final storm comes and you are safe in your Father's house, you won't regret what he didn't give. You'll be stunned at what he did.

17

God's Loving Pursuit

The Burden of Doubt

*Surely goodness and mercy shall follow me
all the days of my life.*

PSALM 23:6 NKJV

Eric Hill had everything you'd need for a bright future. He was twenty-eight years old and a recent college grad with an athletic frame and a soft smile. His family loved him, girls took notice of him, and companies had contacted him about working for them. Although Eric appeared composed without, he was tormented within. Tormented by voices he could not still. Bothered by images he could not avoid. So, hoping to get away from them all, he got away from it all. On a gray rainy day in February 1982, Eric Hill walked out the back door of his Florida home and never came back.

His sister Debbie remembers seeing him leave, his tall frame ambling down the interstate. She assumed he would return. He didn't. She hoped he would call. He didn't. She thought she could find him. She couldn't. Where Eric journeyed, only God and Eric know, and neither of them has chosen to tell. What we do know is Eric heard a voice. And in that voice was an "assignment." And that assignment was to pick up garbage along a roadside in San Antonio, Texas.

To the commuters on Interstate 10, his lanky form and bearded face became a familiar sight. He made a home out of a hole in a vacant lot. He made a wardrobe out of split trousers and a torn sweatshirt. An old hat deferred the summer sun. A plastic bag on his shoulders softened the winter chill. His weathered skin and stooped shoulders made him look twice his forty-four years. But then, sixteen years on the side of the road would do that to you.

That's how long it had been since Debbie had seen her brother. She might never have seen him again had it not been for two events. The first was the construction of a car dealership on Eric's vacant lot. The second was a severe pain in his abdomen. The dealership took his home. The pain nearly took his life.

EMS found him curled in a ball on the side of the road, clutching his stomach. The hospital ran some tests and found that Eric had cancer. Terminal cancer. Another few months and he would be dead. And with no known family or relatives, he would die alone.

His court-appointed attorney couldn't handle this thought. "Surely someone is looking for Eric," he reasoned. So the lawyer scoured the Internet for anyone in search of a brown-haired, adult male with the last name Hill. That's how he met Debbie.

His description seemed to match her memory, but she had to know for sure.

So Debbie came to Texas. She and her husband and two children rented a hotel room and set out to find Eric. By now he'd been released from the hospital, but the chaplain knew where he was. They found him sitting against a building not far from the interstate. As they approached, he stood. They offered fruit; he refused. They offered juice; he declined. He was polite but unimpressed with this family who claimed to be his own.

His interest perked, however, when Debbie offered him a pin to wear, an angel pin. He said yes. Her first time to touch her brother in sixteen years was the moment he allowed her to pin the angel on his shirt.

Debbie intended to spend a week. But a week passed, and she stayed. Her husband returned home, and she stayed. Spring became summer, and Eric improved, and still she stayed. Debbie rented an apartment and began homeschooling her kids and reaching out to her brother.

It wasn't easy. He didn't recognize her. He didn't know her. One day he cursed her. He didn't want to sleep in her apartment. He didn't want her food. He didn't want to talk. He wanted his vacant lot. He wanted his "job." Who was this woman anyway?

But Debbie didn't give up on Eric. She understood that he didn't understand. So she stayed.

I met her one Sunday when she visited our congregation. When she shared her story, I asked what you might want to ask. "How do you keep from giving up?"

"Simple," she said. "He's my brother."

I told her that her pursuit reminded me of another pursuit—that her heart reminded me of another heart. Another kind heart who left home in search of the confused. Another compassionate soul who couldn't bear the thought of a brother or sister in pain. So, like Debbie, he left home. Like Debbie, he found his sibling.

And when Jesus found us, we acted like Eric. Our limitations kept us from recognizing the One who came to save us. We even doubted his presence—and sometimes we still do.

How does he deal with our doubts? He follows us. As Debbie followed Eric, God follows us. He pursues us until we finally see him as our Father, even if it takes *all the days of our lives.*

"Surely goodness and mercy shall follow me all the days of my life; and I will dwell in the house of the LORD forever" (Ps. 23:6 NKJV).

This must be one of the sweetest phrases ever penned. Can we read it from a few other translations?

"Goodness and love unfailing, these will follow me all the days of my life, and I shall dwell in the house of the LORD my whole life long" (NEB).

"I know that your goodness and love will be with me all my life; and your house will be my home as long as I live" (TEV).

"Your beauty and love chase after me every day of my life. I'm back home in the house of YAHWEH for the rest of my life" (MSG).

To read the verse is to open a box of jewels. Each word sparkles and begs to be examined in the face of our doubts: *goodness, mercy, all the days, dwell in the house of the LORD, forever.* They sweep in on insecurities like a SWAT team on a terrorist.

Look at the first word: *surely*. David didn't say, "*Maybe* goodness and mercy shall follow me." Or "*Possibly* goodness and mercy shall follow me." Or "*I have a hunch* that goodness and mercy shall follow me." David could have used one of those phrases. But he didn't. He believed in a sure God, who makes sure promises and provides a sure foundation. David would have loved the words of one of his great-great-grandsons, the apostle James. He described God as the one "with whom there is never the slightest variation or shadow of inconsistency" (James 1:17 PHILLIPS).

Our moods may shift, but God's doesn't. Our minds may change, but God's doesn't. Our devotion may falter, but God's never does. Even if we are faithless, he is faithful, for he cannot betray himself (2 Tim. 2:13). He is a sure God. And because he is a sure God, we can state confidently, "Surely goodness and mercy shall follow me all the days of my life."

And what follows the word *surely*? "Goodness and mercy." If the Lord is the shepherd who leads the flock, goodness and mercy are the two sheepdogs that guard the rear of the flock. Goodness *and* mercy. Not goodness alone, for we are sinners in need of mercy. Not mercy alone, for we are fragile, in need of goodness. We need them both. As one man wrote, "Goodness to supply every want. Mercy to forgive every sin. Goodness to provide. Mercy to pardon."[1]

Goodness and mercy—the celestial escort of God's flock. If that duo doesn't reinforce your faith, try this phrase: "all the days of my life."

What a huge statement. Look at the size of it! Goodness and mercy follow the child of God each and every day! Think of the days that lie ahead. What do you see? Days at home with only toddlers? God will be at your side. Days in a dead-end job? He will walk you through. Days of loneliness? He will take your hand. Surely goodness and mercy shall follow me—not some, not most, not nearly all—but all the days of my life.

And what will he do during those days? (Here is my favorite word.) He will "follow" you.

What a surprising way to describe God! We're accustomed to a God who remains in one place. A God who sits enthroned in the heavens and rules and ordains. David, however, envisions a mobile and active God. Dare we do the same? Dare we envision a God who follows us? Who pursues us? Who chases us? Who tracks us down and wins us over? Who follows us with "goodness and mercy" all the days of our lives?

Isn't this the kind of God described in the Bible? A God who follows us? There are many in the Scriptures who would say so. You have to go no farther than the third chapter of the first book before you find God in the role of a seeker. Adam and Eve are hiding in the bushes, partly to cover their bodies, partly to cover their sin. But does God wait for them to come to him? No, the words ring in the garden: "Where are you?" (Gen. 3:9). With that question God began a quest for the heart of humanity that continues up to and through the moment you read these words.

Moses can tell you about it. He was forty years in the desert when he looked over his shoulder and saw a bush blazing. God had followed him into the wilderness.

Jonah can tell you about it. He was a fugitive on a boat when he looked over his shoulder and saw clouds brewing. God had followed him onto the ocean.

The disciples of Jesus knew the feeling of being followed by God. They were rain soaked and shivering when they looked over their shoulders and saw Jesus walking toward them. God had followed them into the storm.

An unnamed Samaritan woman knew the same. She was alone in life and alone at the well when she looked over her shoulder and heard a Messiah speaking. God had followed her through her pain.

John the Apostle was banished on Patmos when he looked over his shoulder and saw the skies begin to open. God had followed him into his exile.

Lazarus was three days dead in a sealed tomb when he heard a voice, lifted his head, and looked over his shoulder and saw Jesus standing. God had followed him into death.

Peter had denied his Lord and gone back to fishing when he heard his name and looked over his shoulder and saw Jesus cooking breakfast. God had followed him in spite of his failure.

God is the God who follows. I wonder . . . have you sensed him following you? We often miss him. Like Eric, we don't know our Helper when he is near. But he comes.

Through the kindness of a stranger. The majesty of a sunset. The mystery of romance. Through the question of a child or the commitment of a spouse. Through a word well spoken or a touch well timed, have you sensed his presence?

If so, then release your doubts. Set them down. Be encumbered by them no longer. You are no candidate for insecurity. You are no longer a client of timidity. You can trust God. He has given his love to you; why don't you give your doubts to him?

Not easy to trust, you say? Maybe not, but neither is it as difficult as you think. Try these ideas:

Trust your faith and not your feelings. You don't feel spiritual each day? Of course you don't. But your feelings have no impact on God's presence. On the days you don't feel close to God, trust your faith and not your feelings. Goodness and mercy shall follow you all the days of your life.

Measure your value through God's eyes, not your own. To everyone else, Eric Hill was a homeless drifter. But to Debbie, he was a brother. There are times in our lives when we are gangrels—homeless, disoriented, hard to help, and hard to love. In those seasons remember this simple fact: God loves you. He follows you. Why? Because you are family, and he will follow you all the days of your life.

See the big picture, not the small. Eric's home was taken. His health was taken. But through the tragedy, his family was returned to him. Perhaps your home and health have been threatened as well. The immediate result might be pain. But the long-term result might be finding a Father you never knew. A Father who will follow you all the days of your life.

By the way, the last chapter in Eric Hill's life is the best one. Days before he died he recognized Debbie as his sister. And, in doing so, he discovered his home.

We will as well. Like Eric, we have doubted our Helper. But like Debbie, God has followed us. Like Eric, we are quick to turn away. But like Debbie, God is slow to anger and determined to stay. Like Eric, we don't accept God's gifts. But like Debbie, God still gives them. He gives us his angels, not just pinned on a lapel, but placed on our path.

And most of all, God gives us himself. Even when we choose our hovel over his house and our trash over his grace, still he follows. Never forcing us. Never leaving us. Patiently persistent. Faithfully present. Using all of his power to convince us that he is who he is and that he can be trusted to lead us home.

His goodness and mercy will follow us all the days of our lives.

18

Almost Heaven

The Burden of Homesickness

I will dwell in the house of the LORD forever.

PSALM 23:6 NKJV

For the last twenty years, I've wanted a dog. A big dog. But there were always problems. The apartment was too small. The budget was too tight. The girls were too young. But most of all, Denalyn was unenthusiastic. Her logic? She'd already married one slobbering, shedding beast, why put up with a second? So we compromised and got a small dog.

I like Salty, but small dogs aren't really dogs. They don't bark; they yelp. They don't eat; they nibble. They don't lick you; they sniff you. I like Salty, but I wanted a real dog. A man's-best-friend type of dog. A fat-pawed, big-eating, slurp-you-on-the-face type of dog you could saddle or wrestle or both.

I was alone in my passion until Sara was born. She loves dogs. And the two of us were able to sway the household vote. Denalyn gave in, and Sara and I began the search. We discovered a woman in South Carolina who breeds golden retrievers in a Christian environment. From birth the dogs are surrounded by inspirational music and prayers. (No, I don't know if they tithe with dog biscuits.) When the trainer told me that she had read my books, I got on board. A woman with such good taste is bound to be a good breeder, right?

So we ordered a pup. We mailed the check, selected the name Molly, and cleared a corner for her dog pillow. The dog hadn't even been born, and she was named, claimed, and given a place in the house.

Can't the same be said about you? Long before your first whimper, your Master claimed you, named you, and hung a reserved sign on your room. You and Molly have more in common than odor and eating habits. (Just teasing.)

You're both being groomed for a trip. We prefer the terms *maturation* and *sanctification* to *weaning* and *training,* but it's all the same. You're being prepared for your Master's house. You don't know the departure date or flight number, but you can bet your puppy chow that you'll be seeing your Owner someday. Isn't this the concluding promise of David?

"And I will dwell in the house of the LORD forever" (Ps. 23:6 NKJV).

Where will you live forever? In the house of the Lord. If his house is your "forever house," what does that make this earthly house? You got it! Short-term housing. This is not our home. "Our homeland is in heaven" (Phil. 3:20).

This explains the homesickness we feel.

Have you ever longed to be home? May I share a time when I did? I was spending the summer of my nineteenth year working in northern Georgia. The folks in that region are very nice, but no one is too nice to a door-to-door salesman. There were times that summer when I was so lonely for home I felt my bones would melt.

One of those occasions came on the side of a country road. The hour was late, and I was lost. I'd stopped to pull out a flashlight and a map. To my right was a farmhouse. In the farmhouse was a family. I knew it was a family because I could see them. Right through the big plate-glass window, I could see the mother and father and boy and girl. Norman Rockwell would have placed them on a canvas. The mom was spooning out food, and the dad was telling a story, and the kids were laughing, and it was all I could do to keep from ringing the doorbell and asking for a place at the table. I felt so far from home.

What I felt that night, some of you have felt ever since . . .

your husband died.

your child was buried.

you learned about the lump in your breast or the spot in your lung.

Some of you have felt far from home ever since your home fell apart.

The twists and turns of life have a way of reminding us—we aren't home here. This is not our homeland. We aren't fluent in the languages of disease and death. The culture confuses the heart, the noise disrupts our sleep, and we feel far from home.

And, you know what? That's OK.

Homesickness is one of the burdens God doesn't mind if we carry. We, like Molly, are being prepared for another house. And we, like the parakeet from Green Bay, know we aren't there yet.

Pootsie was her name. She escaped from her owner and came into the keeping of the humane society. When no one else claimed her, Sue Gleason did. They hit it off. They talked and bathed together, becoming fast friends. But one day the little bird did something incredible. It flew over to Mrs. Gleason, put her beak in her ear, and whispered, "Fifteen hundred South Oneida Street, Green Bay."

Gleason was dumbfounded. She researched and found that the address existed. She went to the house and found a seventy-nine-year-old man named John Stroobants.

"Do you have a parakeet?" she asked.

"I used to; I miss him terribly."

When he saw his Pootsie, he was thrilled. "You know, he even knows his phone number."[1]

The story isn't as crazy as you might think. You have an eternal address fixed in your mind as well. God has "set eternity in the hearts of men" (Eccles. 3:11 NIV). Down deep you know you are not home yet.

So be careful not to act like you are. Don't lower the duffel bag too soon. Would you hang pictures on the wall of a Greyhound bus? Do you set up a bedroom at the roadside rest stop? Do you load your king-size bed on a commercial flight?

Would you treat this world like home? It isn't. The greatest calamity is not to feel far from home when you are, but to feel right at home when you are not. Don't quench, but rather, stir this longing for heaven.

God's home is a *forever* home. "And I will dwell in the house of the LORD forever" (Ps. 23:6 NKJV).

My friends Jeff and Carol just adopted two small children. Christopher, the older, is only three, but he knows the difference between Jeff's house and the foster home from which he came. He tells all visitors, "This is my forever home."

Won't it be great when we say the same? Couldn't we use a forever home? This home we're in won't last forever. Birthdays remind us of that.

During the writing of this book I turned forty-six. I'm closer to ninety than I am to infancy. All those things they say about aging are coming true. I'm patting myself less on the back and more under the chin. I have everything I had twenty years ago, except now it's all lower. The other day I tried to straighten out the wrinkles in my socks and found out I wasn't wearing any. I can relate to Dave Barry's description of aging:

> . . . dental problems, intestinal malfunctions, muscle deterioration, emotional instability, memory lapses, hearing and vision loss, impotence, seizures, growths, prostate problems, greatly reduced limb function, massive coronary failure, death, and, of course, painful hemorrhoidal swelling.[2]

Aging. It's no fun. The way we try to avoid it, you'd think we could. We paint the body, preserve the body, protect the body. And well we should. These bodies are God's gifts. We should be responsible. But we should also be realistic. This body must die so the new body can live. "Flesh and blood cannot have a part in the kingdom of God. Something that will ruin cannot have a part in something that never ruins" (1 Cor. 15:50).

Aging is God's idea. It's one of the ways he keeps us headed homeward. We can't change the process, but we can change our attitude. Here is a thought. What if we looked at the aging body as we look at the growth of a tulip?

Do you ever see anyone mourning over the passing of the tulip bulb? Do gardeners weep as the bulb begins to weaken? Of course not. We don't purchase tulip girdles or petal wrinkle cream or consult plastic-leaf surgeons. We don't mourn the passing of the bulb; we celebrate it. Tulip lovers rejoice the minute the bulb weakens. "Watch that one," they say. "It's about to blossom."

Could it be heaven does the same? The angels point to our bodies. The more frail we become, the more excited they become. "Watch that lady in the hospital," they say. "She's about to blossom." "Keep an eye on the fellow with the bad heart. He'll be coming home soon."

"We are waiting for God to finish making us his own children, which means our bodies will be made free" (Rom. 8:23).

Are our bodies now free? No. Paul describes them as our "earthy bodies" (Phil. 3:21 MSG). Or as other translations state:

"our lowly body" (NKJV)

"the body of our humble state" (NASB)

"these weak mortal bodies" (NLT)

"our vile body" (KJV)

"our simple bodies" (NCV)

You could add your own adjective, couldn't you? Which word describes your body? My *cancerous* body? My *arthritic* body? My *deformed* body? My *crippled* body? My *addicted* body? My *ever-expanding* body? The word may be different, but the message is the same: These bodies are weak. They began decaying the minute we began breathing.

And, according to God, that's a part of the plan. Every wrinkle and every needle take us one step closer to the last step when Jesus will change our simple bodies into forever bodies. No pain. No depression. No sickness. No end.

This is not our forever house. It will serve for the time being. But there is nothing like the moment we enter his door.

Molly can tell you. After a month in our house she ran away. I came home one night to find the place unusually quiet. Molly was gone.

She'd slipped out unnoticed. The search began immediately. Within an hour we knew that she was far, far from home. Now, if you don't like pets, what I'm about to say is going to sound strange. If you do like pets, you will understand.

You'll understand why we walked up and down the street, calling her name. You'll understand why I drove around the neighborhood at 10:30 P.M. You'll understand why I put up a poster in the convenience store and convened the family for a prayer. (Honestly, I did.) You'll understand why I sent e-mails to the staff, asking for prayers, and to her breeder, asking for advice. And you'll understand why we were ready to toss the confetti and party when she showed up.

Here is what happened. The next morning Denalyn was on her way home from taking the girls to school when she saw the trash truck. She asked the workers to keep an eye out for Molly and then hurried home to host a moms' prayer group. Soon after the ladies arrived, the trash truck pulled into our driveway, a worker opened the door, and out bounded our dog. She had been found.

When Denalyn called to tell me the news, I could barely hear her voice. It was Mardi Gras in the kitchen. The ladies were celebrating the return of Molly.

This story pops with symbolism. The master leaving his house, searching for the lost. Victories in the midst of prayer. Great things coming out of trash. But most of all: the celebration at the coming home. That's something else you have in common with Molly—a party at your homecoming.

By that moment only one bag will remain. Not guilt. It was dropped at Calvary. Not the fear of death. It was left at the grave. The only lingering luggage will be this God-given longing for home. And when you see him, you'll set it down. Just as a returning soldier drops his duffel when he sees his wife, you'll drop your longing when you see your Father. Those you love will shout. Those you know will applaud. But all the noise will cease when he cups your chin and says, "Welcome home." And with scarred hand he'll wipe every tear from your eye. And you will dwell in the house of your Lord—forever.

Conclusion

I fell asleep in the Louvre.

The most famous museum in the world. The best-known building in Paris. Tourists are oohing and aahing, and that's me, nodding and snoring. Seated on a bench. Back to the wall. Chin to my chest. Conked out.

The crown jewels are down the hall. Rembrandt is on the wall. Van Gogh is one floor up. The *Venus de Milo* is one floor down. I should have been star struck and wide eyed.

Denalyn was. You'd have thought she was at Foley's Red Apple sale. If there was a tour, she took it. If there was a button to push, she pushed it. If there was a brochure to read, she read it. She didn't even want to stop to eat.

But me? I gave the *Mona Lisa* five minutes.

Shameful, I know.

I should have been more like the fellow next to me. When I dozed off, he was transfixed on a seventeenth-century Dutch artist's rendering of a flower. When I awoke, the guy was still staring. I closed my eyes again. When I opened them, he hadn't moved.

I leaned toward him and tried to sound reflective. "Awesome, eh?" No response. "The shades are masterful." Still no reply. "Do you think it's a number painting?" He sighed and said nothing, but I knew what he was thinking, *Uncultured klutz.*

He's right. I was. But it wasn't my fault. I like seventeenth-century art as much as the next guy . . . well, maybe not that much. But at least I can usually stay awake.

But not that day. Why did I fall asleep at the Louvre?

Blame it on the bags, baby; blame it on the bags. I was worn out from lugging the family luggage. We checked more suitcases than the road show of the *Phantom of the Opera.*

I can't fault my wife and daughters. They learned it from me. Remember, I'm the one who travels prepared for an underwater wedding and a bowling tournament. It's bad enough for one person to travel like that, but five? It'll wear you out.

You think I'll ever learn to travel light?

I tell you what. Let's make a pact. I'll reduce the leather bags, and we'll both reduce the emotional ones. After all, it's one thing to sleep through the Louvre but quite another to sleep through life.

We can, you know. Do we not dwell in the gallery of our God? Isn't the sky his canvas and humanity his magnum opus? Are we not encircled by artistry? Sunsets burning. Waves billowing.

And isn't the soul his studio? The birthing of love, the bequeathing of grace. All around us miracles pop like fireflies—souls are touched, hearts are changed, and . . .

Yawn. We miss it. We sleep through it. We can't help it. It's hard work carrying yesterday's guilt around. This burlap bag of worry has my neck in a knot. The dread of death is enough to break a back.

It's also enough to make you miss the magic of life. Many miss it every Sunday. Good, well-meaning folks sitting in church, fighting to keep the eyes—if not of their heads at least of their hearts—awake.

And what do we miss? We miss God parting the heavens to hear us sing. Shouldn't we be stretching heavenward, tiptoed on our pews?

What do we miss? God is meeting us in communion! Shouldn't we be distributing, along with the wafers and wine, ammonia sticks so we could awaken each other from our faints of awe?

What do we miss? God's Word. Should we not hold it like nitroglycerin? Shouldn't we be wide-awake? We should, but we dragged that trunk of dissatisfaction all over town last week. And, besides that, we couldn't sleep last night; we kept rolling over on our duffel bag of disappointments.

Then let's get rid of the bags! Once and for all, let's give our luggage to him. Let's take him at his word! "Come to me, all of you who are weary and carry heavy burdens, and I will give you rest" (Matt. 11:28 NLT).

Rest from the burden of a small god. Why? Because I have found **the Lord.**

Rest from doing things my way. Why? Because **the Lord is my Shepherd.**

Rest from endless wants. Why? Because **I shall not want.**

Rest from weariness. Why? Because **he makes me to lie down.**

Rest from worry. Why? Because **he leads me.**

Rest from hopelessness. Why? Because **he restores my soul.**

Rest from guilt. Why? Because **he leads me in the paths of righteousness.**

Rest from arrogance. Why? Because of **his name's sake.**

Rest from the valley of death. Why? Because **he walks me through it.**

Rest from the shadow of grief. Why? Because **he guides me.**

Rest from fear. Why? Because **his presence comforts me.**

Rest from loneliness. Why? Because **he is with me.**

Rest from shame. Why? Because **he has prepared a place for me in the presence of my enemies.**

Rest from my disappointments. Why? Because **he anoints me.**

Rest from envy. Why? Because **my cup overflows.**

Rest from doubt. Why? Because **he follows me.**

Rest from homesickness. Why? Because **I will dwell in the house of my Lord forever.**

And tomorrow, when out of habit you pick your luggage back up, set it down again. Set it down again and again until that sweet day when you find you aren't picking it back up.

And on that day, when you feel the load lifted, when you've taken a step toward traveling light, when you have the energy to ponder the mysteries of life, do me a favor. Walk down the hall and turn to the left. Wait your turn behind the scarlet ropes. Take a good, long look at the *Mona Lisa,* and tell me, what's the big deal about her anyway?

Notes

Chapter 2: The Middle C of Life

1. Or, in Hebrew, fifty-four words describe the first one.
2. Around A.D. 200 Christian scholars began writing the vowels for *Adonai* beneath the Tetragrammaton (YHWH), reminding the reader to say "Adonai." The word was still unpronounceable until German scholars in the middle of the nineteenth century inserted the vowels of *Adonai* between the *Yahweh* consonants creating the name *Jehovah*—a name that had never existed in any language.
3. Nathan Stone, *Names of God* (Chicago: Moody Press, 1944), 20.
4. Donald W. McCullough, *The Trivialization of God: The Dangerous Illusion of a Manageable Deity* (Colorado Springs: NavPress, 1995), 66.
5. Ibid., 54.

Chapter 3: I'll Do It My Way

1. With appreciation to Rick Reilly and his chapter on Jean Van de Velde, "*Mon Dieu!* Better Safe Than Sorry!" in *The Life of Reilly* (New York: Total Sports Illustrated, 2000), 175–77.

Chapter 4: The Prison of Want

1. Randy C. Alcorn, *Money, Possessions, and Eternity* (Wheaton, Ill.: Tyndale Publishers, 1989), 55.

2. Chris Seidman, *Little Buddy* (Orange, Calif.: New Leaf Books, 2001), 138. Used with permission.

3. Rick Atchley, "I Have Learned the Secret," audiotape 7 of the 1997 Pepperdine Lectures (Malibu, Calif., 1997). Used with permission.

4. Used with permission.

Chapter 5: I Will Give You Rest

1. Robert Sullivan, "Sleepless in America," *Life,* February 1998, 56–66 and *Prime Time Live,* 2 March 1998.

2. Sullivan, "Sleepless," 63.

3. Ibid.

4. Phillip Keller, *A Shepherd Looks at Psalm 23* (Grand Rapids, Mich.: Zondervan Publishing, 1970; reprint, in *Phillip Keller: The Inspirational Writings,* New York: Inspirational Press, 1993), 28–29 (page citations are to the reprint edition).

5. Helmut Thielicke, *Encounter with Spurgeon,* trans. John W. Doberstein (Philadelphia: Fortress Press, 1963; reprint, Grand Rapids, Mich.: Baker Book House, 1975), 220 (page citation is to the reprint edition).

Chapter 6: Whaddifs and Howells

1. Og Mandino, *The Spellbinder's Gift* (New York: Fawcett Columbine, 1995), 70–71.

2. From "Worrier and Warrior," a sermon by Ted Schroder, Christ Episcopal Church, San Antonio, Texas, on 10 April 1994.

3. See Psalm 119:105.

Chapter 9: Get Over Yourself

1. Rick Reilly, *The Life of Reilly* (New York: Total Sports Illustrated, 2000), 73.

2. Paul Lee Tan, *Encyclopedia of 7700 Illustrations* (Rockville, Md.: Assurance Publishers, 1979), 211.

3. Ibid., 1100.

4. William J. Bennett, ed., *The Spirit of America: Words of Advice from the Founders in Stories, Letters, Poem and Speeches* (New York: Touchstone, 1997), 161.

Chapter 10: I Will Lead You Home

1. Phillip Keller, *A Shepherd Looks at Psalm 23* (Grand Rapids, Mich.: Zondervan Publishing, 1970; reprint, in *Phillip Keller: The Inspirational Writings,* New York: Inspirational Press, 1993), 70 (page citation is to the reprint edition).

2. F. W. Boreham, *Life Verses: The Bible's Impact on Famous Lives,* vol. 2 (Grand Rapids, Mich.: Kregel Publications, 1994), 211.

Chapter 11: When Mourning Comes

1. Michael P. Green, ed., *Illustrations for Biblical Preaching* (Grand Rapids, Mich.: Baker Book House, 1989), 91.

Chapter 14: The Crowing Rooster and Me

1. Charles W. Slemming, *He Leadeth Me: The Shepherd's Life in Palestine* (Fort Washington, Pa.: Christian Literature Crusade, 1964), quoted in Charles R. Swindoll, *Living Beyond the Daily Grind, Book 1: Reflections on the Songs and Sayings in Scripture* (Nashville: W Publishing Group, 1988), 77–78.

Chapter 15: Slippery Sheep and Healed Hurts

1. "Paul was in prison several times: Philippi (Acts 16:23); Jerusalem (Acts 23:18); Caesarea (Acts 23:33; 24:27; 25:14); and Rome (Acts 28:16, 20, 30)." Robert B. Hughes and J. Carl Laney, *New Bible Companion* (Wheaton, Ill.: Tyndale House Publishers, 1990), 681.

2. Phillip Keller, *A Shepherd Looks at Psalm 23* (Grand Rapids, Mich.: Zondervan Publishing, 1970; reprint, in *Phillip Keller: The Inspirational Writings,* New York: Inspirational Press, 1993), 99 (page citation is to the reprint edition).

Chapter 16: Jam Session

1. F. B. Meyer, *The Shepherd Psalm* (Grand Rapids, Mich.: Kregel Publications, 1991), 115.
2. From a sermon entitled "God's Antidote to Your Hurt" by Rick Warren.

Chapter 17: God's Loving Pursuit

1. F. B. Meyer, *The Shepherd Psalm* (Grand Rapids, Mich.: Kregel Publications, 1991), 125.
2. Though originally written for this book, this story initially appeared in *The Gift for All People.* Thanks to Multnomah Publishing for allowing us to use it in *Traveling Light.*

Chapter 18: Almost Heaven

1. Calvin Miller, *Into the Depths of God: Where Eyes See the Invisible, Ears Hear the Inaudible, and Minds Conceive the Inconceivable* (Minneapolis: Bethany House, 2000), 217.
2. Dave Barry, *Dave Barry Turns 40* (New York: Crown, 1990), quoted in Helen Exley, *A Spread of Over 40s Jokes* (New York: Exley Giftbooks, 1992).

Study Guide

Traveling Light

Prepared by Steve Halliday

1

The Luggage of Life

Traveling Back

1. *The bags we grab are not made of leather; they're made of burdens. The suitcase of guilt. A sack of discontent. You drape a duffel bag of weariness on one shoulder and a hanging bag of grief on the other. Add on a backpack of doubt, an overnight bag of loneliness, and a trunk of fear. Pretty soon you're pulling more stuff than a skycap. No wonder you're so tired at the end of the day. Lugging luggage is exhausting.*

   A. Which of the "bags" listed here trouble you the most? Why?

   B. Have you left any luggage behind? How did it feel to do so?

2. *God is saying to you, "Set that stuff down! You're carrying burdens you don't need to bear."*

   A. Why do you think we carry burdens we don't need to bear?

   B. What keeps you from setting down burdens you needn't bear?

3. *Traveling light means trusting God with the burdens you were never intended to bear.*

   A. What does it mean to trust God with a burden? How does one do this?

   B. What have you learned from observing others with their "luggage"?

Traveling Up

1. Read Psalm 23.

   A. What pictures leap to mind when you read this psalm?

   B. What memories does this psalm conjure up for you?

C. What part of this psalm means the most to you? Why?

D. How does this psalm teach us to give up personal burdens?

2. Read Matthew 11:28–30.

A. To whom are these words addressed? Does this include you?

B. What promise does Jesus give to those who respond to his invitation?

C. Are you taking advantage of Jesus' invitation? Why or why not?

3. Read 1 Peter 5:7.

A. What does this verse instruct us to do? (How are we to obey?)

B. What reason does Peter give for obeying this command?

C. What benefit can we expect to receive when we obey?

Traveling On

1. Set aside at least a half-hour for prayer, and ask the Lord to reveal any burdens you need to lay down. Pray with a piece of paper and a pen in hand, and write down any burdens the Lord brings to mind. Show your completed list to your closest friend, and ask him or her to pray with you that God will show you how to release these burdens.

2. What burdens are your loved ones needlessly bearing? What can you do to help them lay down those unnecessary burdens?

2

The Middle C of Life

The Burden of a Lesser God

Traveling Back

1. *With his very first words in [Psalm 23], David sets out to deliver us from the burden of a lesser deity.*

   A. What lesser deities hold an attraction for your acquaintances?

   B. Why would anyone settle for a lesser deity?

2. Max says that many people settle for one of three lesser deities: God as a genie in a bottle, as a sweet grandpa, or as a busy dad.

   A. Describe in your own words each of these lesser deities. What seems attractive about them?

   B. Have any of these three lesser deities appealed to you? Why or why not?

3. *God is the "One who is" and the "One who causes." Why is that important? Because we need a big God. And if God is the "One who is," then he is an unchanging God.*

   A. Why do we need a big God? Why do we need an unchanging God?

   B. What would be different about your life if God were smaller than he is? How would you feel if he changed capriciously?

4. *Unchanging. Uncaused. Ungoverned. These are only a fraction of God's qualities, but aren't they enough to give you a glimpse of your Father? Don't we need this kind of shepherd? Don't we need an unchanging shepherd?*

   A. How do you answer Max's questions?

   B. Give an example of how God has been an unchanging shepherd in your life.

Traveling Up

1. Read Exodus 3:13–17; 6:2–8.

   A. What do you learn about God from his name?

   B. What do you learn about God from his track record?

   C. What do you learn about God's concern for his people?

2. Read Psalm 102:25–27; 139:7–12.

   A. What do you learn about God from these passages? How do these verses affect your view of God?

3. Read 1 Timothy 6:13–16.

   A. What do you learn about God from this text?

   B. How does Paul suggest we respond to this God?

4. Read Isaiah 40:21–31.

   A. What does this text reveal about God?

   B. What does God think of pretenders to his throne?

   C. How does God intend for this majestic picture of him to encourage our weary hearts?

Traveling On

1. Do a study on the false gods described in Scripture. Start with names such as "Chemosh," "Baal," "Asherah," and the generic "gods." Do other research, perhaps in a good Bible dictionary, to discover something about these "lesser gods." How do they compare to the God of Jesus?

2. Spend some time meditating and concentrating on the attributes of the real God of the Bible. Consider using a daily devotional such as *How Great Thou Art* (Sister, Ore.: Multnomah, 1999), which focuses for a full year on the majesty and greatness of God.

3

I'll Do It My Way

The Burden of Self-Reliance

Traveling Back

1. *We humans want to do things our way. Forget the easy way. Forget the common way. Forget the best way. Forget God's way. We want to do things our way.*

   A. What is it about us that causes us to desire our own way?

   B. When we rely on ourselves rather than God, what is the result?

2. *When David, who was a warrior, minstrel, and ambassador for God, searched for an illustration of God, he remembered his days as a shepherd. . . . And the way he cared for the sheep reminded him of the way God cares for us. David rejoiced to say, "The Lord is my shepherd," and in so doing he proudly implied, "I am his sheep."*

   A. Why do you think David chose to picture God through the image of a shepherd? Why not use another image?

   B. Do you proudly think of yourself as a sheep? Explain.

3. *Will you humor me and take a simple quiz? See if you succeed in self-reliance. Raise your hand if any of the following describe you.*

   You can control your moods.
   You are at peace with everyone.
   You have no fears.
   You need no forgiveness.

   A. Describe someone you know who believes he or she fits one of the previous four statements.

B. Which of these four areas of life cause you the most struggles? Explain.

C. Why is it that the ones who most need a shepherd resist him so?

Traveling Up

1. Read Jeremiah 17:5–8.

   A. What does the Lord think of someone who relies on himself (v. 5)?

   B. What is the result of relying on yourself (v. 6)?

   C. How does the Lord feel about those who trust in him (v. 7)?

   D. What is the result of trusting in God (v. 8)?

2. Read Deuteronomy 8:10–18.

   A. What are we to do in times of prosperity (v. 10)?

   B. In what way can prosperity create a spiritual threat (vv. 11–14)?

   C. Why is it always foolish to believe that we are self-sufficient (vv. 15–18)?

3. Read 1 Corinthians 4:6–7.

   A. What does it mean to "not go beyond what is written" (v. 6 NIV)? Why does the Bible warn us to "not go beyond what is written"?

   B. How would you answer Paul's three questions in verse 7?

Traveling On

1. Consciously get out of your comfort zone, and do something that requires you to rely on another person. Make it as exotic as a parachute jump or as mundane as asking directions to a place you've never visited.

2. Read the classic *A Shepherd Looks at Psalm 23* by Phillip Keller to gain a better picture of what it means to be a sheep in the fold of God.

4

The Prison of Want

The Burden of Discontent

Traveling Back

1. *The prison of want. You've seen her prisoners. They are "in want." They want something. They want something bigger. Nicer. Faster. Thinner. They want.*

   A. Are you in prison?

   B. What things in life are most likely to send you to this prison? Describe them.

2. *David has found the pasture where discontent goes to die. It's as if he is saying, "What I have in God is greater than what I don't have in life."*

   A. What do you have in God? List the first ten things that come to mind.

   B. Can you say that what you have in God is greater than what you don't have in life? Explain.

3. *Are you hoping that a change in circumstances will bring a change in your attitude? If so, you are in prison, and you need to learn a secret of traveling light.*

   A. Answer the question above and explain your answer.

   B. What is this secret of traveling light? How does one master it?

4. *What is the one thing separating you from joy? How do you fill in this blank: "I will be happy when ___________________"? When I am healed. When I am promoted. When I am married. When I am single. When I am rich. How would you finish that statement?*

   A. Answer the question above.

B. How does this thing separate you from joy? How long has it been doing so? How can you deprive it of its power over you?

Traveling Up

1. Read Luke 12:13–21.
   A. What warning does Jesus give in verse 15? What declaration does he make?
   B. What error did the rich man make in the parable Jesus told?
   C. What does it mean to be "rich toward God" (v. 21)? Are you rich toward God? Explain.
2. Read Philippians 4:10–13.
   A. Why did Paul "rejoice greatly in the Lord" (v. 10 NIV)?
   B. What secret does Paul describe in verse 12? How did he gain access to this secret? Do you know this secret? Explain.
   C. How does verse 13 relate to the context of the passage? How does it relate specifically to contentment?
3. Read 1 Timothy 6:3–10.
   A. How does Paul characterize those who teach that godliness is a means to financial gain (v. 5)?
   B. What does Paul say *is* "great gain" (v. 6 NIV)?
   C. What reason does Paul give for his statement (vv. 7–8)?
   D. What warning does Paul give in verses 9–10? Why do so many people ignore this warning? What do you think of his warning? Explain.

Traveling On

1. Make a list of at least a dozen things you possess, whether spiritual or material, that came to you as a result of your relationship with God.
2. Do a Bible study on contentment. Use a good concordance to look up words such as *content* and *contented,* then study the verses that you find. Also see what a good Bible dictionary or encyclopedia has to say on the topic. What do you learn?

5

I Will Give You Rest

The Burden of Weariness

Traveling Back

1. *People with too much work and too little sleep step over to the baggage claim of life and grab the duffel bag of weariness. You don't carry this one. You don't hoist it onto your shoulder and stride down the street. You drag it as you would a stubborn St. Bernard.*

   A. What sorts of things tend to make you weary?

   B. How do you normally deal with weariness? What did you do the last time weariness struck hard?

2. *In our book, busyness is next to godliness. We idolize Thomas Edison, who claimed he could live on fifteen-minute naps. Somehow we forget to mention Albert Einstein, who averaged eleven hours of sleep a night.*

   A. How often do you tell others, "I'm really busy right now"? What keeps you so busy?

   B. How much sleep do you normally get? Is it sufficient for you to function well? Explain.

3. *God's message is plain: "If creation didn't crash when I rested, it won't crash when you do." Repeat these words after me: It is not my job to run the world.*

   A. Name some of the reasons you have heard (or used yourself) for not getting adequate rest.

   B. Why do you think God so emphasized the fourth commandment, about resting on the Sabbath day?

4. *In a world rocky with human failure, there is a land lush with divine mercy. Your Shepherd invites you there. He wants you to lie down. Nestle*

deeply until you are hidden, buried, in the tall shoots of his love, and there you will find rest.

A. What is your favorite way of nestling deeply "in the tall shoots of his love"? Describe what most refreshes you.

B. What is keeping you from resting in God's love right now?

Traveling Up

1. Read Exodus 20:8–11.

A. What does it mean to keep the Sabbath day "holy"?

B. What does God command Israel in verses 9–10?

C. What reason does God give in verse 11 for his command?

D. Why do you think God so highly values our rest?

2. Read Isaiah 30:15–18.

A. According to verse 15, Israel's salvation consisted in what? How did the nation respond to this direction?

B. What response is described in verse 16? How do we often respond in a similar way?

C. What is the result of ignoring God's command to rest (v. 17)?

D. Despite our foolishness, how does the Lord treat us (v. 18)?

3. Read Hebrews 4:1–11.

A. What does the writer warn us about in verse 1?

B. What keeps people from entering God's rest (vv. 2–6)?

C. When is the best time to obey God's command (v. 7)?

D. What kind of rest is the writer describing in verse 9?

E. How do we "labour" to enter God's rest (v. 11 KJV)?

Traveling On

1. What activities or events keep you busy? Try an experiment to judge the accuracy of your assumptions. Keep a "busyness journal"

for one week, recording the things that occupy your time. Write down not only what you did but also how long each took. Then at the end of the week evaluate your journal. Are you busy doing the things that matter most? Or do you need to make some changes?

2. How much sleep do you get? Keep a chart for one month, accurately recording the amount and quality of your sleep. Do the results surprise you? What changes, if any, do you need to make?

6

Whaddifs and Howells

The Burden of Worry

Traveling Back

1. *Worry is the burlap bag of burdens. It's overflowing with "whaddifs" and "howells." "Whaddif it rains at my wedding?" "Howell I know when to discipline my kids?" "Whaddif I marry a guy who snores?" "Howell we pay our baby's tuition?"*

   A. What "whaddifs" trouble you the most?

   B. What "howells" give you the most grief?

   C. How do you typically deal with these "whaddifs" and "howells"?

2. *Worry divides the mind. The biblical word for* worry (merimnao) *is a compound of two Greek words,* merizo *("to divide") and* nous *("the mind"). Anxiety splits our energy between today's priorities and tomorrow's problems. Part of our mind is on the now; the rest is on the not yet. The result is half-minded living.*

   A. What practical things can we do to keep from spending today's energies on tomorrow's problems?

   B. What issues are most likely to nudge you toward half-minded living? Why?

3. *God leads us. God will do the right thing at the right time. And what a difference that makes.*

   A. How has God led you in the past? Describe at least one incident.

   B. Do we believe that God will do the right thing at the right time? How would our lives change if we really believed this?

C. What in your life would change *right now* if you believed this fully?

4. *Meet today's problems with today's strength. Don't start tackling tomorrow's problems until tomorrow. You do not have tomorrow's strength yet. You simply have enough for today.*

   A. How many of the things you have worried about actually have come to pass?

   B. What issues that should be dealt with today are you avoiding by trying to tackle tomorrow's problems?

Traveling Up

1. Read Matthew 6:25–34.

   A. What reason does Jesus give for refusing to worry (vv. 25–27)?

   B. Why should worry not trouble Christians in the same way it troubles nonbelievers (vv. 31–32)?

   C. If we are not to worry, what are we to do (v. 33)? What does this mean in practical terms?

   D. What additional reason for not worrying does Jesus give in verse 34?

2. Read Philippians 4:6–8.

   A. How does Paul recommend that we combat worry?

   B. According to Paul, what will we enjoy when we follow his counsel?

   C. Rather than worry, what kinds of things should fill our minds (v. 8)?

3. Read Hebrews 4:14–16.

   A. Describe the high priest pictured in this passage.

   B. How is verse 16 designed to combat our worry?

Traveling On

1. Make a list of the things in life that worry you the most. Then, one by one, commit these items to the Lord in prayer. As you pray for each concern, tear it off your sheet of paper and throw it in the trash.

2. Use a good concordance to do a word study on worry. Look up terms such as *worry, worried, anxious,* and *anxiety,* and study the verses that you find. What do you learn about how to combat worry?

7

It's a Jungle Out There

The Burden of Hopelessness

Traveling Back

1. *Hopelessness is an odd bag. Unlike the others, it isn't full. It is empty, and its emptiness creates the burden. Unzip the top and examine all the pockets. Turn it upside down and shake it hard. The bag of hopelessness is painfully empty.*

   A. Describe a time when you felt hopeless. What made you feel that way?

   B. What in your life right now threatens your hope? How will you deal with it?

2. *If you have only a person but no renewed vision, all you have is company. If he has a vision but no direction, you have a dreamer for company. But if you have a person with direction—who can take you from this place to the right place—ah, then you have one who can restore your hope.*

   A. Why does it take a competent guide to restore hope?

   B. Do you have such a guide? Explain.

3. *God, your rescuer, has the right vision. He also has the right direction. He made the boldest claim in the history of man when he declared, "I am the way."*

   A. What did Jesus mean when he said, "I am the way"?

   B. Why wasn't it arrogant of Jesus to say that he was *the* way? Then what about Muhammad, the Dalai Lama, or spiritual leaders of other faiths?

4. *We ask God, "Where are you taking me? Where is the path?" And he, like the guide, doesn't tell us. Oh, he may give us a hint or two, but that's*

all. If he did, would we understand? Would we comprehend our location? No, like the traveler, we are unacquainted with this jungle. So rather than give us an answer, Jesus gives us a far greater gift. He gives us himself.

A. How does it make you feel that God almost never tells us what lies ahead for us? Do you wish he did things differently? Explain.

B. In what ways has Jesus guided you in the past? How are you depending upon his guidance right now?

Traveling Up

1. Read Psalm 121.

   A. From where did the psalmist expect his hope to arrive (v. 2)?

   B. How much sleep does God get each night (vv. 3–4)? Why is this important?

   C. What kinds of things is the Lord said to watch over in verses 5–8? How can this give you hope?

2. Read Psalm 33:16–22.

   A. What *cannot* save a king or a warrior (vv. 16–17)? Why are these things vain hopes?

   B. On whom does the Lord fix his eyes (v. 18)? What difference does this make?

   C. What does it mean to "wait in hope" (v. 20 NIV)? How can you put your hope in the Lord?

3. Read Romans 8:18–25.

   A. Why should we avoid attaching too much importance to our present sufferings (v. 18)?

   B. Why do we need hope in the first place (vv. 19–23)?

   C. How does Paul define real hope (v. 24)?

   D. Why is it always too soon to give up hope (v. 25)?

Traveling On

1. Take a guided tour of a place you've never visited. During the tour, consciously remind yourself of how your Savior desires to guide you through life. What unexpected discoveries or parallels do you uncover?

2. Do a Bible study on hope. Use a good concordance to look up the word *hope* and its derivatives, like *hoping, hoped, hopeful,* etc. What do you learn?

8

A Heavenly Exchange

The Burden of Guilt

Traveling Back

1. *God is never wrong. He has never rendered a wrong decision, experienced the wrong attitude, taken the wrong path, said the wrong thing, or acted the wrong way. He is never too late or too early, too loud or too soft, too fast or too slow. He has always been and always will be right. He is righteous.*

   A. Has it ever felt as if God made a mistake with your life? If so, how did you deal with this feeling?

   B. Who is the most "righteous" person you know? What makes you say this about him or her?

2. *The weight of weariness pulls you down. Self-reliance misleads you. Disappointments discourage you. Anxiety plagues you. But guilt? Guilt consumes you. So what do we do? Our Lord is right, and we are wrong. His party is for the guiltless, and we are anything but. What do we do?*

   A. Answer the question above.

   B. How do you deal with disappointments? With anxiety? Guilt?

3. *It was, at once, history's most beautiful and most horrible moment. Jesus stood in the tribunal of heaven. Sweeping a hand over all creation, he pleaded, "Punish me for their mistakes. See the murderer? Give me his penalty. The adulteress? I'll take her shame. The bigot, the liar, the thief? Do to me what you would do to them. Treat me as you would a sinner." And God did.*

   A. Why did innocent Jesus request to take the punishment due to murderers, adulterers, and other sinners?

B. Have you allowed Jesus to take on himself your own sin? Explain.

4. *The path of righteousness is a narrow, winding trail up a steep hill. At the top of the hill is a cross. At the base of the cross are bags. Countless bags full of innumerable sins. Calvary is the compost pile for guilt.*

   A. In what way is Calvary "the compost pile for guilt"?

   B. If you have set your bag of guilt at the foot of Calvary, describe how this came to be. If you have not already done so, why not?

Traveling Up

1. Read Romans 3:9–18.

   A. What does it mean to be "under sin" (NIV)? Who is "under sin" (v. 9)?

   B. List the characteristics of being "under sin" (vv. 10–17).

   C. How does verse 18 summarize all the characteristics you just listed?

2. Read Isaiah 45:21–25.

   A. How does God describe himself in verse 21?

   B. What command does God give in verse 22?

   C. What prediction does God give in verses 23–24?

   D. What promise does God give in verse 25? To whom is he referring?

3. Read Romans 5:6–11 and 1 Peter 3:18.

   A. According to Romans 5:6, for whom did Christ die?

   B. What drove Christ to die for us (v. 8)?

   C. What is the difference between being "justified" and "saved" (v. 9 NIV)?

   D. What is the normal response of one who has been "reconciled" (v. 11 NIV)? Is this your response? Explain.

Traveling On

1. Read a contemporary book by an author who exchanged his or her guilt for the forgiveness of God. How does this remind you of your own need for forgiveness?

2. Is there someone in your life whom you need to forgive but haven't? Remember Jesus' words: "But if you do not forgive men their sins, your Father will not forgive your sins" (Matthew 6:15 NIV). Commit today to forgive this person—and if possible, let him or her know what you've done.

9

Get Over Yourself

The Burden of Arrogance

Traveling Back

1. *God . . . doesn't dislike arrogance. He doesn't disapprove of arrogance. He's not unfavorably disposed toward arrogance. God hates arrogance. What a meal of maggots does for our stomach, human pride does for God's.*

   A. Why do you think God dislikes human pride?

   B. Would you consider yourself a prideful person? Would others agree with you? Explain.

2. *God . . . hates arrogance because we haven't done anything to be arrogant about. Do art critics give awards to the canvas? Is there a Pulitzer for ink? Can you imagine a scalpel growing smug after a successful heart transplant? Of course not. They are only tools, so they get no credit for the accomplishments.*

   A. In what way are we "tools" in God's hands?

   B. Is there any room at all for taking pride in one's accomplishments? Explain.

3. *Why does God have anything to do with us?* For his name's sake. *No other name on the marquee. No other name up in lights. No other name on the front page. This is all done for God's glory.*

   A. Why isn't it vain of God to associate with us for *his* name's sake?

   B. What is meant by "God's glory"? Why is God's glory so important?

4. Consider several ways to cultivate humility and kill ungodly pride:

- Assess yourself honestly.
- Don't take success too seriously.
- Celebrate the significance of others.
- Don't demand your own parking place.
- Never announce your success before it occurs.
- Speak humbly.
- Live at the foot of the cross.

A. Who can help you assess yourself honestly? What does such an assessment reveal?

B. How can you celebrate the significance of others? Who in your immediate circle do you need to celebrate right now?

C. How can you "live at the foot of the cross"? What does this mean?

Traveling Up

1. Read Proverbs 16:5, 18–19.

A. What does the Lord think of the proud (v. 5)? How will he respond to them?

B. What is the outcome of pride (v. 18)?

C. What contrast is made in verse 19? Why is this true?

2. Read Isaiah 57:15–19; 66:2.

A. How does the Lord describe himself in verse 15? With whom is he pleased to live?

B. Why will God not "accuse forever" (v. 16)?

C. How will the Lord respond to those who turn to him in faith (vv. 18–19)?

D. Whom does God esteem, according to Isaiah 66:2? Why does the Lord delight in men and women like this?

3. Read Philippians 2:3–11.

   A. What does verse 3 instruct us not to do? What should we do instead?

   B. What overall instruction do we receive in verse 5?

   C. How did Jesus follow this instruction during his earthly ministry (vv. 6–8)?

   D. How will God reward Jesus for his faithfulness (vv. 9–11)?

   E. In what way are we to emulate Jesus' example? How are you doing in this regard? Explain.

Traveling On

1. Watch a classic movie such as *Citizen Kane* to see how even Hollywood sometimes recognizes the deadly poison of human pride. How does pride ultimately destroy the person who lets it control him or her?

2. Do a Bible study on how God does everything for the sake of his name. Look up references to "the name," "my name," "his name," etc. What do you discover?

10

I Will Lead You Home

The Burden of the Grave

Traveling Back

1. *Someday our Shepherd . . . will take us to the mountain by way of the valley. He will guide us to his house through the valley of the shadow of death.*

   A. Do you think of your own death, or do you avoid the thought? Explain.

   B. Has a believer you were close to ever died? If so, describe how the Shepherd guided him or her through the valley of the shadow of death.

2. *David grants us two important reminders that can help us surrender our fear of the grave.* We all have to face it. . . . *And though his first reminder sobers us, his second reminder encourages us:* We don't have to face death alone.

   A. If you were to face your own death tomorrow, would you be ready? Explain.

   B. Do you feel as though you would be facing death alone? Explain.

3. *Don't face death without facing God. Don't even speak of death without speaking to God. He and he alone can guide you through the valley. Others may speculate or aspire, but only God knows the way to get you home. And only God is committed to getting you there safely.*

   A. Name a few ways in which God helps his children face death.

   B. How can we be certain God is committed to getting us to heaven safely?

4. *[Jesus] may send missionaries to teach you, angels to protect you, teachers to guide you, singers to inspire you, and physicians to heal you, but he sends no one to take you. He reserves this job for himself.*

   A. When Jesus comes to take you home, what do you think you might say to him first?

   B. Why do you think Jesus insists on coming in person to get you? How does this make you feel?

Traveling Up

1. Read Psalm 116:15; 139:16.

   A. What does Psalm 116:15 say is "precious" to God? Why is this so?

   B. What claim does Psalm 139:16 make? Does this give you comfort? Explain.

2. Read 1 Thessalonians 4:13–18.

   A. What do you learn from this passage about those who die in Christ?

   B. How are these words intended to "encourage" us? Why are we instructed to repeat these words to others?

3. Read 2 Corinthians 5:1–10.

   A. What does Paul mean by "earthly tent" (v. 1 NIV)? Why use this picture?

   B. What is life like in this "tent"? How does Paul contrast life in the "heavenly dwelling" (v.2 NIV)?

   C. What token has God given us to assure us that what he says will one day happen, will actually happen (v. 5)?

   D. How is the information in this passage supposed to make us "confident" (v. 6 NIV)?

   E. What preference does Paul express in verse 8? Why does he prefer this?

   F. How is verse 10 both a promise and a warning?

Traveling On

1. Visit a nearby cemetery, and spend at least an hour reading the gravestones to remind yourself both of death's reality and of the hope believers can have despite its cold embrace.

2. Read Herbert Lockyer's classic book. *Last Words of Saints and Sinners*. How do the deaths of the two groups compare?

11

When Mourning Comes

The Burden of Grief

Traveling Back

1. *The black bag of sorrow is hard to bear. It's hard to bear because not everyone understands your grief. They did at first. They did at the funeral. They did at the graveside. But they don't now; they don't understand. Grief lingers.*

   A. How do you personally deal with sorrow?

   B. How can we help someone whose grief just won't go away?

2. *Only God knows the reasons behind his actions. But here is a key truth on which we can stand.* Our God is a good God.

   A. Why do you think God seldom "explains" his actions in our lives?

   B. How have you personally experienced that God is a good God?

3. *Death is God's way of taking people away from evil. From what kind of evil? An extended disease? An addiction? A dark season of rebellion? We don't know. But we know that no person lives one day more or less than God intends.*

   A. Have you ever thought about death in this way? That it's God's way of taking people away from evil? How do you respond to this idea?

   B. How can the idea of God's sovereignty bring comfort in a time of death? How can the doctrine be used to increase someone's pain?

4. *God will lead you* through, *not around, the valley of the shadow of death. And, by the way, aren't you glad it's just a shadow?*

A. If God really loves us, why doesn't he lead us *around* the valley of the shadow of death? Why lead us *through* it?

B. Is death merely a shadow for you? Explain.

Traveling Up

1. Read Lamentations 3:31–33.

   A. How can verse 31 give you hope when you find yourself engulfed in grief?

   B. What do you learn about God in verse 32?

   C. Why is it important that God does not "willingly" bring us grief (v. 33 NIV)? Why does he bring us grief at all?

2. Read John 16:20–22.

   A. What two promises did Jesus give his disciples in verse 20?

   B. What illustration did Jesus use in verse 21 to picture his promises of verse 20? What can we learn from this illustration?

   C. What promise does Jesus give in verse 22? How certain is this promise? On what is it based? How can it continue to help you today when you face grief?

3. Read 1 Peter 1:3–9.

   A. What great blessing does Peter describe in verses 3–4? Do you share in this blessing? Explain.

   B. What kind of shield are we promised in verse 5?

   C. Does genuine faith exempt one from grief (v. 6)? Why or why not?

   D. How do trials and the grief they bring fit in with the Christian life (v. 7)?

   E. What blessing comes to those who believe in Christ (v. 8)?

   F. What blessing does faith ultimately bring to those who exercise it (v. 9)?

Traveling On

1. Interview someone you know to be gifted in the art of comforting the grieving. Look for someone whom others seek out in a time of loss. Ask the person what he or she does at these times. What do you learn?

2. Do a Bible study on the words *tear* and *tears*. What do you learn?

12

From Panic to Peace

The Burden of Fear

Traveling Back

1. *Jesus flat on the ground? Face in the dirt? Extended hands gripping grass? Body rising and falling with sobs? Face as twisted as the olive trees that surround him? What do we do with this image of Jesus? Simple. We turn to it when we look the same.*

   A. Describe the last time you felt the way Jesus is described above.

   B. How does it help us to know that Jesus felt this way?

2. *When you feel the panic, don't focus on the people; focus on the opening. Good counsel in golf. Good counsel in life. Rather than focus on the fear, focus on the solution.*

   A. What kind of situations make you most fearful?

   B. When you face one of these frightening events, how can you "focus on the opening"? What "solution" can you call upon?

3. *Don't avoid life's Gardens of Gethsemane. Enter them. Just don't enter them alone. And while there, be honest. Pounding the ground is permitted. Tears are allowed. And if you sweat blood, you won't be the first. Do what Jesus did; open your heart.*

   A. How do we try to avoid life's Gardens of Gethsemane? Describe the last time you tried to avoid one.

   B. Is it easy or hard for you to express your emotions like this? Explain.

4. *Don't measure the size of the mountain; talk to the One who can move it. Instead of carrying the world on your shoulders, talk to the One who holds the universe on his. Hope is a look away.*

   A. How do we often try to "measure the size of the mountain"? Why is this a bad idea?

   B. In what way is hope "a look away"? How can prayer help to restore our hope? Does it help restore yours? Explain.

Traveling Up

1. Read Psalm 56:3–4.

   A. How does the psalmist deal with his own fears? Do you follow his example? Explain.

   B. Why is the psalmist unafraid of "mortal man" (v. 4 NIV)? Is this a statement of ignorance or something else? Explain.

2. Read Isaiah 41:10–14.

   A. Why does God tell Israel not to fear (v. 10)?

   B. What promise does God give in verses 11–12?

   C. What reason does God give for his promise in verse 13?

   D. What command and promise does God give in verse 14? How can his words encourage you today?

3. Read 1 John 4:16–19.

   A. On what should we rely when we are afraid (v. 16)?

   B. How does John describe God in verse 16? What difference does this make?

   C. How can we have "confidence on the day of judgment" (v. 17 NIV)?

   D. What antidote to fear does John give in verse 18? How does this antidote work?

   E. How is this antidote to be shared? How does this show that we really have the antidote?

Traveling On

1. In your journal write about a time you had "garden" experiences. Explain what situation took you there, how you felt, what prayers you prayed, and how God ministered to you.

2. Read *Foxe's Book of Martyrs* to see how many of God's choicest saints overcame their fear even as they faced death.

13

Silent Nights and Solitary Days

The Burden of Loneliness

Traveling Back

1. *By now you've learned that you don't have to be alone to feel lonely.*

   A. What's the difference between being alone and feeling lonely?

   B. Do you avoid being alone? Explain.

   C. How often, in a normal week, would you say you feel lonely?

2. *Loneliness is not the absence of faces. It is the absence of intimacy. Loneliness doesn't come from being alone; it comes from feeling alone.*

   A. How would you define nonsexual intimacy? With how many friends can you speak intimately? Are you satisfied with this number? Explain.

   B. How do you deal with loneliness? When you feel lonely, what do you do?

3. *Could it be that loneliness is not a curse but a gift? A gift from God? . . . I wonder if loneliness is God's way of getting our attention.*

   A. Do you agree that loneliness can be a gift from God? Explain.

   B. Why might God want to get your attention through loneliness? To what might he want to call your attention?

4. *God changes your* n *into a* v. *You go from* lonely *to* lovely. *When you know God loves you, you won't be desperate for the love of others.*

   A. How does assurance of God's love for you, personally, change everything?

   B. Does knowledge of God's love eliminate the need for intimate friends? Explain.

C. What's the difference between desiring the love of others and being desperate for it?

Traveling Up

1. Read Psalm 88.

   A. How would you describe the man who wrote this psalm?

   B. Why do you think God included this psalm in the Bible?

   C. Have you ever felt as the psalmist did in verses 13–14? Explain.

   D. Most psalms do not end as this one does (v. 18). Why do you think it ends like this? Is this a comfort to you? Explain.

2. Read Deuteronomy 31:6–8.

   A. What command does God give the Israelites in verse 6? What encouragement does he give them?

   B. Why do you suppose that Moses repeats to Joshua both the command and the encouragement in verses 7–8? What does this suggest to you about dealing with your own fears?

3. Read John 14:16–18; Matthew 28:16–20.

   A. What request did Jesus say he would make of the Father in John 14:16?

   B. What promise did Jesus make in John 14:18? How is he fulfilling this promise today?

   C. How can we take courage from Jesus' words in Matthew 28:18?

   D. What encouragement can we get from Jesus' final words in Matthew 28:20? Are you relying on this promise? Why or why not?

Traveling On

1. Examine your schedule, and find an entire day when you can plan to get alone, just you and God. Go to a retreat center, a solitary spot, a place in the woods, any place where you can spend a whole

day in solitude. Bring your Bible, and make no other plans than to spend the day alone with God.

2. Get a group of your believing friends together, and spend a few hours visiting some of your church's shut-ins, whether at their homes or in care centers. Relieve their loneliness for a while.

14

The Crowing Rooster and Me

The Burden of Shame

Traveling Back

1. *Is Peter the only person to do the very thing he swore he'd never do? "Infidelity is behind me!" "From now on, I'm going to bridle my tongue." "No more shady deals. I've learned my lesson." Oh, the volume of our boasting. And, oh, the heartbreak of our shame.*

   A. Describe a time when you followed Peter's example and did the very thing you swore you'd never do. What happened?

   B. Why do you think we engage in such foolish boasting? What do we think we'll gain?

2. *We weep as Peter wept, and we do what Peter did. We go fishing. We go back to our old lives. We return to our pre-Jesus practices. We do what comes naturally, rather than what comes spiritually. And we question whether Jesus has a place for folks like us.*

   A. Have you ever "gone fishing" or returned to your pre-Jesus practices after a spiritual failure? If so, how did you feel at the time?

   B. Why do we question whether Jesus has a place for folks like us? Have you ever felt this way? Explain.

3. *Jesus prepared a table in the presence of the enemy. Judas was allowed to see the supper, but he wasn't allowed to stay there.* You are not welcome here. This table is for my children. You may tempt them. You may trip them. But you will never sit with them. *This is how much he loves us.*

A. Why do you think Jesus allowed Judas to see the supper? Why not banish him before the disciples gathered?

B. What does the Lord's Supper mean to you personally? What goes through your mind during the service?

4. *The same Jesus who'd prepared a meal for Peter had prepared one for me. The same Shepherd who had trumped the devil trumped him again. The same Savior who had built a fire on the shore stirred a few embers in my heart.* "Every one *of you drink this." And so I did. It felt good to be back at the table.*

A. Why do you think Jesus prepared a meal for Peter, who denied him, but not for Judas, who betrayed him? What was the difference?

B. How do the stories of both Peter and Max show true repentance? How does Jesus always respond to true repentance? Why is this important to understand?

Traveling Up

1. Read Joel 2:25–27.

A. What promise does God make to his people who repent (v. 25)?

B. Why do you think God twice says in verses 26–27 that his people will never again be shamed? Why does God care about getting rid of shame?

2. Read 2 Timothy 2:15–16.

A. What instruction is given in verse 15? How can you comply with this command?

B. How can we avoid being ashamed, according to verse 15?

C. How does verse 16 continue to tell us how to avoid being ashamed?

3. Read Hebrews 12:2–3.

A. What are we instructed to do in verse 2? How can this keep us from being ashamed?

B. How did Jesus react to the shame of the cross? Why was there shame at the cross?

C. How are we to benefit from the example of Jesus on the cross?

Traveling On

1. Think of Max's story and how shame kept him from fellowship with God. Be honest with yourself, and ask if you're dealing with anything similar. If so, follow Max's courageous example, and admit this "shameful thing" to a trusted and godly friend. Break its power over you by confessing and forsaking it—and be glad at the Lord's table once more.

2. If you ever have the opportunity, attend a Seder prepared by someone who can explain the Messianic significance of this ancient Jewish meal. Enrich your appreciation of the Lord's Supper.

15

Slippery Sheep and Healed Hurts

The Burden of Disappointment

Traveling Back

1. *A disappointment is a missed appointment. What we hoped would happen, didn't. We wanted health; we got disease. We wanted retirement; we got reassignment. Divorce instead of family. Dismissal instead of promotion.*

   A. What disappointments have you had to face recently?

   B. What do you do with your disappointments?

2. *Just like sheep, we have wounds, but ours are wounds of the heart that come from disappointment after disappointment. If we're not careful, these wounds lead to bitterness. And so just like sheep, we need to be treated.*

   A. How do repeated disappointments lead to bitterness?

   B. What kinds of things have made you bitter? How do you deal with bitterness?

3. *The large portion of our problems are not lion-sized attacks, but rather the day-to-day swarm of frustrations and mishaps and heartaches.*

   A. What little things in life tend to frustrate you the most?

   B. What help can you offer to someone plagued with a swarm of mishaps or heartaches?

4. *Jesus tends to his sheep. And he will tend to you. If you will let him. How? How do you let him? The steps are so simple. First, go to him. Second, assume the right posture. Bow before God. Third, trust in him.*

   A. How can you "go to" Jesus? What does it mean to "go to" him?

   B. Why is it necessary to "bow" before God? What does this mean?

C. What does it mean to "trust" in God? How do we do this, practically speaking?

Traveling Up

1. Read Psalm 22:2–5.

   A. What disappointment did David suffer in verse 2? Have you ever felt like this? Explain.

   B. How did David combat his disappointment in verses 3–5?

   C. What was the result of the ancestors' trust described in verses 4–5? How is this meant to encourage us?

   D. Consider that this is the psalm Jesus quoted while hanging on the cross. What do you think the psalm taught him about disappointment?

2. Read Romans 5:1–5.

   A. How do we gain peace with God (v. 1)?

   B. What benefit does this peace gain us (v. 2)? How should this make us feel?

   C. What relationship does sufferings have to hope (vv. 3–5)?

   D. Why does hope not disappoint us (v. 5)? How does this matter to us on a day-to-day level?

3. Read Psalm 147:1–3.

   A. How did the Israelites deal with their disappointments (v. 1)?

   B. What encouragement does God give his people in verse 3?

   C. How do you think God heals the brokenhearted? What has he done in your own life?

Traveling On

1. Make a list of your biggest disappointments in life. Write them down. Then take each one, in order, to God in prayer. Give them to him explicitly, one by one.

2. Make a new commitment to get involved in regular prayer. Set a time. Set a place. Set a specific period. Prepare a list of concerns and thanks to bring to God. Then do it.

16

Jam Session

The Burden of Envy

Traveling Back

1. *Jealousy sets her cross hairs on the one who has more.*

   A. Describe a time when you felt jealous of someone. What prompted your jealousy?

   B. Why do most of us want "more"? What keeps us from being content with what we have?

2. *If focusing on our diminishing items leads to envy, what would happen if we focused on the unending items? If awareness of what we don't have creates jealousy, is it possible that an awareness of our abundance will lead to contentment?*

   A. Answer both of the preceding questions.

   B. Try to itemize the "unending items" that you possess. What's on your list?

   C. Try to list your "abundance." What does this tell you about God's provision?

3. *God is not a miser with his grace. Your cup may be low on cash or clout, but it is overflowing with mercy. You may not have the prime parking place, but you have sufficient pardon.*

   A. How often do you ponder God's grace to you? His mercy?

   B. How has God been gracious to you this week? This month? This year?

4. *One thing is certain. When the final storm comes and you are safe in your Father's house, you won't regret what he didn't give. You'll be stunned at what he did.*

A. Try to imagine the day you arrive safe in your Father's house. Look around. What has he given you?

B. How can meditating on your eternal future with God help you to deal with what exists today?

Traveling Up

1. Read Proverbs 14:30; 23:17.

   A. With what does Proverbs 14:30 contrast envy? How is this significant?

   B. In what ways do believers sometimes envy "sinners" (Prov. 23:17)?

   C. What does it mean to be "zealous for the fear of the LORD" (NIV)?

2. Read James 3:13–4:5.

   A. What in verse 13 does James contrast with "bitter envy" in verse 14?

   B. Where does envy come from (v. 15)?

   C. What always accompanies envy (v. 16)?

   D. What causes fights and quarrels among spiritual brothers (4:1)?

   F. God himself is said to "envy" in 4:5 (NIV). How does this differ from human envy?

3. Read Titus 3:3–7.

   A. How does Paul describe his pre-Christian life (v. 3)? What do you think he envied?

   B. How did God deliver us from envy (vv. 4–5)?

   C. To what extent did God pour out his Holy Spirit on us (v. 6)? How is this meant to nip envy in the bud?

   D. What was the purpose of God's saving us (v. 7)? How can meditating on this truth destroy envy?

Traveling On

1. Draw a line down a sheet of paper, creating two columns. On the left side, list some of the things you envy in others. On the right side, list what God has supplied you in abundance and, if possible, include a Scripture reference. For example, in the left column you might say "I wish I had better health," and beside it, in the right column, you might list "God will give me a glorious, eternal body (Phil. 3:20–21)."

2. Make a date to serve dinner at a local rescue mission or homeless shelter. Try not to schedule your visit at Thanksgiving or Christmas (since such service organizations usually have more than enough help during those two holidays). And be thankful for what God has given you.

17

God's Loving Pursuit

The Burden of Doubt

Traveling Back

1. *When Jesus found us, we acted like Eric. Our limitations kept us from recognizing the One who came to save us. We even doubted his presence—and sometimes we still do.*

   A. Do you ever doubt God's presence? If so, why?

   B. How do our limitations keep us from recognizing the One who came to save us? How can we overcome these limitations?

2. *If the Lord is the shepherd who leads the flock, goodness and mercy are the two sheepdogs who guard the rear of the flock.*

   A. How does "goodness" differ from "mercy"? How are they the same?

   B. Where in your life do you most need God's goodness and mercy right now? Why don't you take the time to talk to him about your need?

3. *Trust your faith and not your feelings. . . . Measure your value through God's eyes, not your own. . . . See the big picture, not the small.*

   A. How do we sometimes trust our feelings and not our faith? How can we stop making this mistake?

   B. Take a few minutes to describe your value in God's eyes. What has he said about you in the Bible?

   C. How can we see the big picture, not the small?

4. *Most of all, God gives us himself. Even when we choose our hovel over his house and our trash over his grace, still he follows. Never forcing us.*

Never leaving us. Patiently persistent. Faithfully present. Using all of his power to convince us that he is who he is and that he can be trusted to lead us home.

A. How do you know God has given you himself? How can you be sure of this?

B. How has God used his power to convince you he is who he is? What most convinces you that God can be trusted to lead you home?

Traveling Up

1. Read James 1:5–8.

A. To whom is verse 5 addressed? Do you qualify? Explain.

B. What promise does verse 5 make?

C. What condition is placed in verse 6 on the promise of verse 5?

D. To what does James compare someone who doubts God's promise? Why is this picture appropriate?

E. What warning is given in verses 7 and 8? In what way are these individuals "double-minded" (NIV)? How can one correct such a serious problem?

2. Read Jude 20–22.

A. What instruction is given in verse 20? How is this instruction to be carried out?

B. What instruction is given in verse 21? What future event empowers us to follow this instruction?

C. What instruction is given in verse 22? Why do you think the command was given? How can we comply with this command?

3. Read Romans 14:19–23.

A. Describe the command in verse 19. What is the purpose of this command? How well do you fulfill it? Explain.

B. How is it possible to destroy someone for the sake of food (v. 20)?

C. How does verse 21 relate to doubt?

D. What command is given in verse 22? What blessing is available? What does this blessing mean?

E. How is verse 23 an effective guideline for the entire Christian life? What rule is laid out here?

Traveling On

1. Realize that there is a great difference between doubt and questions. Doubt disbelieves in the promises and good character of God; questions merely wonder how God might pull off some incredible feat. To get a "feel" for the difference between doubt and questions, study the vastly different ways God responded to Zechariah in Luke 1:5–20 and Mary in Luke 1:26–38. They asked similar questions ("How can I be sure of this?" versus "How will this be?" [NIV]) regarding miraculous pregnancies, but one was judged and the other blessed. Why?

2. Read Os Guinness's book *God in the Dark* for a clear and helpful discussion on doubt.

18

Almost Heaven

The Burden of Homesickness

Traveling Back

1. *The twists and turns of life have a way of reminding us—we aren't home here. This is not our homeland. We aren't fluent in the languages of disease and death. The culture confuses the heart, the noise disrupts our sleep, and we feel far from home. And, you know what? That's OK.*

   A. Why do we often forget that this is not our real home?

   B. In what ways do you feel like a foreigner on this earth? Are you OK with that? Explain.

2. *Homesickness is one of the burdens God doesn't mind if we carry. We . . . are being prepared for another house. And we . . . know we aren't there yet.*

   A. Do you feel "homesick" for heaven? Explain.

   B. How is God preparing you for "another house"?

3. *The greatest calamity is not to feel far from home when you are, but to feel right at home when you are not.*

   A. Could it be that much of the disappointment we feel in life comes from trying to feel right at home when we're not? Explain.

   B. How can we consciously guard against feeling at home in this world? Name several practical things we can do.

4. *Every wrinkle and every needle take us one step closer to the last step when Jesus will change our simple bodies into forever bodies. No pain. No depression. No sickness. No end.*

   A. How does your own body remind you that this is not your forever home?

B. How would you respond to someone who says this desire for an eternal, painless body is merely wishful thinking and you'd be better off getting all the gusto while you can?

Traveling Up

1. Read Philippians 1:20–23.

   A. Describe Paul's firm expectation in verse 20. What challenge faced him?

   B. In your own words, explain what Paul meant in verse 21.

   C. Describe Paul's dilemma in verse 22. Why was he so torn?

   D. What did Paul mean by "depart" in verse 23 (NIV)? Depart where? Why would this be "better"?

2. Read Philippians 3:17–4:1.

   A. How does Paul describe the enemies of Christ in verses 18–19? What traits characterize them?

   B. Describe the main contrast of these people with believers in Christ (v. 20).

   C. For whom are Christians waiting (vv. 20–21)? What are they waiting for him to do?

   D. What effect should meditating on this truth have on believers (4:1)? Does it have this effect on you? Explain.

3. Read 1 Corinthians 15:50–57.

   A. What two contrasts does Paul make in verse 50? Why should this matter to us? Why is it important?

   B. What "secret" or "mystery" does Paul describe in verses 51–52?

   C. What kind of "clothes" will believers wear in heaven (v. 53)? Why is this important?

   D. Restate the message of verses 54–57 in your own words. Imagine that you are describing this situation to an eight-year-old.

   E. Are you "homesick"? Why or why not?

Traveling On

1. Do a study in the four Gospels and in the Book of Acts on the Lord Jesus' postresurrection body. Describe it. Then realize that our resurrection bodies will look and act similar to his!

2. Read Joni Eareckson Tada's book titled *Heaven*. Joni has lived in a wheelchair for decades since a diving accident at age seventeen, so she expresses a uniquely powerful vision of heaven.

THE GREAT HOUSE OF GOD

A Home for Your Heart

I gladly dedicate this book to my assistant, Karen Hill.

Thank you for thousands of hours of selfless service.

Acknowledgments

I appreciate the following friends for helping, tolerating, resuscitating and/or indulging me during the writing of this book:

Liz Heaney—yet another book, yet another year and still no regrets.

The Oak Hills Church leadership and staff—
I'm out of hibernation! Thanks for covering for me.

The Oak Hills Church—Thanks for ten years (!) of joy.

Steve and Cheryl Green—I don't know what I did to deserve friends like you, but I'm sure glad I did it.

All my friends at Word/Thomas Nelson—
A hearty thanks for a job well done.

To all my minister friends who use my stuff for sermon ideas—Power to you! You deserve a break.

To Laura Kendall—a tip o' the hat for your dip o' the quill. Thanks for your help.

Steve Halliday—for writing the discussion guide.

And to the readers— some of you I'm meeting for the first time, others for the twelfth. You are so gracious to invite me into your home. I'll do my best not to overstay my welcome.

And lastly, to my wife Denalyn—
I guess you could say I love you a little.
A little more every minute of every day. (Happy 40th, honey!)

CHAPTER 1

The Great House of God

A Home for Your Heart

I only ask one thing from the Lord.
This is what I want: let me live in the
Lord's *house all my life.* —Psalm 27:4

I'd like to talk with you about your house. Let's step through the front door and walk around a bit. Every so often it's wise to do a home inspection, you know—check the roof for leaks and examine the walls for bows and the foundation for cracks. We'll see if your kitchen cupboards are full and glance at the books on the shelves in your study.

What's that? You think it odd that I want to look at your house? You thought this was a book on spiritual matters? It is. Forgive me, I should have been clearer. I'm not talking about your visible house of stone or sticks, wood or straw, but your invisible one of thoughts and truths and convictions and hopes. I'm talking about your spiritual house.

You have one, you know. And it's no typical house. Conjure up your fondest notions and this house exceeds them all. A grand castle has been built for your heart. Just as a physical house exists to care for the body, so the spiritual house exists to care for your soul.

You've never seen a house more solid:

the roof never leaks,

the walls never crack,

and the foundation never trembles.

You've never seen a castle more splendid:

the observatory will stretch you,

the chapel will humble you,

the study will direct you,

and the kitchen will nourish you.

Ever lived in a house like this? Chances are you haven't. Chances are you've given little thought to housing your soul. We create elaborate houses for our bodies, but our souls are relegated to a hillside shanty where the night winds chill us and the rain soaks us. Is it any wonder the world is so full of cold hearts?

Doesn't have to be this way. We don't have to live outside. It's not God's plan for your heart to roam as a Bedouin. God wants you to move in out of the cold and live . . . with him. Under his roof there is space available. At his table a plate is set. In his living room a wingback chair is reserved just for you. And he'd like you to take up residence in his house. Why would he want you to share his home?

Simple, he's your Father.

You were intended to live in your Father's house. Any place less than his is insufficient. Any place far from his is dangerous. Only the home built for your heart can protect your heart. And your Father wants you to dwell *in* him.

No, you didn't misread the sentence and I didn't miswrite it. Your Father doesn't just ask you to live *with* him, he asks you to live *in* him. As Paul wrote, "For in him we live and move and have our being" (Acts 17:28 NIV).

Don't think you are separated from God, he at the top end of a great ladder, you at the other. Dismiss any thought that God is on Venus while you are on earth. Since God is Spirit (John 4:23), he is next to you: God himself is our roof. God himself is our wall. And God himself is our foundation.

Moses knew this. "LORD," he prayed, "you have been our home since the beginning" (Ps. 90:1). What a powerful thought: God as your home. Your home is the place where you can kick off your shoes and eat pickles and crackers and not worry about what people think when they see you in your bathrobe.

Your home is familiar to you. No one has to tell you how to locate your bedroom; you don't need directions to the kitchen. After a hard day scrambling to find your way around in the world, it's assuring to come home to a place you know. God can be equally familiar to you. With time you can learn where to go for nourishment, where to hide for protection, where to turn for guidance. Just as your earthly house is a place of refuge, so God's house is a place of peace. God's house has never been plundered, his walls have never been breached.

God can be your dwelling place.

God *wants* to be your dwelling place. He has no interest in being a weekend getaway or a Sunday bungalow or a summer cottage. Don't consider using God as a vacation cabin or an eventual retirement home. He wants you under his roof now and always. He wants to be your mailing address, your point of reference; he wants to be your home. Listen to the promise of his Son, "If my people love me they will obey my teaching. My father will love them and we will come to them and make our home with them" (John 14:23).

For many this is a new thought. We think of God as a deity to discuss, not a place to dwell. We think of God as a mysterious miracle worker, not a house to live in. We think of God as a creator to call on, not a home to reside in. But our Father wants to be much more. He wants to be the one in whom "we live and move and have our being" (Acts 17:28 NIV).

When Jehovah led the children of Israel through the wilderness, he didn't just appear once a day and then abandon them. The pillar of fire was present all night; the cloud was present all day. Our God never leaves us. "I will be with you always," he promised (Matt. 28:20). Our faith takes a quantum leap when we understand the perpetual presence of the Father. Our Jehovah is the fire of our night and the cloud of our day. He never leaves us.

Heaven knows no difference between Sunday morning and Wednesday afternoon. God longs to speak as clearly in the workplace as he does in the sanctuary. He longs to be worshiped when we sit at the dinner table and not just when we come to his communion table. You may go days without thinking of him, but there's never a moment when he's not thinking of you.

Knowing this, we understand Paul's rigorous goal: "We capture every thought and make it give up and obey Christ" (2 Cor. 10:5). We can fathom why he urges us to "pray without ceasing" (1 Thess. 5:17), "be constant in prayer" (Rom. 12:12), "pray in the Spirit at all times" (Eph. 6:18), "continually offer a sacrifice of praise to God" (Heb. 13:15), and "let heaven fill your thoughts" (Col 4:2 TLB).

David, the man after God's own heart, said: "I'm asking Yahweh for one thing, only one thing: to live with him in his house my whole life long. I'll contemplate his beauty, I'll study at his feet. That's the only quiet secure place in a noisy world" (Ps. 27:4–5 MSG). What is this house of God which David seeks? Is David describing a physical structure? Does he long for a building with four walls and a door through which he can enter but never exit? No. "Our LORD does not live in temples built by human hands" (Acts 17:24). When David says, "I will live in the house of the LORD forever" (Ps. 23:6), he's not saying he wants to get away from people. He's saying that he yearns to be in God's presence, wherever he is.

David longs to be in God's house.

I know what you're thinking: *Sure, Max, but he was David. He was the poet and the prince and giant-killer. He didn't have carpools and diapers and a boss who breathes deadlines like a dragon breathes fire. I'd love to live in God's house, too, but for the time being, I'm stuck in the* real *world.*

Forgive me, but I beg to differ. You aren't stuck in the real world. Just the opposite, you are one step away from the house of God. Wherever you are. Whatever time it is. Whether in the office on Thursday or at soccer practice on Saturday, you are only a decision away from the presence of your Father. You need never leave the house of God. You don't need to change your zip code or your neighborhood; all you need to change is your perception.

When your car is stuck in traffic, you can step into the chapel. When the gust of temptation unbalances your stride, step behind the wall of his strength. When the employees belittle you, take a seat in the porch swing next to your Father; he'll comfort you. Remember, this is no house of stone. You won't find it on a map. You won't find it described in a realtor journal.

But you will find it in your Bible. You've seen the blueprint before. You've read the names of the rooms and recited the layout. You're familiar with the design. But chances are you never considered it to be a house plan. You viewed the verses as a prayer.

Indeed they are. The Lord's Prayer. It would be difficult to find someone who hasn't quoted the prayer or read the words:

Our Father who art in heaven,
Hallowed be thy name.
Thy kingdom come,
Thy will be done,
On earth as it is in heaven.
Give us this day our daily bread;
And forgive us our debts,
As we have forgiven our debtors;
And lead us not into temptation,
But deliver us from evil.
For thine is the kingdom and the power and the glory forever.
Amen.

MATTHEW 6:9–13 RSV

Children memorize it. Parishioners recite it. Students study it . . . but I want to challenge us to do something different. I want us to live in it . . . to view it as the floor plan to our spiritual house. In these verses Christ has provided more than a model for prayer, he has provided a model for living. These words do more than tell us what to say to God; they tell us how to exist with God. These words describe a grand house in which God's children were intended to live . . . with him, forever.

Would you like to take a look around? Me, too. I know the perfect place to begin. In the living room a painting hangs over the mantle. The owner of the house treasures it. He invites all who enter to begin their journey gazing at the picture and learning the truth about our Father.

Chapter 2

The Living Room

When Your Heart Needs a Father

Our Father . . .

"OUR FATHER who is in heaven . . ." With these words Jesus escorts us into the Great House of God. Shall we follow him? There is so much to see. Every room reveals his heart, every stop will soothe your soul. And no room is as essential as this one we enter first. Walk behind him as he leads us into God's living room.

Sit in the chair that was made for you and warm your hands by the fire which never fades. Take time to look at the framed photos and find yours. Be sure to pick up the scrapbook and find the story of your life. But please, before any of that, stand at the mantle and study the painting which hangs above it.

Your Father treasures the portrait. He has hung it where all can see.

Stand before it a thousand times and each gaze is as fresh as the first. Let a million look at the canvas and each one will see himself. And each will be right.

Captured in the portrait is a tender scene of a father and a son. Behind them is a great house on a hill. Beneath their feet is a narrow path. Down from the house the father has run. Up the trail the son has trudged. The two have met, here, at the gate.

We can't see the face of the son; it's buried in the chest of his father. No, we can't see his face, but we can see his tattered robe and stringy hair. We can see the mud on the back of his legs, the filth on his shoulders and the empty purse on the ground. At one time the purse was full of money. At one time the boy was full of pride. But that was a dozen taverns ago. Now both the purse and the pride are depleted. The prodigal offers no gift or explanation. All he offers is the smell of pigs and a rehearsed apology: "Father, I have sinned against God and done wrong to you. I am no longer worthy to be called your son" (Luke 15:21).

He feels unworthy of his birthright. "Demote me. Punish me. Take my name off the mailbox and my initials off the family tree. I am willing to give up my place at your table." The boy is content to be a hired hand. There is only one problem. Though the boy is willing to stop being a son, the father is not willing to stop being a father.

Though we can't see the boy's face in the painting, we can't miss the father's. Look at the tears glistening on the leathered cheeks, the smile shining through the silver beard. One arm holds the boy up so he won't fall, the other holds the boy close so he won't doubt.

"Hurry!" he shouts. "Bring the best clothes and put them on him. Also, put a ring on his finger and sandals on his feet. And get our fat calf and kill it so we can have a feast and celebrate. My son was dead, but now he is alive again! He was lost but now he is found!" (Luke 15:22–24).

How these words must have stunned the young man, "*My son* was dead . . ." He thought he'd lost his place in the home. After all, didn't he abandon his father? Didn't he waste his inheritance? The boy assumed he had forfeited his privilege to sonship. The father, however, doesn't give up that easily. In his mind, his son is still a son. The child may have been out of the house, but he was never out of his father's heart. He may have left the table, but he never left the family. Don't miss the message here. You may be willing to stop being God's child. But God is not willing to stop being your Father.

OUR *ABBA*

Of all his names, *Father* is God's favorite. We know he loves this name most because this is the one he used most. While on earth, Jesus called God "Father" over two hundred times. In his first recorded words Jesus explained, "Didn't you know that I must be in my Father's house?" (Luke 2:49). In his final triumphant prayer he proclaims, "Father, I give you my life" (Luke 23:46). In the Gospel of John alone, Jesus repeats this name 156 times. God loves to be called Father. After all, didn't Jesus teach us to begin our prayer with the phrase, "Our *Abba*"?

It is difficult for us to understand how revolutionary it was for Jesus to call Jehovah *"Abba."* What is a common practice today was unheard of in Jesus' day. New Testament scholar Joachim Jeremias describes how rarely the term was used:

> With the help of my assistants, I have examined the prayer literature of ancient Judaism. . . . The result of this examination was, that in no place in this immense literature is this invocation of God as "*Abba,* Father" to be found. *Abba* was an everyday word. It was a homely family-word. No Jew would have dared to address God in this manner, yet Jesus did it always in all his prayers which are handed down to us, with one single exception: the cry from the cross, "My God, my God, why have you forsaken me?" In the Lord's prayer, Jesus authorizes his disciples to repeat the word *Abba* after him. He gives them a share in his sonship. He empowers his disciples to speak with their heavenly father in such a familiar and trusting way.[1]

The first two words of the Lord's Prayer are affluent in significance: *"Our Father"* reminds us we are welcome in God's house because we have been adopted by the owner.

GOD'S MISSION: ADOPTION

When we come to Christ, God not only forgives us, he also adopts us. Through a dramatic series of events, we go from condemned orphans with no hope to adopted children with no fear. Here is how it happens. You come before the judgment seat of God full of rebellion and mistakes. Because of his justice he cannot dismiss your sin, but because of his love he cannot dismiss you. So, in an act which stunned the heavens, he punished himself on the cross for your sins. God's justice and love are equally honored. And you, God's creation, are forgiven. But the story doesn't end with God's forgiveness.

> For you have not received a spirit of slavery leading to fear again, but you have received a spirit of adoption as sons by which we cry out "Abba! Father!" The Spirit himself bears witness with our Spirit that we are children of God (Rom. 8:15–16 NASB).

> But when the fullness of time came, God sent forth His Son, born of a woman, born under the Law, in order that He might redeem those who were under the Law, that we might receive the adoption as sons (Gal. 4:4–5 NASB).

It would be enough if God just cleansed your name, but he does more. He gives you *his* name. It would be enough if God just set you free, but he does more. He takes you home. He takes you home to the Great House of God.

Adoptive parents understand this more than anyone. I certainly don't mean to offend any biological parents—I'm one myself. We biological parents know well the earnest longing to have a child. But in many cases our cribs were filled easily. We decided to have a child and a child came. In fact, sometimes the child came with no decision. I've heard of unplanned pregnancies, but I've never heard of an unplanned adoption.

That's why adoptive parents understand God's passion to adopt us. They know what it means to feel an empty space inside. They know what it means to hunt, to set out on a mission, and take responsibility for a child with a spotted past and a dubious future. If anybody understands God's ardor for his children, it's someone who has rescued an orphan from despair, for that is what God has done for us.

God has adopted you. God sought you, found you, signed the papers and took you home.

GOD'S MOTIVE: DEVOTION

As a minister I have had the privilege of witnessing—up close—the emotion of adoption. On one occasion a lady in another state who had heard me speak called and asked if I knew any prospective adoptive parents. Her pregnant daughter was seeking a home for her unborn child. I put her in touch with a family from our congregation and took a front row seat as the drama unfolded.

I saw the joy at the possibility and the heartbreak at the roadblocks. I watched the resolve in the eyes of the father and the determination in the eyes of the mother. They would travel as far as it took and spend every penny they had. They wanted to adopt that child. And they did. Only moments after his birth, the infant was placed in their arms. And this is no exaggeration: They smiled for a month after they brought their son home. I'd see them in the church hallway; they'd be smiling. I'd see them in the parking lot, smiling. From the pulpit I could see them in the congregation, cradling the baby and smiling. I think if I'd preached a sermon on the agony of hell, they would have smiled through every sentence. Why? Because the child they had longed for had come into their home.

Let me ask you, why did this couple adopt that child? They had a happy marriage. They were financially secure and gainfully employed. What did they hope to gain? Did they adopt the baby so they might have a little extra cash or sleep? You know better. Their supply of both diminished the minute they brought the child home. Then why? Why do people adopt children? As you are thinking, let me tell you why God does.

Delight in these words:

> Long ago, before God made the world, God chose us to be his very own, through what Christ would do for us; he decided then to make us holy in his eyes, without a single fault we who stand before him covered in his love. His unchanging plan has always been to adopt us into his own family by sending Jesus Christ to die for us. *And he did this because he wanted to* (Eph. 1:3–5 TLB, emphasis mine).

And you thought God adopted you because you were good-looking. You thought he needed your money or your wisdom. Sorry. God adopted you simply because he wanted to. You were in his good will and pleasure. Knowing full well the trouble you would be and the price he would pay, he signed his name next to yours and changed your name to his and took you home. Your *Abba* adopted you and became your Father.

May I pause here for just a second? Most of you are with me . . . but a couple of you are shaking your heads. I see those squinty eyes. You don't believe me, do you? You're waiting for the fine print. There's got to be a gimmick. You know life has no free lunch, so you're waiting for the check.

Your discomfort is obvious. Even here in God's living room, you never unwind. Others put on slippers, you put on a front. Others relax, you stiffen. Always on your best behavior, ever anxious that you'll slip up and God will notice and out you'll go.

I understand your anxiety. Our experience with people has taught us that what is promised and what is presented aren't always the same. And for some, the thought of trusting a heavenly Father is doubly difficult because your earthly father disappointed or mistreated you.

If such is the case, I urge you: Don't confuse your heavenly Father with the fathers you've seen on earth. Your Father in heaven isn't prone to headaches and temper tantrums. He doesn't hold you one day and hit you the next. The man who fathered you may play such games, but the God who loves you never will. May I prove my point?

GOD'S METHOD: REDEMPTION

Let's return to the verses that describe your adoption. Read them a second time and see if you can find the verb which precedes the word *adoption* in both verses.

> For you have not received a spirit of slavery leading to fear again, but you have received a spirit of adoption as sons by which we cry out "Abba! Father!" The Spirit himself bears witness with our Spirit that we are children of God (Rom. 8:15–16 NASB).

> But when the fullness of time came, God sent forth His Son, born of a woman, born under the Law, in order that He might redeem those who were under the Law, that we might receive the adoption as sons (Gal. 4:4–5 NASB).

Find it? Not too hard to see, is it? Before the word *adoption* is the word *receive.*

Could Paul have used another phrase? Could he have said, "You have earned the spirit of adoption"? Or "that we might earn our adoption as sons"? I suppose he could have, but we wouldn't have bought it. You and I both know that an adoption is not something we earn; it's something we receive. To be adopted into a family is not a feat one achieves, but rather a gift one accepts.

The parents are the active ones. Adoption agencies don't train children to recruit parents; they seek parents to adopt children. The parents make the call and fill out the papers and endure the interviews and pay the fee and wait the wait. Can you imagine prospective parents saying, "We'd like to adopt Johnny, but first we want to know a few things. Does he have a house to live in? Does he have money for tuition? Does he have a ride to school every morning and clothes to wear every day? Can he prepare his own meals and mend his own clothes?"

No agency would stand for such talk. Its representative would lift her hand and say, "Wait a minute. You don't understand. You don't adopt Johnny because of what he has; you adopt him because of what he needs. He needs a home."

The same is true with God. He doesn't adopt us because of what we have. He doesn't give us his name because of our wit or wallet or good attitude. Paul states it twice because he is doubly concerned that we understand that adoption is something we receive, not something we earn.

Which is *so good* to know. Why? Think carefully about this. If we can't earn our adoption by our stellar performance, can we lose it through our poor performance?

When I was seven years old, I ran away from home. I'd had enough of my father's rules and decided I could make it on my own, thank you very much. With my clothes in a paper bag, I stormed out the back gate and marched down the alley. Like the prodigal son, I decided I needed no father. Unlike the prodigal son, I didn't go far. I got to the end of the alley and remembered I was hungry, so I went back home.

But though the rebellion was brief, it was rebellion nonetheless. And had you stopped me on that prodigal path between the fences and asked me who my father was, I just might have told you how I felt. I just might have said, "I don't need a father. I'm too big for the rules of my family. It's just me, myself and my paper bag." I don't remember saying that to anyone, but I remember thinking it. And I also remember rather sheepishly stepping in the back door and taking my seat at the supper table across from the very father I had, only moments before, disowned.

Did he know of my insurrection? I suspect he did. Did he know of my denial? Dads usually do. Was I still his son? Apparently so. (No one else was sitting in my place.) Had you gone to my father after you had spoken to me and asked, "Mr. Lucado, your son says he has no need of a father. Do you still consider him your son?" what would my dad have said?

I don't have to guess at his answer. He called himself my father even when I didn't call myself his son. His commitment to me was greater than my commitment to him.

I didn't hear the rooster crow like Peter did. I didn't feel the fish belch like Jonah did. I didn't get a robe and a ring and sandals like the prodigal did. But I learned from my father on earth what those three learned from their Father in heaven. Our God is no fair-weather Father. He's not into this love-'em-and-leave-'em-stuff. I can count on him to be in my corner no matter how I perform. You can, too.

May I show you something? Look at the bottom of the painting. See the words etched in gold? The Apostle Paul penned them, but your Father inspired them.

> Neither death, nor life, nor angels, nor ruling spirits, nothing now, nothing in the future, no powers, nothing above us, nothing below us, nor anything else in the world will ever be able to separate us from the love of God that is in Christ Jesus our Lord (Rom. 8:38–39).

Your Father will never turn you away. The doors of this room are never closed. Learn to linger in the living room of God's house. When the words of others hurt you or your own failures distress you, step in here. Gaze at this painting and be reminded of your God: It is right to call him Holy; we speak truth when we call him King. But if you want to touch his heart, use the name he loves to hear. Call him *Father.*

CHAPTER 3

The Foundation

Where Trust Begins

Our Father who is . . .

THE MOST ESSENTIAL WORD in the Lord's prayer is also the shortest. Be careful you don't miss it. A lot of people do. The word is so brief, it'll sneak right past you if you aren't careful.

Without it, the Great House of God cannot stand. Remove it and the house tumbles to the ground.

What is the word? I'll give you a hint. You just read it.

Where is it? You just read it.

Is it in this sentence? It is. It's also in the answer I just gave.

Come on, Max, is this a joke?

Would I kid you? (By the way, the word was in your question. See it?)

Is. "Our Father who *is* in heaven."

God is. Not God *was*. Not God *will be*. Not God *could be* or *should be*, but God *is*. He is the God of the present tense. And he is the foundation of his own house.

THE MORTAR OF FAITH

I write these words on an airplane. A late airplane. An airplane different from the one I was originally assigned. My first flight was canceled due to a mechanical difficulty. A few dozen not-so-happy campers and I were transferred to another plane. As we checked in for the new flight, I heard many of my fellow passengers ask the attendant, "Is this plane okay? Any mechanical flaws with this 747?" We were full of questions about the plane's ability to fly, but the ticket agent had no questions about our ability to do the same.

Not once were we asked, "How about you? Can you fly? Can you flap your arms and get airborne?" Of course, these are bizarre questions. My ability to fly is not important. My strength is immaterial. I'm counting on the plane to get me home.

Need I make the connection? Your achievements, however noble they may be, are not important. Your credentials, as starry as they may be, are of no concern. God is the foundation of this house. The key question in life is not "How strong am I?" but rather "How strong is God?" Focus on his strength, not yours. Occupy yourself with the nature of God, not the size of your biceps.

That's what Moses did. Or at least that's what God told Moses to do. Remember the conversation at the burning bush? The tone was set in the first sentence. "Take off your sandals because you are standing on holy ground" (Exod. 3:5). With these eleven words Moses is enrolled in a class on God. Immediately the roles are defined. God is holy. Approaching him on even a quarter-inch of leather is too pompous. And as we read further we discover that no time is spent convincing Moses what Moses can do, but much time is spent explaining to Moses what God can do.

You and I tend to do the opposite. We would explain to Moses how he is ideally suited to return to Egypt. (Who better understands the culture than a former prince?) Then we'd remind Moses how perfect he is for wilderness travel. (Who knows the desert better than a shepherd?) We'd spend time reviewing with Moses his resumé and strengths. (Come on Moses, you can do it. Give it a try.)

But God doesn't. The strength of Moses is never considered. No pep talk is given, no pats on the backs are offered. Not one word is spoken to recruit Moses. But many words are used to reveal God. The strength of Moses is not the issue; the strength of God is.

Shall we pause for application? Let's repeat that last sentence and let you fill in a blank. Replace the name of Moses with your name.

> The strength of ______________ is not the issue; the strength of God is.

You aren't the force behind the plane nor the mortar within the foundation; God is. I know you know that in your head, but do you know that in your heart? Would you like to? Let me show you some of the boulders which support this mighty house. Let me buttress your confidence in God's house by sharing with you some of his names.

WHAT'S IN A NAME?

Understanding the names of God is no quick study—after all, there are more than eighty names for God in the Old Testament alone. But if you want a place to begin, let me entice you with a few of the compound names given God by some of the heroes of the faith. Each of them reveals a different rock of God's character.

Maybe you are wondering how a study of the names of God can help you understand him. Let me explain. Imagine that you and I are having a conversation in 1978. You approach me on the college campus where I was a student and ask, "Do you know Denalyn Preston?" I would have answered, "Let me think. Oh, I know Denalyn. She's an acquaintance of mine. She's that cute girl who likes to ride bikes and wear overalls to class." That's all I knew about her.

But go forward a year. Now we are in Miami, Florida, where I am a minister and Denalyn is a school teacher. "Do you know Denalyn Preston?" "Of course, I do. She's a friend. I see her every Sunday."

Ask me again a year later, "Denalyn Preston? Sure I know her. She can't take her eyes off of me." (Just kidding, honey.)

Fast forward twelve months. "Who doesn't know Denalyn Preston?" I would answer. "You think she might be willing to go out on a date with me?"

Six months later, "Of course I know her—I can't quit thinking about her. We're going out again next week."

Two months later, "Do I know Denalyn Preston? I'm going to marry her next August!"

Now it's August of 1981. "Do I know Denalyn Preston? No,

but I know Denalyn *Lucado.* She's my wife, and quit bugging us—we're on our honeymoon."

In three years my relationship with Denalyn evolved. And with each change came a new name. She went from *acquaintance* to *friend* to *eye-popping beauty* to *date* to *fiancée* and *wife.* Of course the names have only continued. Now she is *confidante, mother of my children, life-long partner, boss* (just kidding, again). The more I know her the more names I give her.

And the more God's people came to know him, the more names they gave him. Initially, God was known as *Elohim.* "In the beginning God [*Elohim*] created" (Gen. 1:1). The Hebrew word *Elohim* carries with it the meaning "strong one or creator" and appears thirty-one times in the first chapter of Genesis, where we see his creative power.[1]

As God revealed himself to his children, however, they saw him as more than a mighty force. They saw him as a loving Father who met them at every crossroad of their lives.

Jacob, for example, came to see God as *Jehovah-raah,* a caring shepherd. "Like a shepherd," Jacob told his family, "God has led me all my life" (Gen. 48:15).

The phrase was surely a compliment to God, for Jacob was a less-than-cooperative sheep. Twice he tricked his brother, at least once he suckered his blind father. He out-crossed his double-crossing father-in-law by conning him out of his livestock and then, when the fellow wasn't looking, made like a Colt out of Baltimore in the middle of the night, sneaking off with anything that wasn't nailed down.

Jacob was never a candidate for the most well-behaved sheep award, but God never forgot him. He gave him food in the famine, forgiveness in his failures, and faith in his final years. Ask Jacob to describe God in a word, and his word would be *Jehovah-raah,* the caring shepherd.

Abraham had a different name for God: *Jehovah-jireh,* the Lord who provides. It's ironic that Abraham would call God "provider," since Abraham was well provided for already. He lived in a split-level tent with a four-camel garage. Life was good in Ur. "But life will be better in Canaan," he told his family. So off they went. When they asked, "Where will we live?" Abraham answered, "God will provide." And God did. When they got caught in an Egyptian scandal, the people wondered, "How will we get out?" Abraham assured them, "God will provide." And he did. When they split up the land and nephew Lot took the grassland and left Uncle Abraham with the rocks, the people wondered, "How will we survive?" Abraham knew the answer: "God will provide." And he did. And when Abraham and Sarah stood next to the empty crib and she wondered how he'd ever be the father of thousands, he'd put his arm around her, whispering, "The Lord will provide."

And God did. And Abraham bounced his firstborn on his hundred-year-old bony knees. Abraham learned that God provides. But even Abraham must have shook his head when God asked him to sacrifice his own son on Mt. Moriah.

Up the mountain they went. "Where is the lamb we will burn as a sacrifice?" his son asked (Gen. 22:7). One wonders how the answer made it past the lump in Abraham's throat: "God will give us the lamb for the sacrifice, my son" (v. 8). *Jehovah-jireh,* the Lord will provide. Abraham tied up his son and placed him on the altar and raised the knife, and the angel stayed his hand. Abraham had proven his faith. He heard a rustling in the thicket and saw a ram caught by his horns in a bush. He offered it as a sacrifice and gave the mountain a name, *Jehovah-jireh,* the Lord provides.

And then there is Gideon. The Lord came to Gideon and told him he was to lead his people in victory over the Midianites. That's like God telling a housewife to stand up to her abusive husband or a high school student to take on drug peddlers or a preacher to preach the truth to a congregation of Pharisees. "Y-y-you b-b-better get somebody else," we stammer. But then God reminds us that he knows we can't, but he can, and to prove it he gives a wonderful gift. He brings a spirit of peace. A peace before the storm. A peace beyond logic, or as Paul described it, "A peace which passes understanding" (Phil. 4:7). He gave it to David after he showed him Goliath; he gave it to Saul after he showed him the gospel; he gave it to Jesus after he showed him the cross. And he gave it to Gideon. So Gideon, in turn, gave the name to God. He built an altar and named it *Jehovah-shalom,* the Lord is peace (Judges 6:24).

At least a couple of the boulders beneath the house knew the chisel of Moses. On one he carved the name *Jehovah-rophe.* You'll find the English translation in Exodus 15:26: "I am the Lord who heals you." Here is the setting. Over a million Israelites have been liberated from captivity and follow Moses into the desert. Their jubilation over liberation soon becomes frustration over dehydration. (Don't groan. I worked ten minutes on that sentence and fought two editors to keep it in.) They walked three days through a land void of shade, streams, houses, and greenery. Their only neighbors were the sun and serpents.

They finally came upon a lake, but the water was brackish, bitter, and dangerous. I'm sure it wasn't funny at the time, but you've got to chuckle about what happens next. "So Moses cried out to the LORD and the LORD showed him a tree" (Exod. 15:25). Moses is begging for water and God gives him wood?

Let's pause and total the damage. Three days in the desert sun. Hopes raised at the sight of a lake. Hopes dashed at the taste of the water. Moses, cotton-mouthed and parched-lipped, asks for relief . . . and God shows him a tree?

Moses responds by throwing the tree into the lake. Maybe he did it out of aggravation: "Here is what I think of this tree stuff." Or maybe out of inspiration: "You're in charge, God." Whatever the reason, the water is purified, the Israelites' thirst is satisfied, and God is glorified. (That sentence only took five minutes.) In this case, God himself reveals his name: "I am the LORD who heals you" (Exod. 15:26).

The operative word here is *I*. God is the one who heals. He may use a branch of medicine and a branch of a hospital or a branch of a live oak tree, but he is the one who takes the poison out of the system. He is *Jehovah-rophe.*

He is also *Jehovah-nissi,* the Lord my banner. In the heat of battle, soldiers feared getting separated from their army. For that reason a banner was carried into the conflict, and if a fighter found himself alone, the raised flag would signal safety. When the Amalekites (the big bad guys) attacked the Israelites (the little good guys), Moses went up on the mountain and prayed. As long as his hands were up, the Israelites prevailed. But when his hands were down, the Amalekites won. Moses was no dummy—he kept his hands up. The Israelites won, the Amalekites ran, and Moses built an altar for God and chiseled a new name on a stone—*Jehovah-nissi*—the Lord my banner (see Exod. 17:8–16).

These are just a few of the names of God which describe his

character. Study them, for in a given day, you may need each one of them. Let me show you what I mean.

When you are confused about the future, go to your *Jehovah-raah,* your caring shepherd. When you are anxious about provision, talk to *Jehovah-jireh,* the Lord who provides. Are your challenges too great? Seek the help of *Jehovah-shalom,* the Lord is peace. Is your body sick? Are your emotions weak? *Jehovah-rophe,* the Lord who heals you, will see you now. Do you feel like a soldier stranded behind enemy lines? Take refuge in *Jehovah-nissi,* the Lord my banner.

Meditating on the names of God reminds you of the character of God. Take these names and bury them in your heart.

God is

the shepherd who guides,

the Lord who provides,

the voice who brings peace in the storm,

the physician who heals the sick, and

the banner that guides the soldier.

And most of all, he . . . is.

CHAPTER 4

The Observatory

A Heavenly Affection

Our Father who is in heaven . . .

A FEW MORNINGS BACK I was jogging through my neighborhood. I've been known to miss some important dates, but even I could not miss the significance of that day. It was the first day of school. Reminders were everywhere: newscast interviews, stores packed with parents, yellow buses awakened from summer slumber and rumbling down the streets. My own family had spent the previous evening packing backpacks and preparing lunches.

It was no surprise to me, then, to see a pretty little girl step out of her house wearing new clothes and a backpack. She couldn't have been over five or six years of age and was walking toward the curb to wait for her bus. "Have a great first day of school," I greeted as I jogged past.

She stopped and looked at me as if I'd pulled a rabbit out of a hat. "How did you know?!"

She was stunned. From her perspective, I was a genius. Somehow I had miraculously discerned why she was up so early and where she was going. And she was impressed.

"Oh, I just know those kind of things," I shouted back to her. (No need to burst her bubble.)

You, on the other hand, are not so easily impressed. You know how I knew. You understand the difference between a child and a grownup. Adults live in a different world than children. Remember how your parents amazed you? Remember how your dad could identify any car that passed? Weren't you impressed at your mom's ability to turn flour and milk and eggs into a cake? As my parents discussed the Sunday sermon, I can remember thinking, *I didn't understand a word the guy said.*

What's the difference? Simple. By virtue of training and study and experience, adults occupy a different domain. How much more is this true of God. Take the difference between the girl and me, amplify it a million times over, and we begin to see the contrast between us and our Father. Who among us can ponder God without asking the same question the girl did: How did you know?

We ask for grace, only to find forgiveness already offered. (How did you know I would sin?)

We ask for food, only to find provision already made. (How did you know I would be hungry?)

We ask for guidance, only to find answers in God's ancient story. (How did you know what I would ask?)

God dwells in a different realm. "The foolishness of God is higher than human wisdom, and the weakness of God is stronger than human strength" (1 Cor. 1:25). He occupies another dimension. "My thoughts are not like your thoughts. Your ways are not like my ways. Just as the heavens are higher than the earth, so are my ways higher than your ways and my thoughts higher than your thoughts" (Isa. 55:8–9).

Make special note of the word *like*. God's thoughts are not our thoughts, nor are they even *like* ours. We aren't even in the same neighborhood. We're thinking, *Preserve the body;* he's thinking, *Save the soul.* We dream of a pay raise. He dreams of raising the dead. We avoid pain and seek peace. God uses pain to bring peace. "I'm going to live before I die," we resolve. "Die, so you can live," he instructs. We love what rusts. He loves what endures. We rejoice at our successes. He rejoices at our confessions. We show our children the Nike star with the million-dollar smile and say, "Be like Mike." God points to the crucified carpenter with bloody lips and a torn side and says, "Be like Christ."

Our thoughts are not like God's thoughts. Our ways are not like his ways. He has a different agenda. He dwells in a different dimension. He lives on another plane. And that plane is named in the first phrase of the Lord's prayer, *"Our Father who is in heaven."*

THE OBSERVATORY

Having comforted us in the living room and assured us with the foundation, Jesus now leads us upstairs. We ascend to the highest level of the house, stand before a heavy wooden door, and accept God's invitation to enter his observatory.

No telescope is needed in this room. The glass ceiling magnifies the universe until you feel all of the sky is falling around you.

Elevated instantly through the atmosphere, you are encircled by the heavens. Stars cascade past until you are dizzy with their number. Had you the ability to spend a minute on each planet and star, one lifetime would scarcely be enough to begin.

Jesus waits until you are caught up in the splendor of it all, and then he reminds you softly, "Your Father is in heaven."

I can remember as a youngster knowing some kids whose fathers were quite successful. One was a judge. The other a prominent physician. I attended church with the son of the mayor. In Andrews, Texas, that's not much to boast about. Nevertheless the kid had clout that most of us didn't. "My father has an office at the courthouse," he could claim.

Guess what you can claim? "My Father rules the universe."

> The heavens tell the glory of God and the skies announce what his hands have made. Day after day they tell the story; night after night they tell it again. They have no speech or words; they have no voice to be heard. But their message goes out through all the world; their words go everywhere on earth" (Ps. 19:1–5).

Nature is God's workshop. The sky is his resume. The universe is his calling card. You want to know who God is? See what he has done. You want to know his power? Take a look at his creation. Curious about his strength? Pay a visit to his home address: 1 Billion Starry Sky Avenue. Want to know his size? Step out into the night and stare at starlight emitted one million years ago and then read 2 Chronicles 2:6, "No one can really build a house for our God. Not even the highest of heavens can hold him."

He is untainted by the atmosphere of sin,

unbridled by the time line of history,

unhindered by the weariness of the body.

What controls you doesn't control him. What troubles you doesn't trouble him. What fatigues you doesn't fatigue him. Is an eagle disturbed by traffic? No, he rises above it. Is the whale perturbed by a hurricane? Of course not, he plunges beneath it. Is the lion flustered by the mouse standing directly in his way? No, he steps over it.

How much more is God able to soar above, plunge beneath, and step over the troubles of the earth! "What is impossible with man is possible with God" (Matt. 19:26). Our questions betray our lack of understanding:

How can God be everywhere at one time? (Who says God is bound by a body?)

How can God hear all the prayers which come to him? (Perhaps his ears are different from yours.)

How can God be the Father, the Son, and the Holy Spirit? (Could it be that heaven has a different set of physics than earth?)

If people down here won't forgive me, how much more am I guilty before a holy God? (Oh, just the opposite. God is always able to give grace when we humans can't—he invented it.)

How vital that we pray, armed with the knowledge that God is in heaven. Pray with any lesser conviction and your prayers are timid, shallow, and hollow. But spend some time walking in the workshop of the heavens, seeing what God has done, and watch how your prayers are energized.

Speaking of the Father's workshop, let me tell you about a visit I paid to one as an eight-year-old.

GOD'S WORKSHOP

The highlight of my Cub Scout career was the Soap Box Derby. You've heard of people standing on their soap boxes to make a point? We got *inside* our soap boxes to win a trophy. The competition was simple. Construct a motorless wooden go-cart and enter it in a downhill race. Some of the creations were fancy, complete with steering wheel and painted casing. Others were nothing more than a seat on a wooden chassis with four wheels and a rope for steering. My plan was to construct a genuine red roadster like the one in the Scout manual. Armed with a saw and hammer, a stack of lumber, and high ambition, I set out to be the Henry Ford of Troop 169.

I don't know how long my dad watched me before he interrupted my work. Probably not long, since my efforts weren't a pretty sight. The saw kept jamming and the wood kept buckling. The nails tended to bend and the panels didn't fit. At some point Dad mercifully intervened, tapped me on the shoulder, and told me to follow him into his workshop.

The small white frame house on the back of our lot was my dad's domain. I'd never really paid attention to what he did in there. All I knew was what I heard: buzzing saws, pounding hammers, and the whistle of a happy worker. I kept my bike in there, but I never noticed the tools. But then again, I'd never tried to build anything before. Over the next couple of hours that day, he introduced me to the magical world of sawhorses, squares, tape measures, and drills. He showed me how to draw a plan and measure the wood. He explained why it was wiser to hammer first and paint later. I was amazed. What was impossible for me was simple for him. Within an afternoon, we had constructed a pretty decent vehicle. And though I didn't leave the race with a trophy, I did leave with a greater admiration for my father. Why? I'd spent some time in his workshop.

You're following me on this one, aren't you? By showing us the heavens, Jesus is showing us his Father's workshop. He lets us hammer our thumbs just enough times and then taps us on the shoulder and says, "Your Father can handle that for you." And to prove it, he takes us into the Father's workshop. With a sweep of the hands he proudly proclaims: "Our Father is in heaven!"

Behold the sun! Every square yard of the sun is constantly emitting 130,000 horse power, or the equivalent of 450 eight-cylinder automobile engines. And yet our sun, as powerful as it is, is but one minor star in the 100 billion orbs which make up our Milky Way Galaxy. Hold a dime in your fingers and extend it arm's length toward the sky, allowing it to eclipse your vision, and you will block out fifteen million stars from your view.

Consider the earth! Our globe's weight has been estimated at six sextillion tons (a six with twenty-one zeroes). Yet it is precisely tilted at twenty-three degrees; any more or any less and our seasons would be lost in a melted polar flood. Though our globe revolves at the rate of one-thousand miles per hour or twenty-five thousand miles per day or nine million miles per year, none of us tumbles into orbit. Our God who "stretches the northern sky out over the empty space and hangs the earth upon nothing" (Job 26:7) also created an invisible band of gravity to hold us secure.[1]

Now as you stand in the observatory viewing God's workshop, let me pose a few questions. If he is able to place the stars in their sockets and suspend the sky like a curtain, do you think it remotely possible that God is able to guide your life? If your

God is mighty enough to ignite the sun, could it be that he is mighty enough to light your path? If he cares enough about the planet Saturn to give it rings or Venus to make it sparkle, is there an outside chance that he cares enough about you to meet your needs? Or, as Jesus says,

> Look at the birds in the air. They don't plant or harvest or store into barns, but your heavenly Father feeds them. And you know you are worth much more than the birds. . . . Why do you worry about clothes? Look at how the lilies in the field grow. They don't work or make clothes for themselves. But I tell you that even Solomon with his riches was not dressed as beautifully as one of these flowers. God clothes the grass in the field, which is alive today but tomorrow is thrown into the fire. So you can even be sure that God will clothe you. Don't have so little faith! (Matt. 6:25–30)

Why did he do it? A shack would have sufficed, but he gave us a mansion. Did he have to give the birds a song and the mountains a peak? Was he required to put stripes on the zebra and the hump on the camel? Would we have known the difference had he made the sunsets gray instead of orange? Why do stars have twinkles and the waves snowy crests? Why dash the cardinal in red and drape the beluga whale in white? Why wrap creation in such splendor? Why go to such trouble to give such gifts?

Why do you? You do the same. I've seen you searching for a gift. I've seen you stalking the malls and walking the aisles. I'm not talking about the obligatory gifts. I'm not describing the last-minute purchase of drugstore perfume on the way to the birthday party. Forget blue-light specials and discount purchases; I'm talking about that extra-special person and that extra-special gift. I'm talking about stashing away a few dollars a month out of the grocery money to buy him some lizard-skin boots; staring at a thousand rings to find her the best diamond; staying up all night Christmas Eve, assembling the new bicycle. Why do you do it? You do it so the eyes will pop. You do it so the heart will stop. You do it so the jaw will drop. You do it to hear those words of disbelief, "You did this for *me*?"

That's why you do it. And that is why God did it. Next time a sunrise steals your breath or a meadow of flowers leaves you speechless, remain that way. Say nothing and listen as heaven whispers, "Do you like it? I did it just for you."

I'm about to tell you something you may find hard to believe. You're about to hear an opinion that may stretch your imagination. You don't have to agree with me, but I would like you to consider it with me. You don't have to buy it, but at least think about it. Here it is: *If you were the only person on earth, the earth would look exactly the same.* The Himalayas would still have their drama and the Caribbean would still have its charm. The sun would still nestle behind the Rockies in the evenings and spray light on the desert in the mornings. If you were the sole pilgrim on this globe, God would not diminish its beauty one degree.

Because he did it all for you . . . and he's waiting for you to discover his gift. He's waiting for you to stumble into the den, rub the sleep from your eyes, and see the bright red bike he assembled, just for you. He's waiting for your eyes to pop and your heart to stop. He's waiting for the moment between the dropping of the jaw and the leap of the heart. For in that silence he leans forward and whispers: *I did it just for you.*

Find such love hard to believe? That's okay. Remember the little girl who couldn't imagine how I knew she was going to school? Just because she couldn't comprehend it didn't mean I didn't know it. And just because we can't imagine God's giving us sunsets, don't think God doesn't do it. God's thoughts are higher than ours. God's ways are greater than ours. And sometimes, out of his great wisdom, our Father in heaven gives us a piece of heaven just to show he cares.

CHAPTER 5

The Chapel

Where Man Covers His Mouth

Hallowed be thy name . . .

When I lived in Brazil I took my mom and her friend to see Iguacu Falls, the largest waterfalls in the world. Some weeks earlier I'd become an expert on the cataracts by reading an article in *National Geographic* magazine. Surely, I thought, my guests would appreciate their good fortune in having me as a guide.

To reach the lookout point, tourists must walk a winding trail that leads them through a forest. I took advantage of the hike to give an Iguacu nature report to my mom and her friend. So full of information I was, I chattered the entire time. After some minutes, however, I caught myself speaking louder and louder. A sound in the distance forced me to raise my voice. With each turn in the trail, my volume increased. Finally, I was shouting above a roar which was proving to be quite irritating. *Whatever that noise is, I wish they'd shut it off so I could complete my lecture.*

Only after reaching the clearing did I realize that the noise we heard was the waterfalls. My words were drowned out by the force and fury of what I was trying to describe. I could no longer be heard. Even if I could, I no longer had an audience. Even my mother would rather see the splendor than hear my description. I shut my mouth.

There are times when to speak is to violate the moment . . . when silence represents the highest respect. The word for such times is reverence. The prayer for such times is "Hallowed be thy name." And the place for this prayer is the chapel.

If there are walls, you won't notice them. If there is a pew, you won't need it. Your eyes will be fixed on God, and your knees will be on the floor. In the center of the room is a throne, and before the throne is a bench on which to kneel. Only you and God are here, and you can surmise who occupies the throne.

Don't worry about having the right words; worry more about having the right heart. It's not eloquence he seeks, just honesty.

A TIME TO BE SILENT

This was a lesson Job learned. If he had a fault, it was his tongue. He talked too much.

Not that anyone could blame him. Calamity had pounced on the man like a lionness on a herd of gazelles, and by the time the rampage passed, there was hardly a wall standing or a loved one living. Enemies had slaughtered Job's cattle, and lightning had destroyed his sheep. Strong winds had left his partying kids buried in wreckage.

And that was just the first day.

Job hadn't even had time to call Allstate before he saw the leprosy on his hands and the boils on his skin. His wife, compassionate soul that she was, told him to "curse God and die." His four friends came with the bedside manner of drill sergeants, telling him that God is fair and pain is the result of evil, and as sure as two-plus-two equals four, Job must have some criminal record in his past to suffer so.

Each had his own interpretation of God and each spoke long and loud about who God is and why God did what he did. They weren't the only ones talking about God. When his accusers paused, Job gave his response. Back and forth they went . . .

> Job cried out . . . (3:1).
>
> Then Eliphaz the Temanite answered . . . (4:1).
>
> Then Job answered . . . (6:1).
>
> Then Bildad the Shuhite answered . . . (8:1).
>
> Then Job answered . . . (9:1).
>
> Then Zophath the Naamathite answered . . . (11:1).

This verbal ping-pong continues for twenty-three chapters. Finally Job has enough of this "answering." No more discussion-group chit-chat. It's time for the keynote address. He grips the microphone with one hand and the pulpit with the other and launches forth. For six chapters Job gives his opinions on God. This time the chapter headings read: "And Job continued," "And Job continued," "And Job continued." He defines God, explains God, and reviews God. One gets the impression that Job knows more about God than God does!

We are thirty-seven chapters into the book before God clears his throat to speak. Chapter thirty-eight begins with these words: "Then the LORD answered Job."

If your Bible is like mine, there is a mistake in this verse. The words are fine but the printer uses the wrong size type. The words should look like this:

THEN THE LORD ANSWERED JOB!

God speaks. Faces turn toward the sky. Winds bend the trees. Neighbors plunge into the storm shelters. Cats scurry up the trees and dogs duck into the bushes. "Somethin's a-blowin' in, honey. Best get them sheets off the line." God has no more than opened his mouth before Job knows he should have kept his sore one shut.

> I will ask you questions and you must answer me. Where were you when I made the earth's foundation? Tell me if you understand. Who marked off how big it should be? Surely you know! Who stretched a ruler across it? What were the earth's foundations set on, or who put its cornerstone in place while the morning stars sang together and all the angels shouted with joy? (38:3–6)

God floods the sky with queries, and Job cannot help but get the point: Only God defines God. You've got to know the alphabet before you can read, and God tells Job, "You don't even know the ABC's of heaven, much less the vocabulary." For the first time, Job is quiet. Silenced by a torrent of questions.

> Have you ever gone to where the sea begins or walked the valleys under the sea? . . . Have you ever gone to the storehouse for snow or seen the storehouses for hail. . . ? Are you the one who gives the horse his strength or puts the flowing mane on its neck? Do you make the horse jump like a locust? Is it through your wisdom that the hawk flies and spreads its wings toward the south? (38:16, 22; 39:19–20, 26)

Job barely has time to shake his head at one question before he is asked another. The Father's implication is clear: "As soon as you are able to handle these simple matters of storing stars and stretching the neck of the ostrich, then we'll have a talk about pain and suffering. But until then, we can do without your commentary."

Does Job get the message? I think so. Listen to his response. "I am not worthy; I cannot answer you anything, so I will put my hand over my mouth" (40:4).

Notice the change. Before he heard God, Job couldn't speak enough. After he heard God, he couldn't speak at all.

Silence was the only proper response. There was a time in the life of Thomas à Kempis when he, too, covered his mouth. He had written profusely about the character of God. But one day God confronted him with such holy grace that, from that moment on, all à Kempis's words "seemed like straw." He put down his pen and never wrote another line. He put his hand over his mouth.

The word for such moments is reverence.

The room for such moments is the chapel.

The phrase for the chapel is "Hallowed be thy name."

A CUT ABOVE

This phrase is a petition, not a proclamation. A request, not an announcement. Hallowed *be* your name. We enter the chapel and beseech, "Be hallowed, Lord." Do whatever it takes to be holy in my life. Take your rightful place on the throne. Exalt yourself. Magnify yourself. Glorify yourself. You be Lord, and I'll be quiet.

The word *hallowed* comes from the word *holy,* and the word *holy* means "to separate." The ancestry of the term can be traced back to an ancient word which means "to cut." To be holy, then, is to be a cut above the norm, superior, extraordinary. Remember what we learned in the observatory? The Holy One dwells on a different level from the rest of us. What frightens us does not frighten him. What troubles us does not trouble him.

I'm more a landlubber than a sailor, but I've puttered around in a bass boat enough to know the secret for finding land in a storm . . . You don't aim at another boat. You certainly don't stare at the waves. You set your sights on an object unaffected by the wind—a light on the shore—and go straight toward it. The light is unaffected by the storm.

By seeking God in the chapel, you do the same. When you set your sights on our God, you focus on one "a cut above" any storm life may bring.

Like Job, you find peace in the pain.

Like Job, you cover your mouth and sit still.

"Be still, and know that I am God" (Ps. 46:10). This verse contains a command with a promise.

The command?

Be still.

Cover your mouth.

Bend your knees.

The promise? You will *know that I am God.*

The vessel of faith journeys on soft waters. Belief rides on the wings of waiting.

Linger in the chapel. Linger often in the chapel. In the midst of your daily storms, make it a point to be still and set your sights on him. Let God be God. Let him bathe you in his glory so that both your breath and your troubles are sucked from your soul. Be still. Be quiet. Be open and willing. Then you will know that God is God, and you can't help but confess, "Hallowed be thy name."

Chapter 6

THE THRONE

Touching the King's Heart

Thy kingdom come . . .

OUR FAMILY went desk hunting recently. I needed a new one for the office, and we'd promised Andrea and Sara desks for their rooms. Sara was especially enthused. When she comes home from school, guess what she does? She plays school! I never did that as a kid. I tried to forget the classroom activities, not rehearse them. Denalyn assures me not to worry, that this is one of those attention-span differences between genders. So off to the furniture store we went.

When Denalyn buys furniture she prefers one of two extremes—so antique it's fragile or so new it's unpainted. This time we opted for the latter and entered a store of in-the-buff furniture.

Andrea and Sara succeeded quickly in making their selections, and I set out to do the same. Somewhere in the process Sara learned we weren't taking the desks home that day, and this news disturbed her deeply. I explained that the piece had to be painted and they would deliver the desk in about four weeks. I might as well have said four millennia.

Her eyes filled with tears, "But, Daddy, I wanted to take it home today."

Much to her credit she didn't stomp her feet and demand her way. She did, however, set out on an urgent course to change her father's mind. Every time I turned a corner she was waiting on me.

"Daddy, don't you think we could paint it ourselves?"

"Daddy, I just want to draw some pictures on my new desk."

"Daddy, please let's take it home today."

After a bit she disappeared, only to return, arms open wide and bubbling with a discovery. "Guess what, Daddy. It'll fit in the back of the car!"

You and I know that a seven-year-old has no clue what will or won't fit in a vehicle, but the fact that she had measured the trunk with her arms softened my heart. The clincher, though, was the name she called me: "Daddy, can't we please take it home?"

The Lucado family took a desk home that day.

I heard Sara's request for the same reason God hears ours. Her desire was for her own good. What dad wouldn't want his child to spend more time writing and drawing? Sara wanted what I wanted for her, she only wanted it sooner. When we agree with what God wants, he hears us, as well. (See 1 John 5:14.)

Sara's request was heartfelt. God, too, is moved by our sincerity. The "earnest prayer of a righteous man has great power" (James 5:16 TLB).

But most of all, I was moved to respond because Sara called me "Daddy." Because she is my child, I heard her request. Because we are his children, God hears ours. The king of creation gives special heed to the voice of his family. He is not only willing to hear us, he loves to hear us. He even tells us what to ask him.

"Thy kingdom come."

THY KINGDOM COME

We're often content to ask for less. We entered the Great House of God with a satchel full of requests—promotions desired, pay raises wanted, transmission repairs needed, and tuitions due. We'd typically say our prayers as casually as we'd order a burger at the drive-through: "I'll have one solved problem and two blessings, cut the hassles, please."

But such complacency seems inappropriate in the chapel of worship. Here we are before the King of kings. We've just covered our mouths out of reverence for his holiness, now do we open them with the topic of transmissions? Not that our needs don't matter to him, mind you. It's just that what seemed so urgent outside the house seems less significant in here. The pay raise is still needed and the promotion is still desired, but is that where we start?

Jesus tells how to begin. "When you pray, pray like this. 'Our Father who is in heaven, hallowed be thy name. Thy kingdom come.'"

When you say, "Thy kingdom come," you are inviting the Messiah himself to walk into your world. "Come, my King! Take your throne in our land. Be present in my heart. Be present in my office. Come into my marriage. Be Lord of my family, my fears, and my doubts." This is no feeble request; it's a bold appeal for God to occupy every corner of your life.

Who are you to ask such a thing? Who are you to ask God to take control of your world? You are his child, for heaven's sake! And so you ask boldly. "So let us come boldly to the very throne of God and stay there to receive his mercy and to find grace to help us in our times of need" (Heb. 4:16).

A SPIRITUAL DRAMA

A wonderful illustration of this kind of boldness is in the story of Hadassah. Though her language and culture are an atlas apart from ours, she can tell you about the power of a prayer to a king. There are a couple of differences, though. Her request was not to her father, but to her husband, the king. Her prayer wasn't for a desk, but for the delivery of her people. And because she entered the throne room, because she opened her heart to the king, he changed his plans and millions of people in 127 different countries were saved.

Oh, how I'd love for you to meet Hadassah. But since she lived in the fifth century BC, such an encounter is not likely. We'll have to be content with reading about her in the book which bears her name—her other name—the book of Esther.

And what a book it is! Hollywood would have a challenge matching the drama of this story . . . the evil Haman who demanded that all pay him homage . . . the gutsy Mordecai who refused to bow before Haman . . . Mordecai's great words to Esther that she may have been chosen queen for "such a time as this" . . . and Esther's conviction to save her people. "If I perish, I perish," she resolved.

Let's review the central characters.

Xerxes was the king of Persia. He was an absolute monarch over the land from India to Ethiopia. Let Xerxes raise an eyebrow and the destiny of the world would change. In this respect he symbolized the power of God, for our King guides the river of life, and he doesn't even raise an eyebrow.

Haman (whose name sounds like hangman, which you will soon see as more than a curious coincidence) was the right-hand man of Xerxes. Read every word about the man and you'll find nothing good about him. He was an insatiable egotist who wanted the worship of every person in the kingdom. Perturbed by a peculiar minority called the Jews, he decided to exterminate them. He convinced Xerxes that the world would be better with a holocaust and set a date for the genocide of all of Abraham's children.

Haman is a servant of hell and a picture of the devil himself, who has no higher aim than to have every knee bow as he passes. Satan also has no other plan than to persecute the promised people of God. He comes to "steal and kill and destroy" (John 10:10). "He is filled with anger because he knows he does not have much time" (Rev. 12:12). Since the lie in the garden, he has sought to derail God's plan. In this case Satan hopes to destroy the Jews, thereby destroying the lineage of Jesus. For Haman, the massacre is a matter of expediency. For Satan, it is a matter of survival. He will do whatever it takes to impede the presence of Jesus in the world.

That's why he doesn't want you to pray as Jesus taught, "Thy kingdom come."

Esther, Mordecai's adopted daughter, became queen by winning a Miss Persia contest. In one day she went from obscurity to royalty, and in more ways than one she reminds you of you. Both of you are residents of the palace: Esther, the bride of Xerxes and you, the bride of Christ. Both of you have access to the throne of the king, and you both have a counselor to guide and teach you. Your counselor is the Holy Spirit. Esther's counselor was Mordecai.

It was Mordecai who urged Esther to keep her Jewish nationality a secret. It was also Mordecai who persuaded Esther to talk to Xerxes about the impending massacre. You may wonder why she would need any encouragement. Mordecai must have wondered the same thing. Listen to the message he got from Esther: "No man or woman may go to the king in the inner courtyard without being called. There is only one law about this: Anyone who enters must be put to death unless the king holds out his gold scepter. Then that person may live. And I have not been called to go to the king for thirty days" (Esther 4:11).

As strange as it may sound to us, not even the queen could approach the king without an invitation. To enter his throne room uninvited was to risk a visit to the gallows. But Mordecai convinces her to take the risk. If you wonder why I see Mordecai as a picture of the Holy Spirit, watch how he encourages her to do what is right. "Just because you think you live in the king's palace, don't think that out of all the Jewish people you alone will escape. If you keep quiet at this time, someone else will help and save the Jewish people, but you and your father's family will all die. And who knows, you may have been chosen queen for such a time as this" (Esther 4:13–14).

Watch how Esther responds. "Esther put on her royal robes and stood in the inner courtyard of the king's palace, facing the king's hall" (Esther 5:1).

Can't you see her? Right off the cover of *Mademoiselle* magazine? Can't you see King Xerxes? Flipping through his copy of *Car and Chariot.* On either side of him is a burly-chested guard. Behind him is a chattering eunuch. Ahead of him is a long day of cabinet meetings and royal red tape. He lets out a sigh and sinks down into his throne . . . and out of the corner of his eye, he sees Esther.

"When the king saw Queen Esther standing in the courtyard, he was pleased" (5:2). Let me give you my translation of that verse: "When the king saw Queen Esther standing in the courtyard he said, 'a-hubba-hubba-hubba.'" "He held out to her the gold scepter that was in his hand, so Esther went forward and touched the end of it" (5:2).

What follows is the rapid collapse of Satan's deck of cards. Haman schemes to string up Mordecai, the only man who won't grovel at his feet. Esther plans to throw a couple of banquets for Xerxes and Haman. At the end of the second banquet Xerxes begs Esther to ask for something. Esther looks sort of sheepishly at the floor and says, "Well, now that you mention it, there is one eensy weensy favor I've been wanting to ask." And she proceeds to inform the king about the raging anti-Semite who was hell-bent on killing her friends like rats, which meant that Xerxes was about to lose his bride if he didn't act soon, and you don't want that, do you honey?

Xerxes demands the name of the murderer, and Haman looks for the exits. Esther spills the beans, and Xerxes loses his cool. He storms out the door to take a Prozac only to return and find Haman at the feet of Esther. Haman is begging for mercy, but the king thinks he's making a move on the queen. And before Haman has a chance to explain, he's headed to the same gallows he'd built for Mordecai.

Haman gets Mordecai's rope. Mordecai gets Haman's job. Esther gets a good night's sleep. The Jews live to see another day. And we get a dramatic reminder of what happens when we approach our King.

Like Esther, we have been plucked out of obscurity and given a place in the palace.

Like Esther, we have royal robes; she was dressed in cloth, we are dressed in righteousness.

Like Esther, we have the privilege of making our request.

That's what Sara did. Her request wasn't as dramatic as Esther's, but it changed her father's plans. By the way, the living parable of Sara and her desk didn't stop at the store.

On the way home she realized that my desk was still at the store. "I guess you didn't beg, did you, Daddy?" (We have not because we ask not.)

When we unloaded her desk she invited me to christen it with her by drawing a picture. I made a sign which read, "Sara's desk." She made a sign which read, "I love my Daddy." (Worship is the right response to answered prayer.)

My favorite part of the story is what happened the next day. I shared this account in my Sunday sermon. A couple from our church dropped by and picked the desk up, telling us they would paint it. When they returned it a couple of days later, it was covered with angels. And I was reminded that when we pray for God's kingdom to come, it comes! All the hosts of heaven rush to our aid.

Chapter 7

THE STUDY

How God Reveals His Will

Thy will be done . . .

WERE THE SCENE not so common it would be comical. Two heavy-hearted disciples slouching their way home to Emmaus. By the slump in their shoulders, you'd never know today was Resurrection Sunday. By the looks on their faces, you'd think Jesus was still in the tomb. "We were hoping that he would free Israel," they lament (Luke 24:21).

As if he hasn't! How could you be so close to Christ and miss the point? Jesus has just redeemed the world and they are complaining about Rome? Jesus came to deal with sin and death—and they want him to deal with Caesar and soldiers? Jesus came to set us free from hell—and they want to be set free from taxes?

Talk about a miscommunication! They missed the revolution!

I made the same mistake last month. The revolution I missed was nothing like the ones the disciples missed, but I missed it just the same.

The New England colonies were never the same after the Boston Tea Party. Europe was never the same after the Battle of Normandy. The church was never the same after Luther hammered his ninety-five theses on the Wittenburg Door. And my life will never be the same now that e-mail has entered our office.

The avant-garde thinkers on the church staff had been lobbying for this change for months. "Just think," they would say, "just move the cursor and click the mouse and the message is sent."

Easy for them to say. They speak Computer-ese. Not me. Up until recently I thought a *cursor* was a person with foul language and a *mouse* was a rodent you trapped. As far as I knew, *logging-on* was the job of the lumberjack and a *monitor* was the guy who asked you what you were doing roaming the halls during class.

How was I to know that *interface* was a computer term? I thought it was slang for a slam-dunk. (Interface, baby!) Forgive me for lagging behind (or is that "logging behind"?), but a fellow can only handle so much. It happened overnight. I went to sleep in a simple society of sticky-notes and awoke in a paperless culture of e-mail. You can imagine my confusion as everyone started jabbering in this new vocabulary. "I e-mailed you a memo I found at www.confusion.com. Why don't you download your bat.file in my subdirectory and we can interface on the internet?"

What was wrong with, "Did you get my note?"

I miss the old days. I miss the bygone era of pen touching paper and sticky-notes on my door. I long to see handwriting again and to use the "while you were out message" as a coaster for my coffee cup.

But change was inevitable and, digging my heels in the carpet, I was pulled into the netherworld of e-mail. Partly because I was busy but mostly because I was stubborn, I procrastinated learning the system. Every day the computer net mail beeped to alert me about incoming messages. And everyday the number increased. "Max Lucado has 10 unread messages in his box." "Max Lucado has 52 unread messages in his box." "Max Lucado has 93 unread messages in his box."

Finally I gave in. After being carefully tutored and mastering the correct double click of the hamster (I mean the mouse), I found myself gazing inside a room full of information, all waiting for me. There was a letter from Africa, a joke about preachers, a dozen or so announcements about meetings (I had missed—oops!). Within a few minutes I was updated, informed and, I'll admit it, enlightened. As much as I hate to say so, it felt good to get the messages again.

Which is similar to how the two men on the road to Emmaus must have felt. They, too, had missed out on some information. They, too, were confused. They'd missed more than a memo on a committee meeting, however. They'd missed the meaning of the death of Jesus. What should have been a day of joy was to them a day of despair. Why? They didn't know how to understand God's will.

They aren't alone. More than one of us has spent hours staring at the monitor of life wondering what direction to take. We know God has a will for us. "I have good plans for you, not plans to hurt you. I will give you hope and a good future" (Jer. 29:11).

God has a plan and that plan is good. Our question is, how do I access it? Other people seem to receive guidance; how can I? One of the best ways to answer this question is to study the story of these two confused disciples on the road to Emmaus. And I know no better time to answer these questions than now as we enter into the next room in God's Great House and pray, "Thy will be done."

THE STUDY

Just down the hall from the chapel is a room uncluttered by televisions, stereos, and e-mail-infected computers. Envision a study with bookshelves lining the walls, a braided rug on the floor and an inviting fire in the hearth. In front of the fire are two high, wing chairs, one for you and one for your Father. Your seat is empty, and your Father motions for you to join him. Come and sit and ask him whatever is on your heart. No question is too small, no riddle too simple. He has all the time in the world. Come and seek the will of God.

To pray, "Thy will be done" is to seek the heart of God. The word *will* means "strong desire." The study is where we learn what God desires. What is his heart? His passion? He wants you to know it.

Shall God hide from us what he is going to do? Apparently not, for he has gone to great lengths to reveal his will to us. Could he have done more than send his Son to lead us? Could he have done more than give his word to teach us? Could he have done more than orchestrate events to awaken us? Could he have done more than send his Holy Spirit to counsel us?

God is not the God of confusion, and wherever he sees sincere seekers with confused hearts, you can bet your sweet December that he will do whatever it takes to help them see his will. That's what he was doing on the road to Emmaus.

Everybody else was on-line, and they were on foot. They saw the death of Jesus as the death of the movement, and they packed their bags and headed home. And that is where they were going when Jesus appeared to them. How sweet is the appearance of Jesus on the road. Let a lamb take the wrong turn and miss the pasture and our Shepherd, unwilling to let him wander too far, comes to guide him home. How does he do this? How does he reveal his will to us? You might be surprised at the simplicity of the process.

THROUGH THE PEOPLE OF GOD

The first mistake of the duo was to disregard the words of their fellow disciples. God reveals his will through a community of believers. On the first Easter, he spoke through women who spoke to the others. "Today some women among us amazed us. Early this morning they went to the tomb, but they did not find his body there. They came and told us that they had seen a vision of angels who said Jesus was alive" (Luke 24: 22–23).

His plan hasn't changed. Jesus still speaks to believers through believers. "The whole body depends on Christ, and all the parts of the body are joined and held together. Each part does its own work to make the whole body grow and be strong with love" (Eph. 4:15).

While I was driving to my office this morning, my eye saw a traffic light. The sensors within my eye perceived that the color of the light was red. My brain checked my memory bank and announced the meaning of a red light to my right foot. My right foot responded by leaving the accelerator and pressing the brake.

Now what if my body hadn't functioned properly? What if my

eye had decided not to be a part of the body because the nose had hurt its feelings? Or what if the foot was tired of being bossed around and decided to press the gas pedal instead of the brake? Or what if the right foot was in pain, but too proud to tell the left foot, so the left foot didn't know to step in and help? In all instances, a wreck would occur.

God has given each part of the body of Christ an assignment. One way God reveals his will to you is through the church. He speaks to one member of his body through another member. It could happen in a Bible class, a small group, during communion, or during dessert. God has as many methods as he has people.

That, by the way, is why Satan doesn't want you in church. You've noticed, haven't you, that when you're in a spiritual slump, you head out to Emmaus, too. You don't want to be with believers. Or if you do, you sneak in and sneak out of the service, making excuses about meals to prepare or work to do. The truth is, Satan doesn't want you hearing God's will. And since God reveals his will to his children through other children, he doesn't want you in a church. Nor does he want you reading your Bible. Which takes us to another way God reveals his will.

THROUGH THE WORD OF GOD

The disciples disregarded the Word of God. That was their second mistake. Rather than consult the Scriptures, they listened to their fears. Jesus corrects this by appearing to them and conducting a Bible study. We'd expect something a bit more dramatic from one who had just defeated death—turn a tree into a dog or suspend the disciples a few feet in the air. But Jesus sees no need to do more than reacquaint his followers with Scripture.

> "You are foolish and slow to believe everything the prophets said. They said that the Christ must suffer these things before he enters his glory." Then starting with what Moses and the prophets had said about him, Jesus began to explain everything that had been written about himself in the Scriptures. (Luke 24:25–27)

Through the words of the prophets, he used Scripture to reveal his will. Doesn't he do the same today? Open the Word of God and you'll find his will.

> This is God's will, that I should raise up those he has given me. (John 6:39)

> It is God's will that you be born again, that you be "born not of the will of flesh nor of the will of man but of God." (John 1:13)

> It is not God's will that one little one perish. (Matt. 18:14)

> It is my Father's will that everyone who sees the Son and believes on him should have eternal life—that I should raise him at the Last Day. (John. 6:40)

It is his will that the world be saved. Knowing that, then, my task is to align myself with his will. Anytime I find myself choosing between two roads I must ask, "Which road will contribute more to the kingdom of God?"

Sometimes it's obvious. There is no way, for example, that pornography advances the cause of God. It's beyond reason to think that embezzlement enhances the kingdom (even if you tithe on your take). I would take issue with the person who justifies her drug addiction as a way to draw nearer to the mystical side of God.

Other times it's not as clear, but the question is still helpful. Forced to choose between two professions? Will one allow you to have a greater impact for the kingdom? Torn between two churches to attend? Will one afford you a greater chance to glorify God? You wonder if this person is the spouse for you? Ask yourself, Will he or she help me bring glory to God?

His *general* will provides us with guidelines which help us understand his *specific* will for our individual lives.

THROUGH A WALK WITH GOD

> They begged him, "Stay with us; . . . it is almost night."
> So he went in to stay with them. (Luke 24: 29)

We also learn God's will by spending time in his presence. The key to knowing God's heart is having a relationship with him. A *personal* relationship. God will speak to you differently than he will speak to others. Just because God spoke to Moses through a burning bush, that doesn't mean we should all sit next to a bush waiting for God to speak. God used a fish to convict Jonah. Does that mean we should have worship services at Sea World? No. God reveals his heart personally to each person.

For that reason, your walk with God is essential. His heart is not seen in an occasional chat or weekly visit. We learn his will as we take up residence in his house every single day.

If you were to take a name at random out of the phone book

and ask me, "Max, how does Chester Whomever feel about adultery?" I couldn't answer. I don't know Chester Whomever. But if you were to ask me, "Max, how does Denalyn Lucado feel about adultery?" I wouldn't even have to call her. I know. She's my wife. We have walked together long enough that I know what she thinks.

The same is true with God. Walk with him long enough and you come to know his heart. When you spend time with him in his study, you see his passion. Welcome him to enter the gateway of your soul and you'll perceive his will. By the way, did you notice that curious action of Jesus found in verse 28? "They came near the town of Emmaus and Jesus acted as if he were going farther."

Doesn't Jesus want to be with the disciples? Of course he does. But he doesn't want to be where he's not invited. Ever the gentleman, our Lord awaits our invitation. Please note, it was after they gave this invitation that they were "allowed to recognize Jesus" (v. 31).

There is one final way God reveals his will.

THROUGH THE FIRE OF GOD

> When they saw who he was, he disappeared. They said to each other, "It felt like a fire burning in us when Jesus talked to us on the road and explained the Scriptures to us." (vv. 31–32)

Don't you love that verse? They knew they had been with Jesus because of the fire within them. God reveals his will by setting a torch to your soul. He gave Jeremiah a fire for hard hearts. He gave Nehemiah a fire for a forgotten city. He set Abraham on fire for a land he'd never seen. He set Isaiah on fire with a vision he couldn't resist. Forty years of fruitless preaching didn't extinguish the fire of Noah. Forty years of wilderness wandering didn't douse the passion of Moses. Jericho couldn't slow Joshua, and Goliath didn't deter David. There was a fire within them.

And isn't there one within you? Want to know God's will for your life? Then answer this question: What ignites your heart? Forgotten orphans? Untouched nations? The inner city? The outer limits?

Heed the fire within!

Do you have a passion to sing? Then sing!

Are you stirred to manage? Then manage!

Do you ache for the ill? Then treat them!

Do you hurt for the lost? Then teach them!

As a young man I felt the call to preach. Unsure if I was correct in my reading of God's will for me, I sought the counsel of a minister I admired. His counsel still rings true. "Don't preach," he said, "unless you have to."

As I pondered his words I found my answer: "I *have* to. If I don't, the fire will consume me."

What is the fire that consumes you?

Mark it down: Jesus comes to set you on fire! He walks as a torch from heart to heart, warming the cold and thawing the chilled and stirring the ashes. He is at once a Galilean wildfire and a welcome candle. He comes to purge infection and illuminate your direction.

The fire of your heart is the light of your path. Disregard it at your own expense. Fan it at your own delight. Blow it. Stir it. Nourish it. Cynics will doubt it. Those without it will mock it. But those who know it—those who know *him*—will understand it.

To meet the Savior is to be set aflame.

To discover the flame is to discover his will.

And to discover his will is to access a world like none you've ever seen.

CHAPTER 8

The Furnace

Because Someone Prayed

On earth as it is in heaven . . .

I'D LIKE YOU TO THINK about someone. His name is not important. His looks are immaterial. His gender is of no concern. His title is irrelevant. He is important not because of who he is, but because of what he did.

He went to Jesus on behalf of a friend. His friend was sick, and Jesus could help, and someone needed to go to Jesus, so someone went. Others cared for the sick man in other ways. Some brought food, others provided treatment, still others comforted the family. Each role was crucial. Each person was helpful, but none was more vital than the one who went to Jesus.

He went because he was asked to go. An earnest appeal came from the family of the afflicted. "We need someone who will tell

Jesus that my brother is sick. We need someone to ask him to come. Will you go?"

The question came from two sisters. They would have gone themselves, but they couldn't leave their brother's bedside. They needed someone else to go for them. Not just anyone, mind you, for not just anyone could. Some were too busy, others didn't know the way. Some fatigued too quickly, others were inexperienced on the path. Not everyone could go.

And not everyone would go. This was no small request the sisters were making. They needed a diligent ambassador, someone who knew how to find Jesus. Someone who wouldn't quit mid-journey. Someone who would make sure the message was delivered. Someone who was as convinced as they were that Jesus *must* know what had happened.

They knew of a trustworthy person, and to that person they went. They entrusted their needs to someone, and that someone took those needs to Christ.

"So Mary and Martha sent *someone* to tell Jesus, 'Lord, the one you love is sick'" (John 11:3, emphasis mine).

Someone carried the request. Someone walked the trail. Someone went to Jesus on behalf of Lazarus. And because someone went, Jesus responded.

Let me ask you, how important was this person in the healing of Lazarus? How essential was his role? Some might regard it as secondary. After all, didn't Jesus know everything? Certainly he knew that Lazarus was sick. Granted, but he didn't respond to the need until someone came to him with the message. "When Jesus heard this, he said, 'This sickness will not end in death. It is for the glory of God to bring glory to the son of God'" (v. 4).

When was Lazarus healed? After *someone* made the request.

Oh, I know the healing wouldn't unfold for several days, but the timer was set when the appeal was made. All that was needed was the passage of time.

Would Jesus have responded if the messenger had not spoken? Perhaps, but we have no guarantee. We do, however, have an example: The power of God was triggered by prayer. Jesus looked down the very throat of death's cavern and called Lazarus back to life . . . all because someone prayed.

THE FURNACE

In the Great House of God there is a furnace. This furnace affects the whole house, and your prayers fuel the furnace. Your intercession is coal on the fire. Your pleadings are kindling to the flames. The furnace is sturdy, the vents are ready; all that is needed is your prayer.

> Prayer is essential in this ongoing warfare. Pray long and hard. Pray for your brothers and your sisters. (Eph. 6:18 MSG)

In the economy of heaven, the prayers of saints are a valued commodity. John, the apostle, would agree. He wrote the story of Lazarus and was careful to show the sequence: The healing began when the request was made.

This wouldn't be the last time John would make the same point. Read these words, penned later by John. "On the Lord's Day I was in the Spirit and I heard a loud voice behind me that sounded like a trumpet" (Rev. 1:10).

IN THE SPIRIT ON THE LORD'S DAY

We've just moved six decades into the future. John is old now. He's the silver-haired figure stepping through the jagged rocks on a beach. He's looking for a flat place where he can kneel. It is the Lord's day. And John has come to see his Lord.

We don't know who first called this day the Lord's day, but we know why. It was and is his day. It belongs to him. He left his imprint on hell itself that morning. Friday's trial became Sunday's trumpet. This is the Lord's day.

This is also John's spiritual birthday. Decades earlier, on the first Lord's day, John was shaken from his sorrow and sleep by the announcement, "They have taken the Lord out of the tomb and we don't know where they have put him" (John 20:2). On legs much younger and stronger, John sprinted to the empty tomb and the fulfilled promise. Speaking of himself, he later confided, "The other follower, who had reached the tomb first, also went in. He saw and believed" (John 20:8).

After the resurrection came persecution, and the Father scattered his disciples over society like a spring wind scatters dandelions. John, the eyewitness, was placed in Ephesus. There is good reason to believe he spent every Lord's day in the same way he spent the first, leading a friend into the empty tomb of Jesus.

But on this Sunday he has no friend to take to the tomb. He is exiled, banished from his friends. Alone on Patmos. Cut off. With the stroke of a magistrate's pen he was sentenced to pass his days with no companion, with no church.

Rome had stilled the tongue of Peter and silenced the pen of Paul. Now she would break the shepherd's staff of John. No doubt she felt smug in her proscription. One by one, the iron fist of Caesar would crush the fragile work of the Galilean.

If only she had known. But she had no idea. No clue. No concept. For what Rome intended as isolation, heaven ordained as revelation. Rome placed John on Patmos for punishment. Heaven placed John on Patmos for privilege. The same apostle who saw the open grave of Christ was now to glimpse the open door of heaven.

It was the Lord's day, you see. Nothing Rome could do could change that fact. It was the Lord's day in Rome and in Jerusalem. It was the Lord's Day in Egypt and Ethiopia and even along the barren stretches of Patmos. It was the Lord's day. And John was, in his words, "in the Spirit" on the Lord's day. Though he was cut off from man, he was in the very presence of God. Though he was far from friends, he was face-to-face with his Friend. He was praying.

And as he prayed, he again was met by an angel. He again saw what no man had ever seen. The same eyes that saw the resurrected Lord now saw heaven open. And for the next few seconds, minutes, or days, John was caught up in the fury and passion of living in the end of times and in the presence of God.

AND HEAVEN WAS SILENT

Though much could be said about what he saw, let's focus on what he heard. Before John speaks of what he saw, he speaks of what he heard, and what he heard was stunning. "On the Lord's day I was in the Spirit and I heard a voice behind me that sounded like a trumpet" (Rev. 1:10). I can imagine a voice and I can imagine a trumpet, but to imagine the silver-toned trumpet-voice is beyond me. And so we are welcomed to the world of Revelation, a realm where what can't happen on earth always happens in heaven.

For eight chapters we read about the noises of heaven John's ears hear—the glorious, loud, rambunctious, soft, holy sounds of heaven. The angels speak. The thunder booms. The living creatures chant, "Holy, holy, holy," and the elders worship, "You are worthy our Lord and our God to receive glory and honor and power, because you made all things" (4:10). The souls of the martyrs call out, "How long?" (6:10). The earth quakes, and the stars fall like figs in a windstorm. One hundred forty-four thousand people from every nation, tribe, people and language of the earth shout in a loud voice, "Salvation belongs to our God, who sits on the throne and to the lamb" (7:10).

The air is full of sounds—earthquakes, trumpets, proclamations, and declarations. From the first word of the angel there is constant activity and non-stop noise until: "There was silence in heaven for about half an hour . . . " (8:1). Strange this sudden reference to minutes. Nothing else is timed. We are not told the length of the worship or the duration of the songs, but the silence lasted for "about half an hour." "What do you mean, 'about half an hour'?" we want to ask. Did John time it? Why "half an hour"? Why not fifteen minutes or one hour? I don't know. I don't know if John was literal or symbolic. But I do know that, as an orchestra falls silent at the lifting of the conductor's baton, so heaven hushed when the Lamb opened the seventh seal.

As the first six seals revealed how God acts, the seventh revealed how God listens. Look what happens after the seventh seal is opened.

> When the Lamb opened the seventh seal, there was silence in heaven for about half an hour. And I saw the seven angels who stand before God and to whom were given seven trumpets. Another angel came and stood at the altar, holding a golden pan for incense. He was given much incense to offer with the prayers of all God's holy people. The angel put this offering on the golden altar before the throne. The smoke from the incense went up from the angel's hand to God with the prayers of God's holy people. Then the angel filled the incense pan with fire from the altar and threw it on the earth, and there were flashes of lightning, thunder and loud noises, and an earthquake. (8:1–5)

Every song ceased. Every being of the heavenly city hushed. The noise stopped. A sudden stillness fell like a curtain. Why? Why did the Lamb lift his hand for silence? Why did the silver-trumpet voices hush? Because someone was praying. Heaven paused, and Heaven pauses to hear the prayers of . . . someone. A mother for her child. A pastor for a church. A doctor for the diseased. A counselor for the confused. Someone steps up to the furnace with a burden and prays, "Lord, the one you love is sick."

WHEN JESUS HEARD THIS

The phrase the friend of Lazarus used is worth noting. When he told Jesus of the illness he said, "Lord, the one you love is sick." He doesn't base his appeal on the imperfect love of the one in need, but on the perfect love of the Savior. He doesn't say, "The one *who loves you* is sick." He says, "The one *you love* is sick." The power of the prayer, in other words, does not depend on the one who makes the prayer, but on the one who hears the prayer.

We can and must repeat the phrase in manifold ways. "The one you love is tired, sad, hungry, lonely, fearful, depressed." The words of the prayer vary, but the response never changes. The Savior hears the prayer. He silences heaven, so he won't miss a word. He hears the prayer. Remember the phrase from John's gospel? "When Jesus *heard* this, he said, 'This sickness will not end in death'" (John 10:4 emphasis mine).

The Master heard the request. Jesus stopped whatever he was doing and took note of the man's words. This anonymous courier was heard by God.

You and I live in a loud world. To get someone's attention is no easy task. He must be willing to set everything aside to listen: turn down the radio, turn away from the monitor, turn the corner of the page and set down the book. When someone is willing to silence everything else so he can hear us clearly, it is a privilege. A rare privilege, indeed.

So John's message is critical. You can talk to God because God listens. Your voice matters in heaven. He takes you very seriously. When you enter his presence, the attendants turn to you to hear your voice. No need to fear that you will be ignored. Even if you stammer or stumble, even if what you have to say impresses no one, it impresses God—and he listens. He listens to the painful plea of the elderly in the rest home. He listens to the gruff confession of the death-row inmate. When the alcoholic begs for mercy, when the spouse seeks guidance, when the businessman steps off the street into the chapel, God listens.

Intently. Carefully. The prayers are honored as precious jewels. Purified and empowered, the words rise in a delightful fragrance to our Lord. "The smoke from the incense went up from the angel's hand to God." Incredible. Your words do not stop until they reach the very throne of God.

Then, the angel "filled the incense pan with fire from the altar and threw it on the earth" (Rev. 8:5). One call and Heaven's fleet appears. Your prayer on earth activates God's power in heaven, and "God's will is done on earth as it is in heaven."

You are the someone of God's kingdom. You have access to God's furnace. Your prayers move God to change the world. You may not understand the mystery of prayer. You don't need to. But this much is clear: Actions in heaven begin when someone prays on earth. What an amazing thought!

When you speak, Jesus hears.

And when Jesus hears, thunder falls.

And when thunder falls, the world is changed.

All because someone prayed.

Chapter 9

The Kitchen

God's Abundant Table

Give us this day our daily bread . . .

I DID A BIT OF RESEARCH on the culture of the kitchen this week. Here is what I learned: People love to talk about food. If you're ever in need of a conversation prompter, try this one: "Do you know any curious dining practices?" There'll be no shortage of stories. The kitchen seems to be one place where all of us have some experience. In fact, you might say that some people are (ahem) heavyweights in this area. Ask people to relate curious eating habits and they'll give you a mouthful.

Like the uncle who pours syrup on everything he eats. ("Everything?" I asked the same question. *Everything,* I was assured.)

Like the father who puts gravy on his cake and the other father who eats his pie crust first. (Says he likes to save the point till last.)

Like the dad (mine) who crumbled his cornbread in buttermilk. One remembered a verse:

I eat my peas with honey.
I've done it all my life.
It makes them taste funny.
But it keeps them on my knife.[1]

Another remembered an old wives' tale about eating ice cream with the spoon upside down to prevent headaches. More than one person was taught to eat bread after fish and never to drink milk with fish.

I was surprised how many hate to intermingle their servings. "First, I eat all my beans. Then all my corn. Then all my meat." (Correct me if I'm wrong, but aren't they about to be mixed anyway?) One fellow carries this to an extreme. Whereas many segregate their foods so they don't touch while on the plate, he puts each portion on its own saucer.

A history buff reminded me that kitchens in colonial America had a trough in the floor into which the bones would be tossed and near which the dogs would wait. Speaking of dogs, more than one person remembered the childhood days of smuggling unwanted food to their pet and then smiling innocently as mom applauded the clean plate.

Burps are welcome in China. And an empty plate among some Latin cultures only assures your host that you're still hungry. The practice of intersecting the fork and knife on a finished plate was begun by Italian nobility who saw the cross as an act of thanksgiving.[2]

Emily Post would have groaned at some of the earliest writings on etiquette. One written in the 1530s stated: "If you can't swallow a piece of food, turn around discreetly and throw it somewhere."[3]

My favorite table morsel was the story of the man with nine sons. The rule of his kitchen was simple: Dad gets the last piece of chicken. If he doesn't want it, the fastest fork wins. One night, as all ten eyed the final piece on the plate, a thunderstorm caused an electrical blackout. There was a scream in the dark, and when the lights returned, the dad's hand was on the chicken platter with nine forks sticking in it.

Everybody has a kitchen story because everybody has a history in the kitchen. Whether yours was a campfire in the jungle or a culinary castle in Manhattan, you learned early that in this room your basic needs were supplied. A garage is optional. A living room is negotiable. An office is a luxury. But a kitchen? Absolutely essential. Every house has one. Even the Great House of God.

KITCHEN RULES

Or perhaps we should say *especially* the Great House of God. For who is more concerned with your basic needs than your Father in heaven? God is not a mountain guru only involved in the mystical and spiritual. The same hand that guides your soul gives food for your body. The one who clothes you in goodness is the same one who clothes you in cloth. In the school of life, God is both the teacher and the cook. He provides fire for the heart and food for the stomach. Your eternal salvation and your evening meal come from the same hand. There is a kitchen in God's Great House; let's journey downstairs and enjoy its warmth.

The table is long. The chairs are many and the food ample. On the wall hangs a simple prayer: *"Give us this day our daily bread."* The words, though they be brief, raise some good questions. For example, where is the "please"? Dare we saunter into the presence of God and say, "Give us"? Another question concerns the paucity of the prayer. Just bread? Any chance for some spaghetti? And what about tomorrow? Why are we to pray for today's provisions and not those of the future?

Perhaps the best way to answer these questions is to look again at the wall of the kitchen. Beneath the prayer, "Give us this day our daily bread," I can envision two statements. You might call them rules of the kitchen. You've seen such rules before. "No singing at the table." "Wash before you eat." "Carry your plate to the sink." "Max gets double portions of dessert." (I wish!)

God's kitchen has a couple of rules as well. The first is a rule of dependence:

RULE #1: DON'T BE SHY, ASK

The first word in the phrase, "Give us this day our daily bread," seems abrupt. Sounds terse, doesn't it? Too demanding. Wouldn't an "If you don't mind" be more appropriate? Perhaps a "Pardon me, but could I ask you to give . . ." would be better? Am I not being irreverent if I simply say, "Give us this day our daily bread"? Well, you are if this is where you begin. But it isn't. If you have followed Christ's model for prayer, your preoccupation has been his wonder rather than your stomach. The first three petitions are God-centered, not self-centered. "Hallowed be your name . . . your kingdom come . . . your will be done."

Your first step into the house of God was not to the kitchen but to the living room, where you were reminded of your adoption. "Our *Father* who is in heaven." You then studied the foundation of the house, where you pondered his permanence. "Our Father *who is* in heaven." Next you entered the observatory and marveled at his handiwork: "Our Father who is in *heaven*." In the chapel, you worshiped his holiness: "Hallowed be thy name." In the throne room, you touched the lowered scepter and prayed the greatest prayer, "Thy kingdom come." In the study, you submitted your desires to his and prayed, "Thy will be done." And all of heaven was silent as you placed your prayer in the furnace, saying, "on earth as it is in heaven."

Proper prayer follows such a path, revealing God to us before revealing our needs to God. (You might reread that one.) The purpose of prayer is not to change God, but to change us, and by the time we reach God's kitchen, we are changed people. Wasn't our heart warmed when we called him Father? Weren't our fears stilled when we contemplated his constancy? Weren't we amazed as we stared at the heavens?

Seeing his holiness caused us to confess our sin. Inviting his kingdom to come reminded us to stop building our own. Asking God for his will to be done placed our will in second place to his. And realizing that heaven pauses when we pray left us breathless in his presence.

By the time we step into the kitchen, we're renewed people! We've been comforted by our father, conformed by his nature, consumed by our creator, convicted by his character, constrained by his power, commissioned by our teacher, and compelled by his attention to our prayers.

The prayer's next three petitions encompass all of the concerns of our life. "This daily bread" addresses the present. "Forgive our sins" addresses the past. "Lead us not into temptation" speaks to the future. (The wonder of God's wisdom: how he can reduce all our needs to three simple statements.)

First he addresses our need for bread. The term means all of a person's physical needs. Martin Luther defined bread as "Everything necessary for the preservation of this life, including food, a healthy body, house, home, wife and children." This verse urges us to talk to God about the necessities of life. He may also give us the luxuries of life, but he certainly will grant the necessities.

Any fear that God wouldn't meet our needs was left in the observatory. Would he give the stars their glitter and not give us our food? Of course not. He has committed to care for us. We aren't wrestling crumbs out of a reluctant hand, but rather confessing the bounty of a generous hand. The essence of the prayer is really an affirmation of the Father's care. Our provision is his priority.

Turn your attention to Psalm 37.

> Trust in the Lord and do good. Live in the land and feed on truth. Enjoy serving the Lord and he will give you what you want. Depend on the Lord; trust him and he will take care of you. (vv. 3–4)

God is committed to caring for our needs. Paul tells us that a man who won't feed his own family is worse than an unbeliever (1 Tim. 5:8). How much more will a holy God care for his children? After all, how can we fulfill his mission unless our needs are met? How can we teach or minister or influence unless we have our basic needs satisfied? Will God enlist us in his army and not provide a commissary? Of course not.

"I pray that the God of peace will give you everything you need so you can do what he wants" (Heb. 13:20). Hasn't that prayer been answered in our life? We may not have had a feast, but haven't we always had food? Perhaps there was no banquet, but at least there was bread. And many times there was a banquet.

In fact, many of us in the United States have trouble relating to the phrase "Give us this day our daily bread" because our pantries are so packed and our bellies so full we seldom ask for food. We ask for self-control. We don't say, "God let me eat." We say, "God, help me not to eat so much." You won't find books in our stores on surviving starvation, but you'll find shelves loaded with books on losing weight. This doesn't negate the importance of this phrase, however. Just the opposite. For us, the blessed of belly, this prayer has double meaning.

We pray, only to find our prayer already answered! We are like the high school senior who decides to go to college and then learns the cost of tuition. He runs to his father and pleads, "I'm sorry to ask so much, Dad, but I have nowhere else to go. I want to go to college and I don't have a penny." The father puts his arms around the son and smiles and says, "Don't worry, son. The day you were born I began saving for your education. I've already provided for your tuition."

The boy made the request only to find the father had already met it. The same happens to you. At some point in your life it occurs to you that someone is providing for your needs. You take a giant step in maturity when you agree with David's words in 1 Chronicles 29:14: "Everything we have has come from you, and we only give you what is yours already" (TLB). You may be writing a check and stirring the soup, but there's more to putting food on the table than that. What about the ancient symbiosis of the seed and the soil and the sun and the rain? Who created animals for food and minerals for metal? Long before you knew you needed someone to provide for your needs, God already had.

So the first rule in the kitchen is one of dependence. Ask God for whatever you need. He is committed to you. God lives with the self-assigned task of providing for his own, and so far, you've got to admit, he's done pretty well at the job.

The second rule is one of trust.

RULE #2: TRUST THE COOK

My informal survey on eating habits reminded me of the time I pigged out on a Pillsbury Dough tube. When I was a youngster my mom would let me lick the bowl after she used it to stir the cookie dough. I remember thinking how great it would be to make a meal out of the gooey stuff. In college my dream came true.

Four of us friends went to a weekend retreat at a farm. On the way we stopped at a grocery store. As you can imagine, we were careful to select proper vegetables, skim milk, no-fat yogurt—and we stayed away from the sweets. We also drove by the White House and picked up the President and the First Lady to do our laundry. Are you kidding? We filled our basket with nothing but fantasy. And for me, my fantasy was cookie dough! This was going to be a Pillsbury Dough Boy weekend. That night I peeled the plastic off the dough like the peeling off a banana and took a big bite . . . then another . . . then anothuuuther . . . then uhhh-nuuuther. Then . . . yuck. I'd had enough.

That usually happens when we make our own menu. You'll notice this is the first time we've used the word *menu*. The kitchen in God's house is no restaurant. It's not owned by a stranger, it's run by your Father. It's not a place you visit and leave; it's a place to linger and chat. It's not open one hour and closed the next; the kitchen is ever available. You don't eat and then pay; you eat and say thanks. But perhaps the most important difference between a kitchen and a restaurant is the menu. A kitchen doesn't have one.

God's kitchen doesn't need one. Things may be different in your house, but in the house of God, the one who provides the food is the one who prepares the meal. We don't swagger into his presence and demand delicacies. Nor do we sit outside the door and hope for crumbs. We simply take our place at the table and gladly trust him to "Give us this day our daily bread."

What a statement of trust! Whatever you want me to have is all I want. In his book *Victorious Praying,* Alan Redpath translates the phrase, "Give us this day bread suited to our need."[4] Some days the plate runs over. God keeps bringing out more food and we keep loosening our belt. A promotion. A privilege. A friendship. A gift. A lifetime of grace. An eternity of joy. There are times when we literally push ourselves back from the table, amazed at God's kindness. "You serve me a six-course dinner right in front of my enemies. You revive my drooping head; my cup fills with blessing" (Ps. 23:5 MSG).

And then there are those days when, well, when we have to eat our broccoli. Our daily bread could be tears or sorrow or discipline. Our portion may include adversity as well as opportunity.

This verse was on my mind last night during family devotions. I called my daughters to the table and set a plate in front of each. In the center of the table I placed a collection of food: some fruit, some raw vegetables and some Oreo cookies. "Every day," I explained, "God prepares for us a plate of experiences. What kind of plate do you most enjoy?"

The answer was easy. Sara put three cookies on her plate. Some days are like that, aren't they? Some days are "three cookie days." Many are not. Sometimes our plate has nothing but vegetables—twenty-four hours of celery, carrots, and squash. Apparently God knows we need some strength, and though the portion may be hard to swallow, isn't it for our own good? Most days, however, have a bit of it all. Vegetables, which are healthy but dull. Fruit, which tastes better and we enjoy. And even an Oreo, which does little for our nutrition, but a lot for our attitude.

All are important and all are from God. "We know that in everything God works for the good of those who love him" (Rom. 8:28). We, like Paul, must learn the "secret of being happy at anytime in everything that happens, when I have enough to eat and when I go hungry, when I have more than I need and when I do not have enough. I can do all things through Christ, because he gives me strength" (Phil. 4:12).

Perhaps the heart of the prayer is found in the book of Proverbs.

> Give me enough food to live on, neither too much nor too little. If I'm too full, I might get independent, saying, "God, Who needs him?" If I'm poor, I might steal and dishonor the name of my God. (Prov. 30:8–9)

The next time your plate has more broccoli than apple pie, remember who prepared the meal. And the next time your plate has a portion you find hard to swallow, talk to God about it. Jesus did. In the garden of Gethsemane his Father handed him a cup of suffering so sour, so vile, that Jesus handed it back to heaven. "My Father," he prayed, "if it is possible may this cup be taken from me. Yet not as I will, but as you will" (Matt. 26:39).

Even Jesus was given a portion he found hard to swallow. But with God's help, he did. And with God's help, you can too.

CHAPTER 10

THE ROOF

Beneath God's Grace

Forgive us our debts . . .

FORGIVE ME for broaching the issue, but I must.

I realize the topic is personal, but it's time we went public.

I need to talk to you about being overdrawn at the bank.

Your paycheck was late. Your landlord cashed your rent check too quickly. You were going to make a deposit, but your aunt called from Minnesota and by the time you got to the bank it was closed and you didn't know how to make a night deposit.

Regardless of the reason, the result is the same: INSUFFICIENT FUNDS. What an ominous phrase. In the great gallery of famous phrases, "insufficient funds" hangs in the same hallway with "The IRS will audit your account," "A root canal is necessary," and "Let's stop dating and just be friends." INSUFFICIENT FUNDS. (To get the full impact of the phrase, imagine hearing the words spoken by a man with fangs, black cape and a deep voice in a Transylvania castle. "You have insufficient funds.")

You are overdrawn. You gave more than you had to give. You spent more than you had to spend. And guess who has to cough up some cash? Not the bank; they didn't write the check. Not the store; they didn't make the purchase. Not your aunt in Minnesota, unless she's got a soft spot in her heart for you. In the grand scheme of things, you can make all the excuses you want, but a bounced check lands in the lap of the one who wrote it.

What do you do if you don't have any money? What do you do if you have nothing to deposit but an honest apology and good intentions? You pray that some wealthy soul will make a huge deposit in your account. If you're talking about your financial debt, that's not likely to happen. If you're talking about your spiritual debt, however, it already has.

Your Father has covered your shortfall. In God's house you are covered by the roof of his grace.

THE ROOF OF PROTECTION

The roof of a house is seldom noticed. How often do your guests enter your doorway saying, "You have one of the finest roofs I've ever seen!" We've had hundreds of people in and out of our home through the years, and I honestly can't remember one comment about the roof. They might remind me to cut the grass or clean my sidewalk, but compliment my roof? Not yet.

Such disregard is no fault of the builder. He and his crew labored hours, balancing beams and nailing shingles. Yet, in spite of their effort, most people would notice a two-dollar lamp before they would notice the roof.

Let's not make the same mistake. As God covered his Great House, he spared no expense. In fact, his roof was the most costly section of the structure. It cost him the life of his Son. He invites us to study his work by virtue of three words in the center of the prayer. "Forgive our debts."

WE OWE A DEBT WE CANNOT PAY

Debt. The Greek word for debt has no mystery. It simply means "to owe someone something." If to be in debt is to owe someone something, isn't it appropriate for us speak of debt in our prayer, for aren't we all in debt to God?

Aren't we in God's debt when we disobey his commands? He tells us to go south and we go north. He tells us to turn right and we turn left. Rather than love our neighbor, we hurt our neighbor. Instead of seeking his will, we seek our will. We're told to forgive our enemies, but we attack our enemies. We disobey God.

Aren't we in God's debt when we disregard him? He makes the universe and we applaud science. He heals the sick and we applaud medicine. He grants beauty and we credit Mother Nature. He gives us possessions and we salute human ingenuity.

Don't we go into debt when we disrespect God's children? What if I did to you what we do to God? What if I shouted at your child in your presence? What if I called him names or struck him? You wouldn't tolerate it. But don't we do the same? How does God feel when we mistreat one of his children? When we curse at his offspring? When we criticize a co-worker, or gossip about a relative, or speak about someone before we speak to them? Aren't we in God's debt when we mistreat a neighbor?

"Wait a second, Max. You mean every time I do one of these things, I'm writing a check on my heavenly bank account?"

That's exactly what I'm saying. I'm also saying that if Christ had not covered us with his grace, each of us would be overdrawn on that account. When it comes to goodness we would have insufficient funds. Inadequate holiness. God requires a certain balance of virtue in our account, and it's more than any of us has alone. Our holiness account shows insufficient funds, and only the holy will see the Lord; what can we do?

We could try making a few deposits. Maybe if I wave at my neighbor or compliment my husband or go to church next Sunday, I'll get caught up. But how do you know when you've made enough? How many trips do I need to make to the bank? How much credit do I need? When can I relax?

That's the problem. You never can. "People cannot do any work that will make them right with God" (Rom. 4:5). If you are trying to justify your own statement, forget ever having peace. You're going to spend the rest of your days huffing and puffing to get to the drive-through window before the bank closes. You are trying to justify an account you can't justify. May I remind you of the roof of grace which covers you?

"It is God who justifies" (8:33).

GOD PAID A DEBT HE DID NOT OWE

God assigned himself the task of balancing your account. You cannot deal with your own sins. "Only God can take away sins"

(Mark 2:7). Jesus is "The Lamb of God, who takes away the sin of the world." It's not you! (John 1:29).

How did God deal with your debt?

Did he overlook it? He could have. He could have burned the statement. He could have ignored your bounced checks. But would a holy God do that? *Could* a holy God do that? No. Else he wouldn't be holy. Besides, is that how we want God to run his world—ignoring our sin and thereby endorsing our rebellion?

Did he punish you for your sins? Again, he could have. He could have crossed your name out of the book and wiped you off the face of the earth. But would a loving God do that? *Could* a loving God do that? He loves you with an everlasting love. Nothing can separate you from his love.

So what did he do? "God put the world square with himself through the Messiah, giving the world a fresh start by offering the forgiveness of sins. . . . How, you say? In Christ. God put on him the wrong who never did anything wrong, so you could be put right with God" (2 Cor. 5:19–21 MSG).

Don't miss what happened. He took your statement flowing with red ink and bad checks and put his name at the top. He took his statement, which listed a million deposits and not one withdrawal, and put your name at the top. He assumed your debt. You assumed his fortune. And that's not all he did.

He also paid your penalty. If you are overdrawn at a bank, a fine must be paid. If you are overdrawn with God, a penalty must be paid as well. The fine at the bank is a hassle. But the penalty from God is hell. Jesus not only balanced your account, he paid your penalty. He took your place and paid the price for your sins. "He changed places with us and put himself under that curse" (Gal. 3:13).

> That's what Christ did definitively: suffered because of others' sins, the Righteous one for the unrighteous ones. He went through it all— was put to death and then made alive— to bring us to God. (1 Pet. 3:18 MSG)

> But he was wounded for the wrong we did; he was crushed for the evil we did. The punishment, which made us well, was given to him, and we are healed because of his wounds. (Isa. 53:5)

"With one sacrifice, Jesus made perfect forever those who are being made holy" (Heb. 10:14). No more sacrifice needs to be made. No more deposits are necessary. So complete was the payment that Jesus used a banking term to proclaim your salvation. "It is finished!"(John 19:30). *Tetelestai* was a financial term used to announce the final installment, the ultimate payment.

Now, if the task is finished, is anything else required of you? Of course not. If the account is full, what more could you add? Even saying the phrase "forgive our debts" does not earn grace. We repeat the words to remind us of the forgiveness we have, not to attain a forgiveness we need. I'll say more about that in the next chapter, but before moving on may we talk frankly?

For some of you these thoughts about bounced checks and God's grace aren't new, but aren't they precious? Honestly, have you ever been given a gift which compares to God's grace? Finding this treasure of mercy makes the poorest beggar a prince. Missing this gift makes the wealthiest man a pauper.

Again, many of you knew that. I pray the reminder encourages you.

But for others, this is more than good news . . . it is *new* news. You never knew there was a roof of grace. And what a grand roof it is. The tiles are thick and the beams are sturdy. Under it you are shielded from the storms of guilt and shame. Beneath the covering of Christ, no accuser can touch you and no act can condemn you.

Isn't it good to know you don't have to stand outside in the storm anymore?

"But is it big enough for me?" you ask. Well, it was big enough for one who denied Christ (Peter). One who mocked Christ (the thief on the cross). One who persecuted Christ (Paul). Yes, it's big enough for you. Though you've spent a lifetime writing insufficient checks, God has stamped these words on your statement: MY GRACE IS SUFFICIENT FOR YOU.

Picture, if you will, a blank check. The amount of the check is "sufficient grace." The signer of the check is Jesus. The only blank line is for the payee. That part is for you. May I urge you to spend a few moments with your Savior receiving this check? Reflect on the work of his grace. Look toward the roof. Its beams are from Calvary and the nails once held a Savior to the cross. His sacrifice was for you.

Express your thanks for his grace. Whether for the first time or the thousandth, let him hear you whisper, "Forgive us our debts." And let him answer your prayer as you imagine writing your name on the check.

Perhaps I best slip out now and leave the two of you to talk. I'll be waiting in the hallway of the Great House of God.

CHAPTER II

The Hallway

Grace Received, Grace Given

Forgive us our debts as we also have forgiven our debtors . . .
For if you forgive men when they sin against you,
your heavenly Father will also forgive you.
But if you do not forgive men their sins, your
Father will not forgive your sins . . .

I'D LIKE TO TALK to you about bounty hunters, nitro around the neck, one of the greatest principles in the Bible, and okra and anchovy sandwiches. But before I do, let's start with a thought about hit men.

Living in the cross hairs of a hit man is no treat. I should know. I had one after me for three months. He wasn't a Mafia member, nor was he a gang member. He didn't carry a gun with a scope; his weapons were even deadlier. He had a phone number and a commission—track me down and make me pay.

His job? Collect past-due payments for a credit card company.

I hope you'll believe me when I say I had paid my bill. He

certainly didn't believe me. I knew I'd paid the bill—I had the canceled check to prove it. The only problem was that the check was on a boat with all our other belongings somewhere between Miami and Rio. We had just moved to Brazil and our possessions were in transit. I wouldn't have access to my bank statement for three months. He wasn't about to wait that long.

He threatened to ruin my credit, sue the travel agency and call the police; he even said he would tell my mother (the big tattletale). After weeks of calling me collect, he suddenly quit bugging me. No explanation. All I can figure is that he traced the error to north of the equator rather than south, and he left me alone. He also left me amazed. I remember asking Denalyn, "What kind of person would enjoy such a job? His profession is aggravation."

A good day for him means a bad day for everyone he contacts. Don't get me wrong, I understand why such an occupation is necessary. I just wonder what kind of person would want such a job? Who wants to be a missionary of misery? Collectors spend the day making people feel bad. No one wants to take their calls. No one is happy to see them at the door. No one wants to read their letters. Can you imagine what their spouse says as they go to work? "Make 'em squirm, honey." Do their bosses motivate them with the "blood out of a turnip" award? Who is their hero? Godzilla? What a job. Their payday is in your paycheck, and they are out to get it. Can you imagine spending your days like that?

Perhaps you can. Perhaps all of us can. Even the best among us spend time demanding payment. Doesn't someone owe you something? An apology? A second chance? A fresh start? An explanation? A thank you? A childhood? A marriage? Stop and think about it (which I don't encourage you to do for long), and you can make a list of a lot of folks who are in your debt. Your parents should have been more protective. Your children should have been more appreciative. Your spouse should be more sensitive. Your preacher should have been more attentive.

What are you going to do with those in your debt? People in your past have dipped their hands in your purse and taken what was yours. What are you going to do? Few questions are more important. Dealing with debt is at the heart of your happiness. It's also at the heart of the Lord's prayer.

Having reminded us of the grace we have received, Jesus now speaks of the grace we should share.

> Forgive us our debts as we also have forgiven our debtors. . . . For if you forgive men when they sin against you, your heavenly Father will also forgive you. But if you do not forgive men their sins, your Father will not forgive your sins. (Matt. 6:12,14–15 NIV)

Through the center of the Great House of God runs a large hallway. You can't get from one room to another without using it. Want to leave the kitchen and go to the study? Use the corridor. Want to take the stairs to the chapel? Use the corridor. You can't go anywhere without walking the hallway. And you can't walk the hallway without bumping into people.

Jesus does not question the reality of your wounds. He does not doubt that you have been sinned against. The issue is not the existence of pain, the issue is the treatment of pain. What are you going to do with your debts?

Dale Carnegie tells about a visit to Yellowstone Park where he saw a grizzly bear. The huge animal was in the center of a clearing, feeding on some discarded camp food. For several minutes he feasted alone; no other creature dared draw near. After a few moments a skunk walked through the meadow toward the food and took his place next to the grizzly. The bear didn't object and Carnegie knew why. "The grizzly," said, "knew the high cost of getting even."[1]

We'd be wise to learn the same. Settling the score is done at great expense.

THE HIGH COST OF GETTING EVEN

For one thing, you pay a price relationally.

Have you ever noticed in the western movies how the bounty hunter travels alone? It's not hard to see why. Who wants to hang out with a guy who settles scores for a living? Who wants to risk getting on his bad side? More than once I've heard a person spew his anger. He thought I was listening, when really I was thinking, *I hope I never get on his list.* Cantankerous sorts, these bounty hunters. Best leave them alone. Hang out with the angry and you might catch a stray bullet. Debt-settling is a lonely occupation. It's also an unhealthy occupation.

You pay a high price physically.

The Bible says it best. "Resentment kills a fool" (Job 5:2 NIV). It reminds me of an old Amos and Andy routine. Amos asks Andy what that little bottle is he's wearing around his neck. "Nitroglycerine," he answers. Amos is stunned that Andy would be wearing a necklace of nitro, so he asks for an explanation. Andy tells him about a fellow who has a bad habit of poking people in the chest while he's speaking. "It drives me crazy," Andy says. "I'm wearing this nitro so the next time he pokes me, I'll blow his finger off."

Andy's not the first to forget that when you try to get even, you get hurt. Job was right when he said, "You tear yourself to pieces in your anger" (Job 18:4). Ever notice that we describe the people who bug us as a "pain in the neck"? Whose neck are we referring to? Certainly not theirs. We are the ones who suffer.

Sometime ago I was speaking about anger at a men's gathering. I described resentment as a prison and pointed out that when we put someone in our jail cell of hatred, we are stuck guarding the door. After the message a man introduced himself as a former prison inmate. He described how the guard at the gate of a prison is even more confined than a prisoner. The guard spends his day in a four-by-five-foot house. The prisoner has a ten-by-twelve-foot cell. The guard can't leave, the prisoner gets to walk around. The prisoner can relax, but the guard has to be constantly alert. You might object and say, "Yes, but the guard of the prison gets to go home at night." True, but the guard of the prison of resentment doesn't.

If you're out to settle the score, you'll never rest. How can you? For one thing, your enemy may never pay up. As much as you think you deserve an apology, your debtor may not agree. The racist may never repent. The chauvinist may never change. As justified as you are in your quest for vengeance, you may never get a penny's worth of justice. And if you do, will it be enough?

Let's really think about this one. How much justice is enough? Picture your enemy for a moment. Picture him tied to the whipping post. The strong-armed man with the whip turns to you and asks, "How many lashes?" And you give a number. The whip cracks and the blood flows and the punishment is inflicted. Your foe slumps to the ground and you walk away.

Are you happy now? Do you feel better? Are you at peace?

Perhaps for a while, but soon another memory will surface and another lash will be needed and . . . when does it all stop?

It stops when you take seriously the words of Jesus. Read them again: "Forgive us our debts as we also have forgiven our debtors. . . . For if you forgive men when they sin against you, your heavenly Father will also forgive you. But if you do not forgive their sins, your Father will not forgive your sins."

Through this verse we learn the greatest cost of getting even. I've suggested that you pay a high price relationally and physically, but Jesus has a far more important reason for you to forgive. If you don't, you pay a high price spiritually.

Before we discuss what these verses mean, it would be wise to point out what they do not mean. The text does not suggest that we earn God's grace by giving grace. At first blush, the phrase appears to present a type of triangular peace treaty. "If I forgive my enemy, then God will forgive me." A casual reading suggests we earn our forgiveness by offering forgiveness to others. Mercy is a merit which saves me. Such an interpretation is impossible for the simple reason that it conflicts with the rest of Scripture. If we can attain forgiveness by forgiving others (or any other good work), then why do we need a Savior? If we can pay for our sins through our mercy, why did Jesus die for our sins? If salvation is a result of our effort, then why did Paul insist, "You have been saved by grace through believing. You did not save yourselves. It was a gift from God" (Eph. 2:8).

Salvation is a free gift.

The question from the last chapter surfaces again. If we are already forgiven, then why does Jesus teach us to pray, "Forgive us our debts"?

The very reason you would want your children to do the

same. If my children violate one of my standards or disobey a rule, I don't disown them. I don't kick them out of the house or tell them to change their last name. But I do expect them to be honest and apologize. And until they do, the tenderness of our relationship will suffer. The nature of the relationship won't be altered, but the intimacy will.

The same happens in our walk with God. Confession does not create a relationship with God, it simply nourishes it. If you are a believer, admission of sins does not alter your position before God, but it does enhance your peace with God. When you confess, you agree; you quit arguing with God and agree with him about your sin. Unconfessed sin leads to a state of disagreement. You may be God's child, but you don't want to talk to him. He still loves you, but until you admit what you've done, there's going to be tension in the house.

But just as unconfessed sin hinders joy, confessed sin releases it. When we admit sin we are like a first grader standing before the teacher with a messy paper. "I colored outside the lines too many times. Could I start over on a clean sheet?" "Of course," says the teacher. Happy is the first grader who gets a second chance, or as David wrote, "Happy is the person whose sin is forgiven, whose wrongs are pardoned" (Ps. 32:1). So we dash back to our seat and start over.

Would there ever be a case when the teacher would leave you to draw on your soiled paper? There might be. I can think of one example when the teacher might refuse to give you a second chance. Suppose she witnesses your mistreatment of the kid in the next desk. A few minutes earlier she saw him ask you for a piece of paper out of your tablet, and you refused. Though you had plenty to give, you clutched your Big Chief with both hands and refused to share. And now here you are making the same request of her?

Who would blame her if she said, "I tell you what, I'm going to grant you the same kindness you gave your classmate. The way you treat Harry is the way I'll treat you. You're still my student, and I'm still your teacher. I'm not kicking you out of class, but I am going to give you a chance to learn a lesson." Now we're getting down to the nitty-gritty of the verse, for this is exactly what the phrase means: "Forgive us our debts as we have forgiven our debtors."

ONE OF THE GREATEST PRINCIPLES IN THE BIBLE

"Treat me as I treat my neighbor." Are you aware that this is what you are saying to your Father? Give me what I give them. Grant me the same peace I grant others. Let me enjoy the same tolerance I offer. God will treat you the way you treat others.

In any given Christian community there are two groups: those who are contagious in their joy and those who are cranky in their faith. They've accepted Christ and are seeking him, but their balloon has no helium. One is grateful, the other is grumpy. Both are saved. Both are heaven bound. But one sees the rainbow and the other sees the rain.

Could this principle explain the difference? Could it be that they are experiencing the same joy they have given their offenders? One says, "I forgive you," and feels forgiven. The other says, "I'm ticked off," and lives ticked off at the world.

Elsewhere Jesus said:

> Don't judge other people, and you will not be judged.

> Don't accuse others of being guilty, and you will not be accused of being guilty. *Forgive, and you will be forgiven. Give, and you will receive*. You will be given much. Pressed down, shaken together, and running over, it will spill into your lap. The way you give to others is the way God will give to you. (Luke 6:37–38, emphasis mine)

It's as if God sends you to the market to purchase your neighbor's groceries saying, "Whatever you get your neighbor, get also for yourself. For whatever you give him is what you receive."

Pretty simple system. I'm not too bright, but I can figure this one out. I love thick, juicy hamburger meat, so I buy my neighbor thick, juicy hamburger meat. I'm crazy about double-chocolate ice cream, so I buy my neighbor double-chocolate ice cream. And when I drink milk, I don't want the skimpy skim stuff that Denalyn makes me drink. I want Christian milk, just like God made it. So what do I buy my neighbor? Christian milk, just like God made it.

Let's take this a step further. Suppose your neighbor's trash blows into your yard. You mention the mess to him, and he says he'll get to it sometime next week. You inform him that you've got company coming and couldn't he get out of that chair and do some work? He tells you not to be so picky, that the garbage fertilizes your garden. You're just about to walk across the lawn to have a talk when God reminds you, "Time to go to the market and buy your neighbor's groceries." So you grumble and mumble your way to the store, and then it hits you, "I'll get even with the old bum." You go straight to the skim milk. Then you make a beeline to the anchovies and sardines. You march right past the double-chocolate ice cream and head toward the okra and rice.

You make a final stop in the day-old bread section and pick up a crusty loaf with green spots on the edge.

Chuckling, you drive back to the house and drop the sack in the lap of your lazy, good-for-nothing neighbor. "Have a good dinner." And you walk away.

All your brilliant scheming left you hungry, so you go to your refrigerator to fix a sandwich, but guess what you find. Your pantry is full of what you gave your enemy. All you have to eat is exactly what you just bought. We get what we give.

Some of you have been eating sardines for a long time. Your diet ain't gonna change until you change. You look around at other Christians. They aren't as sour as you are. They're enjoying the delicacies of God, and you're stuck with okra and anchovies on moldy bread. You've always wondered why they look so happy and you feel so cranky. Maybe now you know. Could it be God is giving you exactly what you're giving someone else?

Would you like a change of menu? Earlier I referred to a men's conference where I spoke on the topic of anger. A couple of weeks after I returned home I received this letter from a man named Harold Staub.

> Max,
>
> Thank you so much for speaking on forgiveness at Promise Keepers in Syracuse, NY, on June 7 and 8. I was there. Just want you to know I went home, talked to my wife on many subjects about forgiveness—the best two weeks of my life. You see, she went home to be with the Lord on June 24, totally forgiven. How wonderful is his love. Thank you so very much.[2]

When we called Harold to ask his permission to print his letter, he shared the touching details of his final days with his wife. He didn't know she was near death, nor did she. He did know, however, that some unresolved issues lay between them. Upon arriving home, he went to her, knelt before her and asked forgiveness for anything he'd ever done. The gesture opened a floodgate of emotions and the two talked late into the night. The initial effort at reconciliation continued for two weeks. The marriage enjoyed a depth not yet known. When Harold's wife died suddenly of an embolism, he was shocked. But he was ready and now he is at peace.

What about you? Would you like some peace? Then quit giving your neighbor such a hassle. Want to enjoy God's generosity? Then let others enjoy yours. Would you like assurance that God forgives you? I think you know what you need to do.

So, what will you be eating? Chocolate ice cream or okra? It's up to you.

CHAPTER 12

The Family Room

Learning to Live Together

Our . . .

WE ARE MUCH LIKE Ruth and Verena Cady. Since their birth in 1984 they have shared much. Just like any twins, they have shared a bike, a bed, a room, and toys. They've shared meals and stories and TV shows and birthdays. They shared the same womb before they were born and the same room after they were born. But the bond between Ruthie and Verena goes even further. They share more than toys and treats; they share the same heart.

Their bodies are fused together from the sternum to the waist. Though they have separate nervous systems and distinct personalities, they are sustained by the same, singular three-chambered heart. Neither could survive without the other. Since separation is not an option, cooperation becomes an obligation.

They have learned to work together. Take walking, for example. Their mother assumed they would take turns walking forward or backwards. It made sense to her that they would alternate; one facing the front and the other the back. The girls had a better idea. They learned to walk sideways, almost like dancing. And they dance in the same direction.

They've learned to make up for each other's weaknesses. Verena loves to eat, but Ruthie finds sitting at the table too dull. Ruthie may eat only a half cup of fruit a day. No problem, her sister will eat enough for both. It's not unusual for her to have three bowls of cereal, two yogurts and two pieces of toast for breakfast. Ruthie tends to get restless while her sister eats and has been known to throw a bowl of ice cream across the room. This could lead to discipline for her, but also has consequences for her sister.[1]

When one has to sit in the corner, so does the other. The innocent party doesn't complain; both learned early that they are stuck together for the good and the bad. Which is just one of the many lessons these girls can teach those of us who live in God's Great House.

Don't we share the same kitchen? Aren't we covered by the same roof and protected by the same walls? We don't sleep in the same bed, but we sleep under the same sky. We aren't sharing one heart . . . but then again maybe we are; for don't we share the same hope for eternity, the same hurt from rejection, and the same hunger to be loved? Like the Cady twins, don't we have the same Father?

We don't pray to *my* Father or ask for *my* daily bread or ask God to forgive *my* sins. In God's house we speak the language of plurality: "*our* Father," "*our* daily bread," "*our* debts," "*our* debtors," "lead *us* not into temptation," and "deliver *us*."

The abundance of plural pronouns escorts us into one of the most colorful rooms in the house, the family room.

THE FAMILY ROOM

If you'd like a reminder of our Father's creativity, you'll find one here. We all call God "Father" and we all call Christ "Savior," but beyond that, things are quite diverse. Take a walk around the room and see what I mean.

> Shoot some snooker with the bikers at the pool table.
>
> Pick up a Swahili phrase from the tribesmen.
>
> Eavesdrop on the theologians discussing dispensationalism.
>
> Experience worship with a bagpipe, then cross the room and try the same with the accordion.
>
> Ask the missionary if she ever gets lonely and the Bible translator if he ever gets confused.
>
> Hear the testimony of the murderer and the music of the minstrel.

And if you're wondering how those folks from the other denominations got here, ask them. (They may want to ask you the same question.)

Oh, the diversity of God's family.

We are olive-skinned, curly-haired, blue-eyed and black.
We come from boarding schools and ghettos, mansions and shacks.
We wear turbans, we wear robes. We like tamales. We eat rice.
We have convictions and opinions, and to agree would be nice,
but we don't, still we try and this much we know:
'Tis better inside with each other than outside living alone.

Quite a family, wouldn't you agree? From God's perspective we have much in common. Jesus lists these common denominators in his prayer. They are easy to find. Every time we see the word *our* or *us,* we find a need.

WE ARE CHILDREN IN NEED OF A FATHER

During the writing of this book, my daughter Jenna and I spent several days in the old city of Jerusalem. (I've promised to take each of my daughters to Jerusalem when they're twelve years old. Got the idea from Joseph.) One afternoon, as we were exiting the Jaffa gate, we found ourselves behind an orthodox Jewish family—a father and his three small girls. One of the daughters, perhaps four or five years of age, fell a few steps behind and couldn't see her father. "*Abba*!" she called to him. He stopped and looked. Only then did he realize he was separated from his daughter. "*Abba*!" she called again. He spotted her and immediately extended his hand. She took it and I took mental notes as they continued. I wanted to see the actions of an *abba*.

He held her hand tightly in his as they descended the ramp.

When he stopped at a busy street, she stepped off the curb, so he pulled her back. When the signal changed, he led her and her sisters through the intersection. In the middle of the street, he reached down and swung her up into his arms and continued their journey.

Isn't that what we all need? An *abba* who will hear when we call? Who will take our hand when we're weak? Who will guide us through the hectic intersections of life? Don't we all need an *abba* who will swing us up into his arms and carry us home? We all need a father.

WE ARE BEGGARS IN NEED OF BREAD

Not only are we children in need of a father, we are also beggars in need of bread. "Give us this day our daily bread," we pray.

You may not appreciate my using the term *beggar*. You may prefer the word *hungry*. "We are all hungry, in need of bread." Such a phrase certainly has more dignity than the word *beggar*. Who wants to be called a beggar? Didn't you earn the money to buy the bread that sits on your table? Who are you to beg for anything? In fact, you may even find the word *hungry* offensive. To be hungry is to admit a basic need, something we sophisticated people are reluctant to do. Let me think, there must be a better phrase. How about this one? We aren't beggars, nor are we hungry; we are simply "abdominally challenged." There, that's better! "Abdominally challenged, in need of bread." You maintain a sense of independence with that word.

After all, you are ultimately responsible for the food you eat, right? Didn't you create the ground in which the seed was sown? No? Well, at least you made the seed? You didn't? What about the sun? Did you provide the heat during the day? Or the rain, did you send the clouds? No? Then exactly what did you do? You harvested food you didn't make from an earth you didn't create.

Let me see if I have this straight. Had God not done his part, you would have no food on your table. Hmmm, perhaps we best return to the word *beggar*. We are all beggars, in need of bread.

SINNERS IN NEED OF GRACE

We share one other need: We are sinners in need of grace, strugglers in need of strength. Jesus teaches us to pray, "Forgive our debts . . . and lead us not into temptation."

We've all made mistakes and we'll all make some more. The line that separates the best of us from the worst of us is a narrow one, hence we'd be wise to take seriously Paul's admonition:

> Why do you judge your brothers or sisters in Christ? And why do you think you are better than they? We will all stand before the Lord to be judged, because it is written in the Scriptures: "As surely as I live, says the Lord, everyone will bow before me; everyone will say that I am the Lord." (Rom. 14:10)

Your sister would like me to remind you that she needs grace. Just like you need forgiveness, so does she. There comes a time in every relationship when it's damaging to seek justice, when settling the score only stirs the fire. There comes a time when the best thing you can do is accept your brother and offer him the same grace you've been given.

That's what Jenna did.

Earlier I mentioned our recent trip to Israel. I'll conclude by referring to it one more time. She and I boarded a 1:00 A.M. flight in Tel Aviv which would carry us back to the States. Traveling is always hectic, but that night it was especially bad. The plane was packed and we were delayed because of extra-tight airport security. As we boarded, I realized that our seats weren't together. We were separated by an aisle. With no time to seek help from the front desk, I determined to persuade the fellow sitting next to Jenna to swap seats with me. *Surely he'll understand,* I thought. He didn't. He was already nestled down for the ten-hour flight and wasn't about to move. "Please," I begged, "let me sit by my daughter."

"I'm not moving."

"Come on, sir. Let's trade places."

He leaned up and looked at my seat and leaned back. "No thanks," he declined.

Growl. I took my seat and Jenna took hers next to the thoughtless, heartless scoundrel. As the plane prepared for take-off, I dedicated my mind to drawing a mental sketch of the jerk. Wasn't hard. Only a glance or two in his direction and I had him pegged as a terrorist on his way to assassinate the president of our country. By the time the plane was backing up, I was plotting how I'd trip him if he dared walk to the restroom during the flight. No doubt he'd smuggled a gun on board and it would fall to me to apprehend him.

I turned to intimidate him with a snarl and saw, much to my surprise, Jenna offering him a pretzel. What? My daughter fraternizing with the enemy! And even worse, he took it! As if the pretzel were an olive branch, he accepted her gift and they both leaned their seats back and dozed off.

I eventually dozed myself, but not before I'd learned the lesson God had used my daughter to teach me.

In God's house we occasionally find ourselves next to people we don't like. If we could ask them to leave, we would, but we aren't given the option. All of us are here by grace and, at some point, all of us have to share some grace. So the next time you find yourself next to a questionable character, don't give him a hard time . . . give him a pretzel.

CHAPTER 13

The Walls

Satan, God's Servant

And lead us not into temptation,
but deliver us from the evil one . . .

THE SMALL POPULATION of people who saw me play school athletics have never questioned my decision to enter the ministry. I have, however, received a letter reminding me of the time I deep-snapped a football over the punter's head. Another former classmate reminisced with me about the fly ball that slipped out of my glove and allowed the winning run to score. And then there was the time my buddy scored a touchdown on an eighty-yard punt return only to have it called back because his buddy, yours truly, got penalized for clipping. Oh, the pain of such memories. They hurt, not just because I messed up, but because I helped the other team. It's bad to lose; it's worse still to help your opponent win!

My most blatant experience of aiding the opposition occurred in a sixth-grade basketball tournament. I can't remember the exact score when I finally got to play, but I know it was close. I recall a loose ball, a scramble to grab it and complete surprise when my teammate on the bottom of the pile threw it to me. When I saw that no one was between me and the basket, I took off. With the style of an MVP-to-be, I made a lay-up worthy of air-time on ESPN. My surprise at the ease of the basket was surpassed only by my surprise at the silence of the crowd.

No one applauded! Rather than pat me on the back, my team buried their faces in their hands. That's when I realized what I'd done. I'd made a basket on the wrong end of the court—I'd aided the enemy! I'd helped the wrong team. No wonder no one tried to stop me—I was helping their side.

Can you imagine how silly I felt?

If you can, then you can imagine how silly Satan must feel. Such is the pattern of the devil's day. Every time he sets out to score one for evil, he ends up scoring a point for good. When he schemes to thwart the kingdom, he always advances it. May I offer a few examples from the Bible?

BACKFIRES OF HELL

Remember Abraham's wife, Sara? God promised her a child, but she remained childless for decades. Satan used an empty crib to stir up tension and dissension and doubt. Sara would serve as his *prima facie* evidence as to why you can't trust God. In the end, she modeled just the opposite. The thought of this ninety-year-old in the maternity ward has instructed millions that God saves the best for last.

How about Moses? Satan and his hoard howled with delight the day the young prince was run out of Egypt by the very people he wanted to deliver. They thought they'd derailed God's plan, when actually they'd played into God's hand. God used the defeat to humble his servant and the wilderness to train him. The result stood before Pharaoh forty years later, a seasoned Moses who'd learned to listen to God and survive in the desert.

And what about Daniel? The sight of Jerusalem's best young men being led into captivity appeared to be a victory for Satan. Hell's strategy was to isolate the godly young men. Again, the plan boomeranged. What Satan intended as captivity, God used for royalty. Daniel was soon asked to serve in the king's court. The very man Satan sought to silence spent most of his life praying to the God of Israel and advising the kings of Babylon.

And consider Paul. Satan hoped the prison would silence his pulpit, and it did, but it also unleashed his pen. The letters to the Galatians, Ephesians, Philippians, and Colossians were all written in a jail cell. Can't you just see Satan kicking the dirt and snarling his lips every time a person reads those epistles? He helped write them!

Peter is another example. Satan sought to discredit Jesus by provoking Peter to deny him. But the plan backfired. Rather than be an example of how far a fellow can fall, Peter became an example of how far God's grace extends.

Every time Satan scores a basket, the other team gets the points. He's the Colonel Klink of the Bible. Remember Klink? He was the fall guy for Hogan on the television series, *Hogan's Heroes.* Klink supposedly ran a German POW camp during World

War II. Those inside the camp, however, knew better. They knew who *really* ran the camp: the prisoners. They listened to Klink's calls and read his mail. They even gave Klink ideas, all the while using him for their own cause.

Over and over the Bible makes it clear who really runs the earth. Satan may strut and prance, but it's God who calls the shots.

DELIVER US FROM THE EVIL ONE

The next-to-last phrase in the Lord's prayer is a petition for protection from Satan: "And lead us not into temptation, but deliver us from the evil one."

Is such a prayer necessary? Would God ever lead us into temptation? James 1:13 says, "When people are tempted they should not say, 'God is tempting me.' Evil cannot tempt God, and God himself does not tempt anyone." If God does not tempt us, then why pray, "Lead us not into temptation"? These words trouble the most sophisticated theologian.

But they don't trouble a child. And this is a prayer for the child-like heart. This is a prayer for those who look upon God as their *Abba*. This is a prayer for those who have already talked to their Father about provision for today ("Give us our daily bread.") and pardon for yesterday ("Forgive us our debts."). Now the child needs assurance about protection for tomorrow.

The phrase is best understood with a simple illustration. Imagine a father and son walking down an icy street. The father cautions the boy to be careful, but the boy is too excited to slow down. He hits the first patch of ice. Up go the feet and down plops the bottom. Dad comes along and helps him to his feet. The boy apologizes for disregarding the warning and then, tightly holding his father's big hand, he asks, "Keep me from the slippery spots. Don't let me fall again."

The Father is so willing to comply. "The steps of the godly are directed by the Lord. He delights in every detail of their lives. Though they stumble, they will not fall, for the Lord holds them by the hand" (Ps. 37:23–24 TLB). Such is the heart of this petition. It's a tender request of a child to a father. The last few slips have taught us—the walk is too treacherous to make alone. So we place our small hand in his large one and say, "Please, *Abba,* keep me from evil."

THE EVIL ONE

Besides, who else would we trust to deliver us from the Evil One? We have heard of this devil. And what we've heard disturbs us. Twice in Scripture the curtain of time is pulled back and we are granted a glimpse at the most foolish gamble in history. Satan was an angel who was not content to be near God; he had to be above God. Lucifer was not satisfied to give God worship; he wanted to occupy God's throne.

According to Ezekiel both Satan's beauty and evil were unequaled among the angels:

> You were an example of what was perfect, full of wisdom and perfect in beauty. You had a wonderful life, as if you were in Eden, the Garden of God. Every valuable gem was upon you . . . You walked among the gems that shined like fire. Your life was right and good from the day you were created, until evil was found in you. (Ezek. 28:12–15)

The angels, like humans, were made to serve and worship God. The angels, like humans, were given free will. Otherwise how could they worship? Both Isaiah and Ezekiel describe an angel more powerful than any human, more beautiful than any creature, yet more foolish than any being who has ever lived. His pride was his downfall.

Most scholars point to Isaiah 14:13–15 as the description of Lucifer's tumble:

> I will go up to heaven. I will put my throne above God's stars. I will sit on the mountains of the gods, on the slopes of the sacred mountain. I will go up above the tops of the clouds. I will be like God Most High.

You can't miss the cadence of arrogance in the words: "I will . . . I will . . . I will . . . I will . . . I will." Because he sought to be like God, he fell away from God and has spent history trying to convince us to do the same. Isn't that the strategy he used with Eve? "You will be like God," he promised (Gen. 3:5).

He has not changed. He is as self-centered now as he was then. He is as foolish now as he was then. And he is just as limited now as he was then. Even when Lucifer's heart was good, he was inferior to God. All angels are inferior to God. God knows everything, they only know what he reveals. God is everywhere, they can only be in one place. God is all-powerful, angels are only as powerful as God allows them to be. All angels, including Satan, are inferior to God. And this may surprise you: Satan is still a servant to God.

THE DEVIL IS "GOD'S DEVIL"

He doesn't want to be. He doesn't intend to be. He would like nothing more than to build his own kingdom, but he can't. Every time he tries to advance his cause, he ends up advancing God's.

Erwin Lutzer articulates this thought in his book, *The Serpent of Paradise:*

> The devil is just as much God's servant in his rebellion as he was in the days of his sweet obedience. . . . We can't quote Luther too often: The devil is God's devil.
>
> Satan has different roles to play, depending on God's counsel and purposes. He is pressed into service to do God's will in the world; he must do the bidding of the Almighty. We must bear in mind that he does have frightful powers, but knowing that those can only be exercised under God's direction and pleasure gives us hope. Satan is simply not free to wreak havoc on people at will."[1]

Satan doing the bidding of the Almighty? Seeking the permission of God? Does such language strike you as strange? It may. If it does, you can be sure Satan would rather you not hear what I'm about to say to you. He'd much rather you be deceived into thinking of him as an independent force with unlimited power. He doesn't want me to tell you about the walls that surround the Great House of God. Satan cannot climb them, he cannot penetrate them. He has absolutely no power, except that power that God permits.

He'd rather you never hear the words of John, "God's Spirit who is in you, is greater than the devil who is in the world" (1 John 4:4). And he'd certainly rather you never learn how God uses the devil as an instrument to advance the cause of Christ.

How does God use Satan to do the work of heaven? God uses Satan to:

1. *Refine the faithful.* We all have the devil's disease. Even the meekest among us have a tendency to think too highly of ourselves. Apparently Paul did. His resume was impressive: a personal audience with Jesus, a participant in heavenly visions, an apostle chosen by God, an author of the Bible. He healed the sick, traveled the world, and penned some of history's greatest documents. Few could rival his achievements. And maybe he knew it. Perhaps there was a time when Paul began to pat himself on the back. God, who loved Paul and hates pride, protected Paul from the sin. And he used Satan to do it.

> To keep me from becoming conceited because of these surpassingly great revelations, there was given me a thorn in my flesh, a messenger from Satan to torment me. (2 Cor. 12:7)

We aren't told the nature of the thorn, but we are told its purpose—to keep Paul humble. We are also told its origin—a messenger from Satan. The messenger could have been a pain, a problem or a person who was a pain. We don't know. But we do know the messenger was under God's control. Please note verse eight, "Three times I pleaded with the Lord to take it away from me. But he said to me, 'My grace is sufficient for you, my power is made perfect in weakness.' " Satan and his forces were simply a tool in the hand of God to strengthen a servant.

Another example of the devil as God's servant is the temptation of Job. The devil dares to question the stability of Job's faith and God gives him permission to test Job. "All right then," God says, "everything Job has is in your power, but you must not touch Job himself" (Job 1:12). Note that God set both the permission and parameters of the struggle. Job passes the test and Satan complains, stating that Job would have fallen had he been forced to face pain. Again God gives permission and again God gives the parameters. "Job is in your power," he tells Satan, "but you may not take his life" (2:6).

Though the pain and the questions are abundant, in the end Job's faith and health are greater than ever. Again, we may not understand the reason for the test, but we know its source. Read this verse out of the last chapter. The family of Job: "Comforted him and made him feel better about the trouble God *the Lord* had brought on him" (42:11, emphasis mine).

Satan has no power except that which God gives him.

To the first-century church Smyrna, Christ said, "Do not be afraid of what you are about to suffer. I tell you, the devil will put some of you in prison to test you, and you will suffer for ten days. But be faithful, even if you have to die, and I will give you the crown of life" (Rev. 2:10).

Analyze Jesus' words for a minute. Christ informs the church of the persecution, the duration of the persecution (ten days), the reason for the persecution (to test you) and the outcome of the persecution (a crown of life). In other words, Jesus uses Satan to fortify his church.

Colonel Klink blows another one. Satan scores again for the other team. Don't you know that bugs him? Even when he appears to win, he loses. Martin Luther was right on target when he described the devil as God's tool, a hoe used to care for his garden. The hoe never cuts what the gardener intends to save and never saves what the gardener intends to weed. Surely a part of Satan's punishment is the frustration he feels in unwillingly serving as a tool to create a garden for God. Satan is used by God to refine the faithful.

God also uses the devil to:

2. *Awaken the sleeping.* Hundreds of years before Paul, another Jewish leader battled with his ego, but he lost. Saul, the first king of Israel, was consumed with jealousy. He was upstaged by David, the youngest son of a shepherding family. David did everything better than Saul: he sang better, he impressed the women more, he even killed the giants Saul feared. But rather than celebrate David's God-given abilities, Saul grew insanely hostile. God, in an apparent effort to awaken Saul from this fog of jealousy, enlisted the help of his unwilling servant, Satan. "The next day an evil spirit from God rushed upon Saul, and he prophesied in his house" (1 Sam. 18:10).

Observe a solemn principle: There are times when hearts grow so hard and ears so dull that God turns us over to endure the consequence of our choices. In this case, the demon was released to torment Saul. If Saul would not drink from the cup of God's kindness, let him spend some time drinking from the cup of hell's fury. "Let him be driven to despair that he might be driven back into the arms of God."[2]

The New Testament refers to incidents where similar discipline is administered. Paul chastises the church in Corinth for their tolerance of immorality. About an adulterer in the church he says:

> Then hand this man over to Satan. So his sinful self will be destroyed, and his spirit will be saved on the day of the Lord. (1 Cor. 5:5).

Paul gives comparable instruction to Timothy. The young evangelist was dealing with two disciples who'd made a shipwreck of their faith and had negatively influenced others. His instruction to Timothy? "Hymenaeus and Alexander have done that, and I have given them to Satan so they will learn not to speak against God" (1 Tim. 1:20).

As drastic as it may appear, God will actually allow a person to experience hell on earth, in hopes of awakening his faith. A holy love makes the tough choice to release the child to the consequences of his rebellion.

By the way, doesn't this help explain the rampant evil which exists in the world? If God allows us to endure the consequences of our sin and the world is full of sinners, then the world is going to abound in evil. Isn't this what Paul meant in the first chapter of Romans? After describing those who worship the creation rather than the creator, Paul says, "God left them and let them do the shameful things they wanted to do" (Rom. 1:26). Does God enjoy seeing the heartbreak and addictions of his children? No more than a parent enjoys disciplining a child. But holy love makes tough choices.

Remember, discipline should result in mercy, not misery. Some saints are awakened by a tap on the shoulder while others need a two-by-four to the head. And whenever God needs a two-by-four, Satan gets the call. He also gets the call to:

3. *Teach the church.* Perhaps the clearest illustration of how God uses Satan to achieve his purposes is found in the life of

Peter. Listen to the warning Jesus gives to him: "Simon, Simon, Satan has asked to test all of you as a farmer sifts his wheat. I have prayed that you will not lose your faith! Help your brothers be stronger when you come back to me" (Luke 22:31–32).

Again, notice who is in control. Even though Satan had a plan, he had to get permission. "All authority in heaven and on earth has been given to me," Jesus explained, and this is proof (Matt. 28:18 NIV). The wolf cannot get to the sheep without permission of the Shepherd, and the Shepherd will only permit the attack if, in the long term, the pain is worth the gain.

The purpose of this test is to provide a testimony for the church. Jesus was allowing Peter to experience a trial so he could encourage his brothers. Perhaps God is doing the same with you. God knows that the church needs living testimonies of his power. Your difficulty, your disease, your conflict are preparing you to be a voice of encouragement to your brothers. All you need to remember is that:

> No test or temptation that comes your way is beyond the course of what others have had to face. All you need to remember is that God will never let you down; he'll never let you be pushed beyond your limit; he'll always be there to help you come through it. (1 Cor. 10:13)

> You intended evil against me, but God meant it for good. (Gen. 50:20)

Remember, Satan cannot penetrate the walls of the Great House of God.

Is it still hard to imagine how your struggle could lead to any good? Still hard to conceive how your disease or debt or death could be a tool for anything worthwhile? If so then I've got one final example. While not wanting to minimize your struggle, I must say yours is a cakewalk compared to this one. A sinless Savior was covered with sin. The author of life was placed in the cave of death. Satan's victory appeared sure. Finally, the devil had scored on the right end of the court. And not only had he scored, he'd slam-dunked the MVP and left him lying on the floor. The devil had blown it with everyone from Sara to Peter, but this time he'd done it right. The whole world had seen it. The victory dance had already begun.

But all of a sudden there was a light in the tomb and a rumbling of the rock; then Friday's tragedy emerged as Sunday's Savior, and even Satan knew he'd been had. He'd been a tool in the hand of the gardener. All the time he thought he was defeating heaven, he was helping heaven. God wanted to prove his power over sin and death, and that's exactly what he did. And guess who helped him do it? Once again Satan's lay-up becomes a foul-up. Only this time, he didn't give heaven some points, he gave heaven the championship game.

Jesus emerged as the victor and Satan was left looking like a . . . well, I'll let you figure that out. Take the first letter of each of the ways God uses the devil and see if you can find Satan's true identity.

Refine the faithful.

Awaken the sleeping.

Teach the church.

CHAPTER 14

The Chapel

Relying on God's Power

For thine is the kingdom and the power
and the glory forever. Amen.

I CAME ACROSS AN ARTICLE of a lady who reminds me of us. She went up a mountain she should have avoided. No one would have blamed her had she stayed behind. At twelve below zero, even Frosty the Snowman would have opted for the warm fire. Hardly a day for snow skiing, but her husband insisted and she went.

While waiting in the lift line she realized she was in need of a restroom, *dire* need of a restroom. Assured there would be one at the top of the lift, she and her bladder endured the bouncy ride, only to find there was no facility. She began to panic. Her husband had an idea: Why not go into the woods? Since she was wearing an all-white outfit, she'd blend in with the snow. And what better powder room than a piney grove?

What choice did she have? She skied past the tree line and arranged her ski suit at half mast. Fortunately, no one could see her. Unfortunately, her husband hadn't told her to remove her skis. Before you could say, "Shine on harvest moon," she was streaking backwards across the slope, revealing more about herself than she ever intended. (After all, hindsight is 20/20.) With arms flailing and skis sailing, she sped under the very lift she'd just ridden and collided with a pylon.

As she scrambled to cover the essentials, she discovered her arm was broken. Fortunately her husband raced to her rescue. He summoned the ski patrol, who transported her to the hospital.

While being treated in the emergency room, a man with a broken leg was carried in and placed next to her. By now she'd regained her composure enough to make small talk. "So, how'd you break your leg?" she asked.

"It was the darndest thing you ever saw," he explained. "I was riding up the ski lift and suddenly I couldn't believe my eyes. There was this crazy woman skiing backwards, at top speed. I leaned over to get a better look and I guess I didn't realize how far I'd moved. I fell out of the lift."

Then he turned to her and asked, "So how'd you break your arm?"[1]

Don't we make the same mistake? We climb mountains we were never intended to climb. We try to go up when we should have stayed down, and as a result, we've taken some nasty spills in full view of a watching world. The tale of the lady (sorry, I couldn't resist) echoes our own story. There are certain mountains we were never made to climb. Ascend them and you'll end up bruised and embarrassed. Stay away from them and you'll sidestep a lot of stress. These mountains are described in the final phrase of the Lord's prayer, "Thine is the kingdom and the power and the glory forever. Amen."

A RETURN TO THE CHAPEL

Our Lord's prayer has given us a blueprint for the Great House of God. From the living room of our Father to the family room with our friends, we are learning why David longed to "live in the house of the LORD forever" (Ps. 23:6). In God's house we have everything we need: a solid foundation, an abundant table, sturdy walls, and an impenetrable roof of grace.

And now, having seen every room and explored each corner, we have one final stop. Not to a new room, but to one we have visited earlier. We return to the chapel. We return to the room of worship. The chapel, remember, is where we stand before God and confess, "Hallowed be thy name."

The chapel is the only room in the house of God we visit twice. It's not hard to see why. It does us twice as much good to think about God as it does to think about anyone or anything else. God wants us to begin and end our prayers thinking of him. Jesus is urging us to look at the peak more than we look at the trail. The more we focus up there, the more inspired we are down here.

Some years ago a sociologist accompanied a group of mountain climbers on an expedition. Among other things, he observed a distinct correlation between cloud cover and contentment. When there was no cloud cover and the peak was in view, the climbers were energetic and cooperative. When the gray clouds eclipsed the view of the mountaintop, though, the climbers were sullen and selfish.

The same thing happens to us. As long as our eyes are on his majesty there is a bounce in our step. But let our eyes focus on the dirt beneath us and we will grumble about every rock and crevice we have to cross. For this reason Paul urged, "Don't shuffle along, eyes to the ground, absorbed with the things right in front of you. Look up, and be alert to the things going on around Christ—that's where the action is. See things from his perspective" (Col 3:1–2 MSG).

Paul challenges you to "be alert to the things going on around Christ." The Psalmist reminds you to do the same, only he uses a different phrase. "O magnify the LORD with me and let us exalt his name together" (Ps. 34:3).

Magnify. What a wonderful verb to describe what we do in the chapel. When you magnify an object, you enlarge it so that you can understand it. When we magnify God, we do the same. We enlarge our awareness of him so we can understand him more. This is exactly what happens in the chapel of worship—we take our mind off ourselves and set it on God. The emphasis is on him. "*Thine* is the kingdom and the power and the glory forever."

And this is exactly the purpose of this final phrase in the Lord's prayer. These words magnify the character of God. I love the way this phrase is translated in *The Message:*

You're in charge!

You can do anything you want!

You're ablaze in beauty!

Yes! Yes! Yes!

Could it be any simpler? God is in charge! This concept is not foreign to us. When the restaurant waiter brings you a cold hamburger and a hot soda, you want to know who is in charge. When a young fellow wants to impress his girlfriend, he takes her down to the convenience store where he works and boasts, "Every night from five to ten o'clock, I'm in charge." We know what it means to be in charge of a restaurant or a store, but to be in charge of the universe? This is the claim of Jesus.

> God raised him from the dead and set him on a throne in deep heaven, *in charge* of running the universe, everything from galaxies to governments, no name and no power is exempt from his rule. And not just for the time being but forever. He is *in charge* of it all, has the final word on everything. At the center of all this Christ rules the church. (Eph. 1:22–23 MSG, emphasis mine)

There are many examples of Jesus' authority, but I'll just mention one of my favorites. Jesus and the disciples are in a boat crossing the sea of Galilee. A storm arises suddenly and what was placid becomes violent—monstrous waves rise out of the sea and slap the boat. Mark describes it clearly: "A furious squall came up, and the waves broke over the boat so that it was nearly swamped" (Mark 4:37 NIV).

It's very important that you get an accurate picture, so I'm going to ask you to imagine yourself in the boat. It's a sturdy vessel, but no match for these ten-foot waves. It plunges nose first into the wall of water. The force of the waves dangerously tips the boat until the bow seems to be pointing straight at the sky, and just when you fear flipping over backwards, the vessel pitches forward into the valley of another wave. A dozen sets of hands join yours in clutching the mast. All your shipmates have wet heads and wide eyes. You tune your ear for a calming voice, but all you hear are screams and prayers. All of a sudden it hits you—someone is missing. Where is Jesus? He's not at the mast. He's not grabbing the edge. Where is he? Then you hear something—a noise . . . a displaced sound . . . like someone is snoring. You turn and look, and there curled in the stern of the boat is Jesus, sleeping!

You don't know whether to be amazed or angry, so you're both. How can he sleep at a time like this? Or as the disciples asked, "Teacher, don't you care if we drown" (Mark 4:38, NIV)?

If you're a parent of a teenager, you've been asked similar questions. The time you refused to mortgage your house so your daughter could buy the latest style tennis shoes, she asked, "Don't you care if I look out of date?"

When you insisted that your son skip the weekend game and attend his grandparents' golden anniversary, he asked, "Don't you care if I have a social life?"

When you limited the ear piercing to one hole per lobe, the accusation came thinly veiled as a question, "Don't you care if I fit in?"

Do the parents care? Of course they do. It's just that they have a different perspective. What the teenager sees as a storm, mom and dad see as a spring shower. They've been around enough to know these things pass.

So had Jesus. The very storm which made the disciples panic made him drowsy. What put fear in their eyes put him to sleep. The boat was a tomb to the followers and a cradle to Christ. How could he sleep through the storm? Simple, he was in charge of it.

The same happens with you and televisions. Ever doze off with the TV on? Of course you have. But put the same television in the grass hut of a primitive Amazonian Indian who has never seen one and, believe me, he won't sleep. How could anyone sleep in the presence of a talking box! As far as he knows, those little people behind the glass wall might climb out of the box and come after him. There is no way he's going to sleep. And there is no way he's going to let you sleep either. If you doze off, he'll wake you up. Don't you care that we're about to be massacred? Rather than argue with him, what do you do? You just point the remote at the screen and turn it off.

Jesus didn't even need a remote. "He got up, rebuked the wind and said to the waves, 'Quiet! Be still!' Then the wind died down and it was completely calm. He said to his disciples, 'Why are you so afraid? Do you still have no faith'" (Mark. 4:39–40, NIV)?

Incredible. He doesn't chant a mantra or wave a wand. No angels are called, no help is needed. The raging water becomes a stilled sea, instantly. Immediate calm. Not a ripple. Not a drop. Not a gust. In a moment the sea goes from a churning torrent to a peaceful pond. The reaction of the disciples? Read it in verse 41: "They were in absolute awe, staggered. 'Who is this anyway?' they asked. 'Wind and sea at his beck and call!'" (MSG).

They'd never met a man like this. The waves were his subjects and the winds were his servants. And that was just the beginning of what his sea mates would witness. Before it was over, they would see fish jump into the boat, demons dive into pigs, cripples turn into dancers, and cadavers turn into living, breathing people. "'He even gives orders to evil spirits and they obey him!'" the people proclaimed (Mark 1:27).

Is it any wonder the disciples were willing to die for Jesus?

Never had they seen such power, never had they seen such glory. It was like, well, like the whole universe was his kingdom. You wouldn't have needed to explain this verse to them; they knew what it meant: "Thine is the kingdom and the power and the glory forever."

In fact, it was two of these rescued fishermen who would declare his authority most clearly. Listen to John: "Greater is he who is in you than he who is in the world" (1 John 4:4). Listen to Peter: "Jesus has gone into heaven and is at God's right hand ruling over angels, authorities and powers" (1 Pet. 3:22).

It's only right that they declare his authority. And it's only right that we do the same. And that is exactly what this phrase is, a declaration. A declaration of the heart. A declaration God deserves to hear. Doesn't he? Doesn't he deserve to hear us proclaim his authority? Isn't it right for us to shout from the bottom of our hearts and at the top of our voice, "Thine is the kingdom and the power and the glory forever!" Isn't it right for us to stare at these mountain peaks of God and worship him?

Of course it is. Not only does God deserve to hear our praise, we need to give it.

MOUNTAINS YOU WEREN'T MADE TO CLIMB

There are certain mountains only God can climb. The names of these mountains? You'll see them as you look from the window of the chapel in the Great House of God. "Thine is the kingdom, and the power and the glory forever." A trio of peaks mantled by the clouds. Admire them, applaud them, but don't climb them.

It's not that you aren't welcome to try, it's just that you aren't able. The pronoun is *thine,* not *mine; thine* is the kingdom, not *mine* is the kingdom. If the word *Savior* is in your job description, it's because you put it there. Your role is to help the world, not save it. Mount Messiah is one mountain you weren't made to climb.

Nor is Mount Self-Sufficient. You aren't able to run the world, nor are you able to sustain it. Some of you think you can. You are self-made. You don't bow your knees, you just roll up your sleeves and put in another twelve-hour day . . . which may be enough when it comes to making a living or building a business. But when you face your own grave or your own guilt, your power will not do the trick.

You were not made to run a kingdom, nor are you expected to be all-powerful. And you certainly can't handle all the glory. Mount Applause is the most seductive of the three peaks. The higher you climb the more people applaud, but the thinner the air becomes. More than one person has stood at the top and shouted, "Mine is the glory!" only to lose their balance and fall.

"Thine is the kingdom and the power and the glory forever." What protection this final phrase affords. As you confess that God is in charge, you admit that you aren't. As you proclaim that God has power, you admit that you don't. And as you give God all the applause, there is none left to dizzy your brain.

Let's let the lady on the slope teach us a lesson: There are certain mountains we weren't meant to climb. Stay below where you were made to be, so you won't end up exposing yourself to trouble.

Chapter 15

A Home for Your Heart

My daughter Sara had a friend over to spend the night recently. There was no school the next day, so we let the two of them stay up as late as they wanted. A bedtime reprieve for a couple of seven-year-olds is like freeing a convict from death row. The two outlasted me. I was dozing in my chair when I awoke and realized it was nearly midnight and they were still awake. "All right, girls," I informed them, "we better go to bed." Groaning the entire time, they changed clothes, brushed their teeth, and climbed in the sack. That's when our little guest asked to call her mom. At first we declined, but then the chin trembled and the eyes misted, and, knowing we were moments away from an explosion, we gave her the phone.

I could envision what was happening on the other end of the line—a phone ringing in the dark, a mom reaching over the slumbering husband to grab the receiver.

The little girl didn't even say hello. "Mommy, I want to come home." With a teddy bear in one hand and the phone in the other, she pleaded her case. She was afraid of waking up in a strange room. This wasn't her house. She wanted her bed, her pillow and most of all, her mommy.

I can't blame her. When I travel, the hardest part of the trip is going to sleep. The pillow never feels right, the sheets are too . . . too stiff? Besides, who knows who slept here last night. The curtains never block the flashing neon light outside the window. I need to get up early, but can I trust the operator to remember the wake-up call? After all, there was that night in Boise when no one called me and . . . off go my thoughts, covering every issue from Denalyn's doctor visit to tomorrow's flight to next spring's income tax. I'd call home, but it's too late. I'd go for a walk, but I might get mugged. I'd order room service, but I already have. I'd go home but, well, I'm supposed to be a grown man. Finally, I sit up in bed and flip on the TV and watch Sports Center until my eyes burn, then eventually doze off.

I can relate to Sara's friend. When it comes to resting your body, there's no house like your own.

I can also relate to the Psalmist, David. When it comes to resting your soul, there is no place like the Great House of God. "I'm asking Yahweh for one thing," he wrote, "only one thing: to live with him in his house my whole life long. I'll contemplate his beauty, I'll study at his feet. That's the only quiet secure place in a noisy world" (Ps. 27:4–5 MSG).

If you could ask God for one thing, what would you request?

David tells us what he would ask. He longs to *live* in the house of God. I emphasize the word live, because it deserves to be emphasized. David doesn't want to chat. He doesn't desire a cup of coffee on the back porch. He doesn't ask for a meal or to spend an evening in God's house. He wants to move in with him . . . forever. He's asking for his own room . . . permanently. He doesn't want to be stationed in God's house, he longs to retire there. He doesn't seek a temporary assignment, but rather lifelong residence.

When David says, "I will live in the house of the Lord forever" (Ps. 23:6), he's saying simply that he never wants to step away from God. He craves to remain in the aura, in the atmosphere, in the awareness that he is in God's house, wherever he is.

The Lord's Prayer is a floor plan of the house of God: a step-by-step description of how God meets our needs when we dwell in him. Everything that occurs in a healthy house is described in this prayer. Protection, instruction, forgiveness, provision . . . all occur under God's roof.

"Then why," you might ask, "don't more people feel protected, forgiven, or instructed?"

My answer is as simple as the question is direct. Most have not learned to dwell in the house. Oh, we visit it. We stop in for the day or even drop by for a meal. But abide here? This is God's desire.

Remember the promise of his Son, "If people love me, they will obey my teaching. My Father will love them and we will come to them and make our home with them" (John 14:23). He wants to be the one in whom "we live and move and have our being" (Acts 17:28 NIV).

Let me conclude with an example of how this prayer can be a home for your heart. I have a long way to go, but I'm trying to learn to dwell in the Great House of God. Over the last seven days I took note of the times I took strength from a part of the house.

> On Monday I was tired, physically drained, so I stepped into the chapel and said, "Thine is the power," and the Father reminded me it was okay to rest.
>
> On Tuesday I had more to do than I had hours to do it. Rather than stress out, I stepped into the kitchen and asked for daily bread. He gave me the strength to get everything done.
>
> On Wednesday I was in the kitchen again. Needing some ideas for a children's book, I stepped up to the table and made a request. By bedtime the manuscript was drafted.
>
> We had a strategic staff meeting this week. We began with a half-hour of prayer and worship during which I stepped into the observatory and then into the chapel. I asked the God who made the heavens to make sure the meeting went well, and he did. I asked the Holy God who is above us to guide us, and he did.
>
> On one occasion I was impatient. I went into the hallway to ask for God's grace, only to find it already given. On another I was tempted, yet at just the right time a person entered the room with a word of wisdom, and I was reminded of the thickness of the wall. And then there was the frustration I felt over a person's opinion. Not knowing how to respond, I stepped into the study and opened the word, and 1 Corinthians 13 reminded me, "Love is patient and kind."

I don't want to leave the wrong impression. There were times when I worried rather than worshipped, there were times when I told God what I had to have rather than trust him to fill my plate. But day by day, I'm learning to live in the Great House of God.

I hope you are, too. Take Paul's advice and "pray without ceasing." Make it your aim never to leave God's house. When you're worried about your bills, step into God's kitchen. When you feel bad about a mistake, look up at the roof. When you call on a new client, whisper a prayer as you enter the office: "Thy kingdom come to this place." When you're in a tense meeting, mentally step into the furnace room and pray, "Let the peace of heaven be felt on earth." When it's hard to forgive your spouse, pull out the check of grace God has given you.

My prayer for you is the same as Paul's: "Let your minds be re-made and your whole nature thus transformed" (Rom. 12:2 NEB). May the Holy Spirit change your mind. May you grow so at ease in the house of God that you never leave it. And when you find yourself in another house, may you do what Sara's friend did—call home. Tell your Father that you can't rest in anyone's house but his. He won't mind the call. In fact, he'll be waiting by the phone.

POSTSCRIPT

His Model, Our Guide

We're Home.

DOESN'T IT FEEL WONDERFUL, knowing we're home where we belong? Here, in the place where our spirit has longed to rest . . . the place where we feel safe and secure.

Could I make a suggestion for your life in God's Great House? Each day, as you awaken in his presence, remember the blueprint. And as you talk to your Father, trace the floor plan in your mind. It's a helpful way to enter his presence. Here's an example of how the Lord's Prayer can guide your prayers:

Our Father

Thank you for adopting me into your family.

who is

Thank you, my Lord,
for being a God of the present tense:
my Jehovah-jireh (the God who provides),
my Jehovah-raah (the caring Shepherd),
my Jehovah-shalom (the Lord is peace),
my Jehovah-rophe (the God who heals),
and my Jehovah-nissi (Lord, my banner).

in heaven,

Your workshop of creation reminds me: If you can make
the skies, you can make sense out of my struggles.

Hallowed be thy name.

Be holy in my heart.
You are a "cut above" all else.
Enable me to set my sights on you.

Thy kingdom come,

Come kingdom!
Be present, Lord Jesus!
Have free reign in every corner of my life.

Thy will be done,

Reveal your heart to me, dear Father.
Show me my role in your passion.
Grant me guidance in the following decisions . . .

On earth as it is in heaven.

Thank you that you silence heaven to hear my prayer.
On my heart are the ones you love.
I pray for . . .

Give us this day our daily bread.

I accept your portion for my life today.
I surrender the following concerns
regarding my well-being . . .

Forgive us our debts,
I thank you for the roof of grace over my head,
bound together with the timbers and nails of Calvary.
There is nothing I can do to earn or add to your mercy.
I confess my sins to you . . .

As we also have forgiven our debtors;
Treat me, Father, as I treat others.
Have mercy on the following friends
who have wounded me . . .

Lead us not into temptation,
Let my small hand be engulfed in yours.
Hold me, lest I fall.
I ask for special strength regarding . . .

Our Father . . . give us . . . forgive us . . . lead us
Let your kindness be on all your church.
I pray especially for ministers near
and missionaries far away.

Thine—not mine—*is the kingdom,*
I lay my plans at your feet.

Thine—not mine—*is the power,*
I come to you for strength.

Thine—not mine—*is the glory,*
I give you all the credit.

Forever. Amen.
Thine—not mine—*is the power.* Amen.

Notes

The Great House of God

CHAPTER 2 *The Living Room*

1. Joachim Jeremias, *The Prayers of Jesus* (New York: SCM Press, 1967), p. 57, as quoted in John Stott, "Has Anyone Told You About the Power of Prayer?" audiotape, All Souls Cassettes, No. E42/1A.

CHAPTER 3 *The Foundation*

1. All information on the names of God was taken from: Nathan Stone, *Names of God* (Chicago: Moody Press, 1944).

CHAPTER 4 *The Observatory*

1. Adapted from Brennan Manning, *The Ragamuffin Gospel* (Portland, OR.: Multnomah Press, 1990), pp. 32–33.

CHAPTER 9 *The Kitchen*

1. Source unknown.
2. Charles Panati, *Panati's Extraordinary Origins of Everyday Things,* (New York: Harper and Row, Publisher, 1987), p. 81.
3. Ibid., p. 86.
4. Alan Redpath, *Victorious Praying,* (Grand Rapids, MI: Revell, 1973), p. 74.

CHAPTER 11 *The Hallway*

1. John MacArthur, "The Pardon of Prayer" audio tape, © 1980 John MacArthur (Word of Grace, Panorama City, CA).
2. Thanks to Harold C. Staub for permission to use this letter.

CHAPTER 12 *The Family Room*

1. K. Hubbard, "A Gift of Grace: The Death of Conjoined Twins Ruth and Verena Cady," *People Weekly*, 5 November 1993, Vol. 36, pp. 42–44.

CHAPTER 13 *The Walls*

1. Erwin Lutzer, *The Serpent of Paradise* (Chicago: Moody Press, 1996), 102.
2. Ibid., 111.

CHAPTER 14 *The Chapel*

1. Lois Lambley, " . . . so how'd you break your arm?" Et Cetera, *North Bend Eagle,* 18 January 1995, p. 4.

Study Guide

Written by Steve Halliday

Chapter 1 The Great House of God

LET US PONDER

1. God can be your dwelling place.
   A. In what way can God be someone's "dwelling place"?
   B. Is God your dwelling place? Explain.
2. You may go days without thinking of God, but there's never a moment when he's not thinking of you.
   A. How often do you estimate that you think of God? What keeps you from thinking about him? How do you overcome this obstacle?
   B. Do you believe God never stops thinking about you? Explain.
3. You are one step away from the house of God. Wherever you are. Whatever time it is.
   A. What does Max mean by "stepping into the house of God?"
   B. Does this image of the Great House of God help you to grasp and utilize the Lord's prayer? If so, how? If not, why not?
4. Christ has provided more than a model for prayer, he has

provided a model for living. These words do more than tell us what to say to God, they tell us how to exist with God.

A. In what way is the Lord's Prayer a model for living?
B. How does the Lord's Prayer tell us how to exist with God?
C. What part of the Lord's Prayer speaks most powerfully to you? Why?

LET US PREPARE

1. Read through the Lord's Prayer in Matthew 6:9–13.
   A. What part of this prayer most encourages you? Why?
   B. What part most convicts you? Why?
   C. Are there any parts you don't understand? If so, what are they? (Then especially look for Max's comments on that part later in the book.)
   D. If you were to assign parts of a house to each part of this prayer, how would you do it?
2. Read Acts 17:24–28.
   A. What picture of God does this passage portray? How does this picture fit into your concept of prayer? Explain.
   B. Note verse 28. How does the concept mentioned here fit with Max's image of the Great House of God?
3. Read Psalm 90:1–2.
   A. What is significant about that?
   B. What kind of requests does Moses make of God in the rest of this psalm (see especially verses 12–17).
4. Read 1 Thessalonians 5:17–18; Romans 12:12; Ephesians 6:18–20; Hebrews 13:15,18–19; Colossians 4:2–4; Philippians 4:6–7.

A. What do you learn about prayer in each of the verses above?

5. How does the pattern of prayer laid out in the Lord's Prayer relate to the passages listed above?

LET US PRAY

1. This week read through the Lord's Prayer in Matthew 6:9–13 at least once each day. Read it meditatively to soak in its rich truth. Then take some time to pray about the concerns that touch your life, based on this pattern prayer.
2. Sit down with a piece of paper and a pen and "take apart" the Lord's Prayer phrase by phrase. Divide the prayer into units that make sense to you—"Our Father," for example, or "hallowed be thy name"—and write a paragraph on how that unit is significant to you. Then take a moment to pray through the whole prayer, especially considering what you have written about its various parts.

The Living Room

Chapter 2 When Your Heart Needs a Father

LET US PONDER

1. You may be willing to stop being God's child. But God is not willing to stop being your Father.
   A. Were you ever "willing" to stop being God's child? If so, explain. What would cause anyone to want to stop being his child?
   B. How do we know God is not willing to stop being our Father? How would you try to explain this to someone who thought it was too good to be true?
2. "Our Father" reminds us we are welcome in God's house because we have been adopted by the owner.
   A. Do you feel welcome in God's house? If so, why? If not, why not?
   B. What is significant about becoming a member of God's family through adoption? Why does the Bible use this term "adopted"?
3. God adopted you simply because he wanted to. You were his good will and pleasure.

   A. Why do you think God would want to adopt any of us? What does he get out of the deal?
   B. In what way are all believers (including you) God's "good will and pleasure"? Why does Max believe this? Do you believe it? Explain.
4. Our God is no fair weather Father. He's not into this love-'em-and-leave-'em stuff. I can count on him to be in my corner no matter how I perform. You can, too.
   A. Why is it important to know that God will never leave us? What does this knowledge do for us?
   B. Do you always *feel* as though God is always in your corner? What might account for these feelings? Are they true? How can we deal with them?

LET US PREPARE

1. Consider the phrase "Our Father."
   A. What does this phrase communicate to you? How does it make you feel? What pictures does it bring to mind?
   B. In what ways is God like a father?
2. Read Luke 15:11–32.
   A. What picture of a father is being presented in this story? Why do you think Jesus would paint such a picture?
   B. With which character in the story do you most closely identify? Why?
   C. Why is verse 20 an especially good picture of our heavenly Father? How can keeping this picture in mind help our prayer lives?
3. Read Romans 8:15–17; Galatians 4:4–7; Ephesians 1:3–8.
   A. According to these passages, how does someone become

a child of God?

B. What rights and privileges are granted to God's children, according to these verses?

C. How do you think this knowledge is supposed to affect our prayer lives? Does it influence the way you pray? Why or why not?

LET US PRAY

1. Spend at least five minutes alone with God, speaking to him about nothing other than what it means to you to be called his child.
2. Get out a concordance and find several of the more than 200 times God is called "Father" in the New Testament. Choose ten of these texts and "pray through" them, speaking to God about his fatherly characteristics as described in the verses you chose.

The Foundation

Chapter 3 Where Trust Begins

LET US PONDER

1. God is the foundation of his own house.
   A. What does it mean that God is the foundation of his own house?
   B. How stable would the house be if God were not its foundation? Explain.
   C. What would happen if God's house were built on the foundation of your own strength? Do we ever act as though this were true? Explain.
2. The key question in life is not "How strong am I?" but rather "How strong is God?"
   A. Why is this the key question in life?
   B. Why is it so easy to reverse the above statements? Do you ever do this? If so, what happens?
   C. This key question depends on your relationship to God. Explain why this is so, and describe how you came into a relationship with him. How would you describe that relationship?

3. Meditating on the names of God reminds you of the character of God. Take these names and bury them in your heart.
   A. Max lists several of God's names. Which one means the most to you? Why?
   B. How does one "bury" the names of God in one's heart? What does this mean? Why is it important? Have you done this? Explain.

LET US PREPARE

1. Consider the phrase "Our Father *who is*."
   A. What does it mean to you that God "is"?
   B. How would you feel if God "wasn't"?
   C. How does God show you, personally, that he "is"?
2. Read Isaiah 6:1–4 and Revelation 4:6–11.
   A. What attribute of God is most prominent in these two passages? Describe this trait in your own words.
   B. How do those who surround God as described in these passages respond to him? Why do they so respond?
   C. Why is it important to keep these thoughts in mind when we address our heavenly Father in prayer?
3. Consider the following Scriptures that give various names of God. How is each one important? For each one, identify what life circumstances would make that trait especially appealing:
   A. Genesis 1:1, Elohim (God the Creator).
   B. Genesis 48:15, Jehovah-raah (Caring Shepherd).
   C. Genesis 22:7–8, Jehovah-jireh (The Lord who Provides).
   D. Judges 6:24, Jehovah-shalom (The Lord is Peace).
   E. Exodus 15:26, Jehovah-rophe (The Lord who Heals You).
   F. Exodus 17:8–16, Jehovah-nissi (The Lord my Banner).

LET US PRAY

1. Take a few moments to confess to God your weakness. Be specific—for example, confess your short temper or your pride or your devotion to things rather than people. Then take at least twice as long to praise God for his strength and faithfulness to you. Thank him for cleansing you through the blood of his Son and for adopting you into his family.
2. Pick one of the names of God listed above and meditate on that name for an entire day. Write the appropriate verse on a card and refer to it frequently throughout the day. Then, before you retire for the night, praise God for showing that trait to you and thank him for acting according to his name.

The Observatory

Chapter 4 A Heavenly Affection

LET US PONDER

1. God dwells in a different realm. He occupies a different dimension.
   A. In what way does God dwell in a different realm and different dimension from us?
   B. If God does not dwell with us, how can he be of help to us?
2. You want to know who God is? See what he has done.
   A. Do you want to know who God is? Why or why not? What difference does it make?
   B. How does seeing what God has done show us who he is? From what you see, who would you say God is? Explain.
3. Spend some time walking in the workshop of the heavens, seeing what God has done, and watch how your prayers are energized.
   A. Why does Max think there is a connection between gazing at the stars and the strength of one's prayer life? Is this connection present in your life? Explain.

B. When was the last time you spent several minutes just observing the heavens? Could you do so tonight?

4. Next time a sunrise steals your breath or a meadow of flowers leaves you speechless, remain that way. Say nothing and listen as heaven whispers, "Do you like it? I did it just for you."
   A. Why is silence often an appropriate response to the feeling of wonder?
   B. Do you think God would have made the world so beautiful if you were the only one on the planet? Explain.

LET US PREPARE

1. Consider the phrase "Our Father who is in heaven."
   A. Does the fact that God is in heaven make him feel distant to you at times? Explain.
   B. What benefits are there in having a God "in heaven"?
2. Read 1 Corinthians 1:25.
   A. What comparison is made in this verse? What is it intended to convey?
   B. How should this verse give us great confidence in prayer?
3. Read Isaiah 55:8–9.
   A. What comparison is made in this verse? What is it intended to convey?
   B. Why should this verse give us great confidence in prayer?
   C. How can this verse help to explain some of our disappointments in prayer?
4. Read Psalm 19:1–6.
   A. How does the universe teach us about God, according to this passage?

5. What did David learn about God from observing the universe? Do you think this knowledge helped or hindered his prayer life? Explain.

LET US PRAY

1. The next cloudless night, take a half hour to do nothing but lie on the ground and gaze up at the sky. What do you see? Try counting the stars. After you have basked in the glory of the heavens for awhile, spend an equal amount of time praising God for what you have just seen. Praise him for his power, for his wisdom, for his grace and his love. Thank him that you have eyes to see his creation and a mind to comprehend some of it. Focus on his glory and majesty and splendor and might. Have a good time of celebrating God Almighty!
2. Take a few minutes to read through Revelation 21–22:6. Remember that the place this passage describes is God's home and is merely a reflection of his majesty and greatness. Then praise him for creating such a beautiful place where we will spend eternity with him. "Pray through" this passage, thanking him for his goodness in providing such a marvelous eternal home for us.

The Chapel

Chapter 5 Where Man Covers His Mouth

LET US PONDER

1. There are times when to speak is to violate the moment . . . when silence represents the highest respect. The word for such times is *reverence*. The prayer for such times is "Hallowed be thy name."
   A. What does "reverence" mean to you? Why is it associated with silence?
   B. How does one "hallow" God's name? From the opposite viewpoint, how does one profane it? In the last week, did you do more of one than the other? Explain.
2. God says to Job, "As soon as you are able to handle these simple matters of storing stars and stretching the neck of the ostrich, then we'll have a talk about pain and suffering. But till then, we can do without your commentary."
   A. If you had been in Job's shoes, do you think you would have reacted much as he did? Why or why not?
   B. In times of trouble, do you ever demand answers of God? If he were to respond to your questions, what do you think he'd say?

3. When you set your sights on God, you focus on one "cut above" any storm life may bring.
   A. How can you set your sights on God? What does this entail?
   B. How does setting one's sights on God help us in the middle of life's storms? Do you have any personal examples of this? If so, describe them.

LET US PREPARE

1. Consider the phrase "hallowed be thy name."
   A. How does a person "hallow" something?
   B. How does the term "hallow" relate to the term "holy"?
2. Read Job 38:3–18.
   A. What is the point of all of God's questions? What lesson does he want Job to learn?
   B. If you were in Job's shoes at this point in the story, how do you think you would react? Why?
   C. What do you learn about God in this passage?
3. Read Job 40:4–5; 42:1–6.
   A. How did Job react to God's speeches? Was this an appropriate response? Why?
   B. What did Job finally learn about God? How did it change his attitude toward his circumstances?
   C. In all of God's speeches, does he answer Job's questions? What is significant about this?
4. Read Psalm 46:10.
   A. What command are we given in this verse? What is the reason for the command?
   B. Is this an easy command for you to obey? Why or why

not? Why is it so crucial? What do we miss when we ignore it?

LET US PRAY

1. Go for a long, leisurely walk someplace where you can be alone with God to enjoy the work of his hands. Be silent as you marvel at his handiwork and creativity. Notice everything you can around you—the colors, the smells, the shapes, the immensity and the smallness of his creation. Then at the end of your walk, break your silence and thank him both for the beauty of his creation and for the ability to walk and take it all in. Speak to him reverently and lovingly, trying to avoid making any requests during your prayer.
2. Slowly and carefully read through Job 38–41. Try to picture as much as you can of all the mysteries God describes. Then also try to put yourself in Job's place—how would you feel if God should deliver such a power-packed message to you? Spend some time alone with God, in silence, basking in his overwhelming majesty and splendor.

Chapter 6 Touching the King's Heart

LET US PONDER

1. When you say, "thy kingdom come," you are inviting the Messiah himself to walk into your world. . . . This is no feeble request; it's a bold appeal for God to occupy every corner of your life.
   - A. Have you ever invited the Messiah to walk into your world? If so, how? If not, why not?
   - B. Does God "occupy every corner of your life" right now? Explain. If not, would you like him to? Explain.
2. For Haman, the massacre is a matter of expediency. For Satan, it is a matter of survival. He will do whatever it takes to impede the presence of Jesus in the world.
   - A. Why was Satan's plan to wipe out the ancient Jews "a matter of survival"? What did he have at stake?
   - B. How do you think Satan tries to impede the presence of Jesus in the world today? How does he do it in your own corner of the world?
3. When we pray for God's kingdom to come, it comes! All the hosts of heaven rush to our aid.

A. If God's kingdom were to come into your workplace, what would happen?

B. In what way do the hosts of heaven rush to our aid when we pray for God's kingdom to come? Have you ever prayed for his kingdom to come, and this didn't seem to happen? Explain. What might we conclude from this?

LET US PREPARE

1. Consider the phrase "thy kingdom come."
   A. When you think of God's coming kingdom, what comes to mind?
   B. Why do you think we should pray that God's kingdom would come?
2. Read Esther 3–9.
   A. What was the calamity facing God's people? Who engineered it? How did he engineer it?
   B. How did God take these terrible circumstances and turn them on their heads? How did what was bad turn into what was good?
   C. What part did Esther play in this drama? What part did Mordecai play? What was the role of the king? From the text's point of view, who is the central character?
   D. Choose one key verse for each of these seven chapters. Why do you think the verses you chose are significant? What do they teach you?
   E. Note that Esther is the only book in the Bible which does not mention God by name. Can you see him in this book anyway? Explain.
3. Read Hebrews 4:14–16.

A. What title is Jesus given in this passage? What does this title tell us about his work on our behalf?
B. What reasons does this passage give us for trusting that Jesus can and will help us (see especially verse 15)?
C. What conclusion is made in verse 16, based on what is said in verses 14–15? Do you take advantage of this? Why or why not?

4. Read Hebrews 12:28.
   A. What kind of "kingdom" are we to receive? How is this significant?
   B. What is to be our response to this promise?
   C. How is God described in this verse? Do you often think of him this way? Explain.

LET US PRAY

1. Get a concordance and look up the word "kingdom" in the Gospel of Matthew (there are more than fifty references). Then take your Bible and read through each of these verses, trying to get a "bird's-eye view" of the kingdom of God. As you read, frequently stop to pray about what you are learning. Remember, you are praying to the king of the kingdom!
2. Spend some time asking God to occupy every corner of your life. What "corners" might you still be withholding from him? Finances? Relationships? Work? School? Recreation? Be as honest with yourself as possible and take inventory of your life. Then invite the King to take control in every area.

The Study

Chapter 7 How God Reveals His Will

LET US PONDER

1. God has a plan and that plan is good. Our question is, how do I access it?
   A. Do you believe God has a plan for you? If so, why? If not, why not?
   B. How do you "access" God's plan for your own life?
2. To pray, "thy will be done" is to seek the heart of God.
   A. Why does praying "thy will be done" indicate that we're seeking the heart of God? How is this prayer to change us?
   B. If you had to describe the "heart of God" to a non-Christian, what would you say?
3. God's *general* will provides us with guidelines that help us understand his *specific* will for our individual lives.
   A. What does Max mean by God's "general" will? What does he mean by God's "specific" will?
   B. How does God's general will help us to discover God's specific will? How do the two "wills" interrelate? Do you

think his specific will ever contradicts or ignores his general will? Explain.

4. Want to know God's will for your life? Then answer this question: "What ignites your heart?" . . . The fire of your heart is the light of your path. Disregard it at your own expense.
   A. Do you want to know God's will for your life? If he were to tell you specifically and audibly right now what his will for you is, would you be willing to do it, no matter what? Explain.
   B. What ignites your own heart? What fills you with enthusiasm? Do you see how that interest can be translated into God's will for your life? Are there any cautions you should observe with this advice? If so, what?

LET US PREPARE

1. Consider the phrase "thy will be done."
   A. What do you already know about the will of God for you? Do you struggle with any part of it? Explain.
   B. Is it easy or hard for you to submit yourself to the will of God? Explain.
2. Max lists four components that work together to help us find God's will:
   - Through the people of God.
   - Through the Word of God.
   - Through our walk with God.
   - Through the fire of God.

   A. In your own words, explain how each of these components "works."
   B. Which of these components do you utilize most frequent-

ly? Which do you tend to overlook? What, if anything, needs to change so that all four can work together for you to find God's will?

3. Read Luke 24:13–35.
   A. What were the two men talking about as they walked to Emmaus? How would you describe their demeanor?
   B. How did Jesus approach the men? Why do you think he approached them like this, and not more directly?
   C. How did the men finally recognize Jesus? Is there anything significant about this? If so, what?
   D. How did the men respond to their encounter? In what way is this a model for us?
4. Read Matthew 7:21, 10:29; John 6:40; Acts 18:21; Romans 12:2; Ephesians 5:17–21; 1 Thessalonians 4:3–8, 5:18.
   A. What do you learn about God's will from these passages?
   B. How eager are you to do the will of God he has already revealed to you? Take time to ask him to help you fulfill his will, whatever it may be for you.

LET US PRAY

1. Get out a concordance and look up the word "will," looking especially for those verses that tell us something about the will of God. Make a list of the items that are specially mentioned as being God's will for all of his children. Then spend some time praying about this list, thanking God for helping you to fulfill his will in those areas in which you are doing well, and asking him for his strength in those areas in which you struggle.

2. Many times we do not know exactly what God's will might be for us; we must follow the Lord's example in the Garden of Gethsemane by telling the Lord our request, then concluding our prayer by asking that "nevertheless, not my will, but your will be done." If there is some issue in your life that fits this model, pray about it right now.

The Furnace

Chapter 8 Because Someone Prayed

LET US PONDER

1. The power of God was triggered by prayer. Jesus looked down the very throat of death's cavern and called Lazarus back to life . . . all because someone prayed.
   A. Why do you think prayer often "triggers" the power of God? Why does this connection exist?
   B. What do you think might have happened in the case of Lazarus had someone not told Jesus about his friend's condition? Explain.
2. The power of prayer does not depend on the one who *makes* the prayer, but on the one who *hears* the prayer.
   A. Do you think Max is right about the statement above? Why or why not?
   B. Does the character of the person who prays have no bearing on the power of the prayer? Explain.
3. One call and heaven's fleet appears. Your prayer on earth activates God's power in heaven, and "God's will is done on earth as it is in heaven."

A. What would your neighborhood look like if God's will were done there as it is in heaven? What would your home look like? What part, if any, do you play in seeing this happen?

B. If it is true that "one call and heaven's fleet appears," then why do you think the Bible so often instructs us to pray "without ceasing"?

4. You are the someone of God's kingdom. You have access to God's furnace. Your prayers move God to change the world.

A. How often do you take advantage of your access to God's furnace? Are you satisfied with this? If not, what would it take for it to change?

B. Take a little time to discuss some of your prayers that helped "change the world," at least in your little corner of the planet.

LET US PREPARE

1. Consider the phrase "on earth as it is in heaven."

A. How is God's will done in heaven? Begrudgingly? Reluctantly? Complainingly? How do the angels do God's will?

B. How do you usually do God's will on earth? Could it be said that you do his will as it is done in heaven? Explain.

2. Read John 11:1–44.

A. Retell the story in your own words.

B. How does Jesus respond when he hears of Lazarus's illness? Is this what you might have expected? Is it what his disciples expected? Explain.

C. How do Mary and Martha respond to Jesus when he finally comes to their town? How does he respond to them?
D. Why do you think Jesus waited to perform this miracle (see especially verses 15, 40, and 42).
E. What does this passage teach you about the will of God?

3. Read Revelation 8:1–5.
A. Describe what is happening in this passage.
B. Is any reason given for the silence of heaven in this passage? If so, what is it?
C. What do you learn about prayer in this passage?

LET US PRAY

1. Get out a concordance and look up the word "hear" wherever it appears in the book of Psalms. Note how often the psalmists declare that God hears their prayers and how often they entreat him to hear. Using their prayers as a model, thank God for hearing you and bring to him any requests you may have.
2. Take stock of the areas of your life over which you exercise substantial control. If God's will is not being done in any of those areas as it would be done in heaven, ask God to help you rectify this. If these areas are going well, thank God for enabling you to do his will.

THE KITCHEN

Chapter 9 God's Abundant Table

LET US PONDER

1. God is not a mountain guru involved only in the mystical and spiritual. The same hand which guides your soul gives food for your body.
   A. Do you know of anyone who thinks of God only as a "mountain guru"? If so, how do they respond to him? What do they do? What don't they do?
   B. Do you ever tend to think that the "mystical and spiritual" is more important (or more godly) than "food for your body"? Explain. What does God say about this?
2. If you have followed Christ's model for prayer, your preoccupation has been his wonder rather than your stomach. The first three petitions are God-centered, not self-centered.
   A. What does it mean to be preoccupied with God's wonder rather than your stomach? How does someone get to this point?
   B. What do you think Jesus was teaching in the Lord's prayer by making the first three petitions God-centered rather

than self-centered? Do your own prayers often follow this model? If not, why not?

3. God lives with the self-assigned task of providing for his own, and so far, you've got to admit, he's done pretty well at the job.
   A. How has God provided for you in this past week? In the past month? In the past year? Since you became a Christian?
   B. Does the knowledge that God promises to provide for you make a difference in the way you live? Why or why not?
4. In the house of God, the one who provides the food is the one who prepares the meal.
   A. What does Max mean in the statement above? What difference does it make?
   B. How has God "prepared the meal" for you? Describe at least one example.

LET US PREPARE

1. Consider the phrase "Give us this day our daily bread."
   A. What do you think is included in the idea of "daily bread"?
   B. Why do you think God tells us to ask every day for what we need that day?
2. Review the two rules Max cites for asking God for our daily bread:
   - Don't be shy, ask.
   - Trust the cook.

   A. Are you ever "shy" about asking God for something? If so, why?

B. Why is it so important to "trust the cook"? How do we show that we sometimes *don't* trust the cook?

3. Read Psalm 37:3–6.

A. What advice is given here about seeking our daily bread?

B. What promise is given us here?

4. Read Matthew 6:25–34.

A. What advice is given here about seeking our daily bread?

B. What illustrations are given to help us understand God's ways?

C. What promise is given to us if we will follow God's way?

LET US PRAY

1. What special needs confront you today? List the pressing needs you have right now (not your special desires, but your needs) and spend some unhurried time with your Lord, asking him to meet the specific needs you bring to him. Then thank him for hearing and trust that he will do what he says.
2. Note that the verse talks about "our" daily needs. What are some of the needs of your loved ones, colleagues or close acquaintances? Make a list of these needs, and pray specifically that God would meet each one. When you are through praying, let these people know that you have been praying for them and ask them to let you know when God meets the need you've prayed about.

The Roof

Chapter 10 Beneath God's Grace

LET US PONDER

1. In God's house you are covered by the roof of his grace.
   - A. What does the term "grace" mean to you?
   - B. How does grace "cover" you? In what way is a roof a good picture of grace? How has it sheltered you in the past week?
2. If Christ had not covered us with his grace, each of us would be overdrawn on that account. When it comes to goodness we would have insufficient funds. Inadequate holiness.
   - A. Was there ever a time where you thought you had sufficient funds to cover your spiritual debts? If so, describe that time. What, if anything, convinced you that you were wrong?
   - B. How much holiness would we need to come into God's presence? How can we acquire such holiness?
3. God assumed your debt. You assumed his fortune. And that's not all he did. He also paid your penalty.
   - A. What does it mean that God "assumed your debt"? How was this done?

B. What does it mean that you "assumed [God's] fortune"? How was this done?

C. How did God pay your penalty?

LET US PREPARE

1. Consider the phrase "Forgive us our debts."
   A. What "debts" have you owed to God? What does this term "debts" include?
   B. Have you asked God to forgive your debts? If so, how? If not, why not?
   C. How is God able to forgive us of our debts?
2. Max develops two primary ideas in this chapter:
   - We owe a debt we cannot pay.
   - God paid a debt he did not owe.

   A. What is the debt we cannot pay? Why can we not pay it?
   B. Why did God pay a debt he did not owe? How did he pay it?
3. Read Isaiah 64:6 and Romans 3:23.
   A. What do these verses tell us about our debt to God?
   B. What is the result of this debt?
4. Read Romans 4:5, 8:33; 2 Corinthians 5:19–21; Galatians 3:13; 1 Peter 3:18.
   A. How did God handle our debt, according to these verses?
   B. What, if anything, do these verses tell us we are required to do to take advantage of what God has done for us?

LET US PRAY

1. Remind yourself of what Christ went through to provide

redemption for us by reading the story of his Passion (Matthew 26:36–28:15; Mark 14:32–16:8; Luke 22:39–24:12; John 18:1–20:9). Take some time to thank him for his grace, especially recalling how he saved you from the just penalty of your own sins.

2. Be in prayer for others you know who do not yet know Christ, that they might also come to know the joy of God's forgiveness. Name these people specifically and ask that God might open a door for his children—perhaps you?—to share the gospel effectively with those who don't yet know him.

The Hallway

Chapter 11 Grace Received, Grace Given

LET US PONDER

1. Dealing with debt is at the heart of your happiness. It's also at the heart of the Lord's prayer.
   A. Why is dealing with debt at the heart of a person's happiness?
   B. Why does Max say that debt is at the heart of the Lord's prayer?
   C. How do you typically deal with "debts" owed to you?
2. Confession does not create a relationship with God, it simply nourishes it.
   A. Why does confession not create a relationship with God? If it doesn't create such a relationship, what does?
   B. How does confession "nourish" a relationship with God? Is this easy or hard for you to do? Explain.
3. In any given Christian community there are two groups: those who are contagious in their joy and those who are cranky in their faith.
   A. Describe someone you know who is contagious in his or her joy.

B. Describe someone you know (without naming the person!) who is cranky in his or her faith.
C. Which type of Christian do you consider yourself? Would others agree?

4. Want to enjoy God's generosity? Then let others enjoy yours.
   A. How can you let others enjoy your generosity this week?
   B. If someone were to judge God's generosity by observing your own, what would they think?

LET US PREPARE

1. Consider the phrase "Forgive us our debts as we also have forgiven our debtors."
   A. This phrase troubles many people; why do you think it does? Does it trouble you? If so, why?
   B. Who are your "debtors"? Have you forgiven them? Explain.
2. Max talks about "the high cost of getting even." What do the following texts tell us about this high cost?
   A. Matthew 18:21–35.
   B. Matthew 6:14–15.
   C. Galatians 5:14–15.
3. Read Luke 6:37–38.
   A. What does this text tell us to avoid?
   B. What does this text tell us to do?
   C. What is the result of our obedience? What is the result of our disobedience?

LET US PRAY

1. Is there anyone in your life whom you have a hard time forgiving? If so, admit this to the Lord. Tell him about your feelings, without trying to justify why you feel that way. Ask him to give you his strength to do what you believe he is asking you to do: to forgive that person. Confess that this is not something you will be able to do on your own strength and that perhaps you even struggle with the desire to grant forgiveness to the person who hurt you. Commit this to the Lord and allow him to bring you to the place you need to be.
2. Is there anyone in your life who may be having a hard time forgiving you for something you have done? If so, ask the Lord to help you ask forgiveness of this person, no matter how hard it might be. After praying for God's strength and direction, approach the person and try to iron out your problems. Strive for peace.

The Family Room

Chapter 12 Learning to Live Together

LET US PONDER

1. We don't pray to *my* Father or ask for *my* daily bread or ask God to forgive *my* sins. In God's house we speak the language of plurality: "our Father," "our daily bread," "our debts," "our debtors," "lead us not into temptation," and "deliver us."
   A. Why do you think Jesus stressed "plurality" in his prayer?
   B. Take stock of your own prayer life. Would you say it is more characterized by "me" prayers or "us" prayers? Explain.
2. We all need a father . . . we are all beggars in need of bread . . . we are sinners in need of grace.
   A. What is your most critical need from your Father? Why?
   B. What kind of "bread" do you most need today? Explain.
   C. What form of grace do you most require right now? Why not ask God to supply it even at this moment?
3. In God's house we occasionally find ourselves next to people we don't like.
   A. What kind of people do you find most difficult to get along with? Why? How do you deal with these folks?

B. Describe a time when you asked God to help you get along with someone you didn't like. What happened?

LET US PREPARE

1. Consider the term "our."
   A. Why do you think Jesus taught us to pray in the plural number rather than in the singular?
   B. Do you make it a habit to pray for others as well as for yourself, or is this something you struggle with? Explain.
2. Max says we all need at least three things:
   - We are children in need of a father.
   - We are beggars in need of bread.
   - We are sinners in need of grace.

   A. In what ways has God shown himself to be a father to you?
   B. In what ways do you recognize that you a beggar in need of bread?
   C. How do you show that you are a sinner in need of grace?
3. Read Romans 12:14–21.
   A. What instruction does this text give us for living with others?
   B. What is the hardest thing in this passage for you to do? Why?
4. Read Romans 14:10–13.
   A. What general rule of thumb does Paul give us here for living with other believers? What is the reason behind this rule of thumb?

B. What motivation does Paul give in verse 11 for obeying his instruction? Is this something you often think about? Should it be? Explain.

LET US PRAY

1. Get together some evening with a few of your closest Christian friends and agree to pray for an hour—with one catch. Agree that each of you will pray for the others, but that you will not pray for yourself.
2. Spend some time alone praying for the people and ministries of your church. Pray for guidance, for protection, for strength, for God's Spirit to lead you all into his love, truth, and service. Try not to pray much about yourself, but instead focus on the people who are growing in Christ with you at your church.

The Walls

Chapter 13 Satan, God's Servant

LET US PONDER

1. Every time Satan sets out to score one for evil, he ends up scoring a point for good. When he schemes to thwart the kingdom he always advances it.
   A. Give a few biblical examples that illustrate the statements above.
   B. Describe a few incidents from your own life that demonstrated the truth of the statements above.
2. Satan may strut and prance, but it's God who calls the shots.
   A. How does Satan "strut and prance"? How does he do this in your own life?
   B. How important is it to know that "God calls the shots"? What practical difference does this make to the way we live?
3. All angels, including Satan, are inferior to God. And, this may surprise you, Satan is still a servant to God.
   A. Why is it important to know that angels are inferior to

God? What would happen if they weren't?

B. In what way is Satan a servant to God?

4. The walls which surround the Great House of God—Satan cannot climb them, he cannot penetrate them. He has absolutely no power, except that power which God permits.

A. What are the "walls" which surround the Great House of God? Of what are they made?

B. Why do you think God permits Satan any power at all?

LET US PREPARE

1. Consider the phrase, "and lead us not into temptation, but deliver us from evil."

A. Why should we pray that God would not lead us into temptation? Is there really any danger of that? If not, what is the purpose of this part of the Lord's Prayer?

B. In what ways has God "delivered you from evil" in the past year?

2. Max says that God uses Satan in three primary ways:

- To refine the faithful
- To awaken the sleeping
- To teach the church

A. How does Satan "refine" the faithful? How has he been used to refine you?

B. How does Satan "awaken the sleeping"? Who are the sleeping? And how does he do this in your own experience?

C. Satan seems an unlikely teacher of the church. What does it mean that he can be used to teach the church? What lessons has your own church learned from him?

3. Read Isaiah 14:12–15 and Ezekiel 28:12–17.
   A. What do these passages teach us about the transformation of Satan into an angel of darkness?
   B. What was Satan's paramount sin, according to Ezekiel? How is this sin still a potent trap for us?
4. Read John 19:1–16.
   A. From a human observer's point of view, who seems to be in control of this scene? Who is really in control? How do you know?
   B. Note especially Jesus' words in verse 11. What does he tell Pilate? In what way are his words equally applicable to any of God's adopted children?

LET US PRAY

1. What are your biggest temptations in life? How do you handle them? Read 1 Corinthians 10:12–13; then ask God to give you the strength and the wisdom to handle in a godly way the temptations that come into your life. Ask him to help you remember that often the best course of action is to flee (2 Timothy 2:22) and to enable you to do what will bring him the most glory. Thank him for his protection and his watchful keeping over you.
2. Take some time to recall the many ways God has "delivered you from evil" since you became a Christian. Recount as many as you can think of, thanking God for his power and praising him for his strength and goodness. Then ask him to continue to deliver you from the temptations and trials that inevitably come your way.

The Chapel

Chapter 14 Relying on God's Power

LET US PONDER

1. The chapel is the only room in the house of God we visit twice. . . . It does us twice as much good to think about God as it does to think about anyone or anything else. God wants us to begin and end our prayers thinking of him.
   A. Why would God have us visit the "chapel," and no other room, twice? What is so special about the chapel?
   B. Do you usually begin and end your prayers by thinking of God? If not, how can you change your normal practice? And why should you?
2. As long as our eyes are on His Majesty, there is a bounce in our step. But let our eyes focus on the dirt beneath us and we will grumble about every rock and crevice we have to cross.
   A. Why is there a "bounce in our step" when we gaze upon His Majesty? Why does this energize us?
   B. What does it mean to "focus on the dirt beneath us"? Why is this so easy to do? How can we prompt ourselves to quit looking at "dirt" and start gazing at God?

3. You were not made to run a kingdom, nor are you expected to be all-powerful. And you certainly can't handle all the glory.
   A. How do we sometimes act as if we were made to run a kingdom? As if we were all-powerful?
   B. Why aren't we equipped to handle all the glory? If we're not, who is? And what makes him so different from us?
4. As you confess that God is in charge, you admit that you aren't.
   A. How easy is it for you to admit that God is in charge and you aren't? Explain.
   B. What are some practical ways to admit we're not in charge and to confess that God is?

LET US PREPARE

1. Consider the phrase "For thine is the kingdom and the power and the glory. Amen."
   A. In what way is this an appropriate ending to the Lord's Prayer?
   B. How do each of the three main terms—"kingdom," "power," and "glory"—focus our attention once more on God? What do each of these terms convey to you?
2. Read Colossians 3:1–4.
   A. On what things are we to set our minds, according to this passage?
   B. What is the reason for doing so?
   C. What promise is given in verse 4?
3. Read Hebrews 12:2–3.
   A. On what are we to fix our eyes, according to this passage? Why?

   B. What happens when we don't comply with this command, according to verse 3? Have you ever experienced such consequences? Explain.

4. Read 1 Corinthians 2:9.
   A. What kind of God do we serve, according to this verse?
   B. How do you respond to the greatness of God's love, as expressed in this verse? How does it make you feel? How does it make you act?

LET US PRAY

Regardless of the time of year when you read this, get a copy of Handel's *Messiah* and play the Hallelujah Chorus. Listen carefully to the words and soak in the surging, powerful music. Then spend some time praising God for who he is and thanking him for what he has done for you. Thank him that he will continue to be a powerful, glorious King in your life and that one day his power and glory and kingdom will be apparent for all the universe to see.

THE GREAT HOUSE OF GOD

Chapter 15 A Home for Your Heart

LET US PONDER

1. If you could ask God for one thing, what would you request?
   A. Answer Max's question above. Why would you ask for this thing?
   B. How different would your answer have been ten years ago? Explain.
2. David craves to remain in the aura, in the atmosphere, in the awareness that he is in God's house wherever he is.
   A. Do you share David's craving? If so, how do you express this craving? If not, why not?
   B. Describe the most unusual place you've ever been in God's house. What happened?
3. Day by day, I'm learning to live in the Great House of God.
   A. Do you live more in God's house than you did five years ago? Explain.
   B. What is so important about the "day by day" phrase above? What is important about the "I'm learning" portion of the statement? What do both of these things imply about living in the Great House of God? How should this be an encouragement to us all?

LET US PREPARE

1. In what way is God "a home for your heart"? How does the Lord's Prayer help you to live in that home?
2. Read Psalm 27:1–5.
   A. What claims does David make in this passage?
   B. What does this passage tell you about David's deepest desires?
   C. What can you learn from David's example here?
3. Read John 14:23.
   A. According to this verse, what is required for us to make our "home" with God?
   B. What promise is given here? Have you taken advantage of this promise? Explain.
4. Read Acts 17:28.
   A. What does this verse tell us about having a relationship with God? Do you have this kind of relationship? If so, describe it.
   B. What does it mean to "live" in God? What does it mean to "move" in God? What does it mean to have one's "being" in God? What does it mean to be one of God's "offspring"?
   C. How is this verse a fitting summary of the main point of *The Great House of God*?

LET US PRAY

1. Read through the entire Lord's Prayer one more time (Matthew 6:9–13). As you read, think through the various "rooms" that exist there. Then pray through the prayer, entering each room and relating each one to the events and challenges and triumphs of your life. Begin with praise, end with praise, and in between make your most urgent requests known to God, both for yourself and for others.